# The Faces of Authoritarianism and Strategies of Dissent in Contemporary Brazil

# MODERN AMERICAS

Modern Americas is a series for books discussing the culture, politics and history of the Americas from the nineteenth century to the present day. It aims to foster national, international, transnational and comparative approaches to topics in the region, including those that bridge geographical and/ or disciplinary divides, such as between the disparate parts of the hemisphere covered by the series (the US, Latin America, Canada and the Caribbean) or between the humanities and social/ natural sciences.

*Series Editors*

Claire Lindsay is Professor of Latin American Literature and Culture, UCL.

Tony McCulloch is Associate Professor in North American Studies at the Institute of the Americas, UCL.

Maxine Molyneux is Emeritus Professor of Sociology at the Institute of the Americas, UCL.

Kate Quinn is Associate Professor in Caribbean History at the Institute of the Americas, UCL.

# The Faces of Authoritarianism and Strategies of Dissent in Contemporary Brazil

Edited by Andreza Aruska de Souza Santos
and Katerina Hatzikidi

**UCL**PRESS

First published in 2025 by
UCL Press
University College London
Gower Street
London WC1E 6BT

Available to download free: www.uclpress.co.uk

Collection © Editors, 2025
Text © Contributors, 2025

The authors have asserted their rights under the Copyright, Designs and Patents Act 1988 to be identified as the authors of this work.

A CIP catalogue record for this book is available from The British Library.

Any third-party material in this book is not covered by the book's Creative Commons licence. Details of the copyright ownership and permitted use of third-party material is given in the image (or extract) credit lines. Every effort has been made to identify and contact copyright holders and any omission or error will be corrected if notification is made to the publisher. If you would like to reuse any third-party material not covered by the book's Creative Commons licence, you will need to obtain permission directly from the copyright owner.

This book is published under a Creative Commons Attribution-NonCommercial 4.0 International licence (CC BY-NC 4.0), https://creativecommons.org/licenses/by-nc/4.0/. This licence allows you to share and adapt the work for non-commercial use providing attribution is made to the author and publisher (but not in any way that suggests that they endorse you or your use of the work) and any changes are indicated. Attribution should include the following information:

de Souza Santos, A.A. and Hatzikidi, K. (eds.). 2025. *The Faces of Authoritarianism and Strategies of Dissent in Contemporary Brazil*. London, UCL Press. https://doi.org/10.14324/111.9781800088207

Further details about Creative Commons licences are available at https://creativecommons.org/licenses/

ISBN: 978-1-80008-818-4 (Hbk)
ISBN: 978-1-80008-819-1 (Pbk)
ISBN: 978-1-80008-820-7 (PDF)
ISBN: 978-1-80008-822-1 (epub)
DOI: https://doi.org/10.14324/111.9781800088207

*The editors dedicate this book to Leo and Ariadne
who came to this world while this work was underway.*

# Contents

| | |
|---|---|
| *List of figures* | ix |
| *List of tables* | xi |
| *List of contributors* | xiii |
| *List of abbreviations* | xv |

1  The faces of authoritarianism: an introduction   1
*Katerina Hatzikidi and Andreza Aruska de Souza Santos*

## Part I: National myth, international pariah?

2  From Bolsonaro to Lula: theoretical and practical challenges in Brazilian politics   31
*Marcos Nobre*

3  The radical right in Brazil: part of a global family   47
*Ariel Goldstein*

## Part II: Small actions, great impacts

4  Bureaucratic resistance and its limits in Bolsonaro's Brazil   65
*Katherine Bersch, Gabriela Lotta and Daniel Thomas*

5  Autonomy as limitless freedom: authoritarian affordances in Brazil's Prevent Senior case   87
*Katerina Hatzikidi*

6  Regimes of truth: disinformation and conflicting on- and offline realities   107
*Lorena G. Barberia, Natália de Paula Moreira and Isabel Seelaender Costa Rosa*

## Part III: God above all

7  Mobilising charismatic evangelical Christianity: spiritual warfare and political activism amid the 2022 Brazilian elections   129
*Manoela Carpenedo*

8 Opacity and anxiety: how disruptive ritual may offer a
clue to certain evangelical affinities with political
authoritarianism 151
*David Lehmann*

**Part IV: Political peripheries at the centre**

9 Corruption models and the appeal of left- and right-wing
politics in rural Brazil 173
*Aaron Ansell*

10 Idealism, pragmatism and disenchantment in Brazilian
elections: politicians and the votes of the poor 193
*Flávio Eiró*

11 Afterword 209
*Flávia Biroli, 13 August 2024*

*Index* 213

# List of figures

| | | |
|---|---|---|
| 6.1 | Bolsonaro's tweets, speeches and key events relating to Covid-19 vaccines in 2020 | 111 |
| 6.2 | Percentage of respondents willing to get vaccinated against Covid-19 in 2020, Brazil | 119 |
| 6.3a | Willingness to be vaccinated against Covid-19 by those approving of Bolsonaro's government, August 2020 | 120 |
| 6.3b | Willingness to be vaccinated against Covid-19 by those approving of Bolsonaro's government, October 2020 | 120 |
| 9.1 | Facebook meme | 181 |

# List of tables

6.1  Positions of Bolsonaro's Covid-19 vaccine tweets and the
     public's engagement in 2020                              114
6.2  Brazilian Government Covid-19 vaccine purchase
     agreements in 2020 and 2021                              116

# List of contributors

**Aaron Ansell** is a cultural anthropologist and Associate Professor of Religion and Culture at Virginia Tech.

**Lorena G. Barberia** is an Associate Professor of Political Science at the University of São Paulo.

**Katherine Bersch** is Frontis W. Johnston Associate Professor of Political Science at Davidson College, Davidson, NC.

**Manoela Carpenedo** is Assistant Professor at the Faculty of Religion, Culture and Society, University Groningen.

**Andreza Aruska de Souza Santos** is Associate Professor and Director of King's Brazil Institute at King's College London.

**Flávio Eiró** is Assistant Professor at the Department of Social and Cultural Anthropology of the Vrije Universiteit Amsterdam, The Netherlands.

**Ariel Goldstein** is a CONICET researcher and author specialising in the intersection of extreme right politics and global issues.

**Katerina Hatzikidi** is a political anthropologist and senior postdoctoral researcher at the ERC-funded PACT: Populism and Conspiracy Theory project at the University of Tübingen.

**David Lehmann** is Emeritus Professor of Social Science, University of Cambridge.

**Gabriela Lotta** is Professor of Public Administration and Government at the Fundação Getulio Vargas, São Paulo, Brazil.

**Natalia de Paula Moreira** is a Postdoctoral Fellow at Wesleyan University, Connecticut.

**Marcos Nobre** is Professor of Political Philosophy at the University of Campinas (Unicamp) and President of the Brazilian Center of Analysis and Planning (Cebrap).

**Isabel Seelaender Costa Rosa** is a research affiliate with the Solidarity Research Network in Public Policy and Society.

**Daniel Thomas** recently completed his Master's degree in Economics at the University of Virginia. He is currently serving as a research fellow in the Economics Department at the University of Maryland.

# List of abbreviations

| | |
|---|---|
| AfD: | Alternative für Deutschland (Alternative for Germany) |
| ANPR: | Associação Nacional dos Procuradores da República (National Association of Attorneys of the Republic, Brazil) |
| ANS: | Agência Nacional de Saúde Suplementar (National Regulatory Agency for Private Health Insurance and Plans) |
| ANVISA: | Agência Nacional de Vigilância Sanitária (Brazilian Health Regulatory Agency) |
| CPAC: | Conservative Political Action Conference |
| CPI: | Comissão Parlamentar de Inquérito (National Congressional Panel) |
| Fidesz: | Federation of Young Democrats |
| IBAMA: | Instituto Brasileiro do Meio Ambiente e dos Recursos Naturais Renováveis (Brazilian Institute of Environment and Renewable Natural Resources) |
| ICMBio: | Instituto Chico Mendes de Conservação da Biodiversidade (Chico Mendes Institute for Biodiversity Conservation) |
| IURD: | Igreja Universal do Reino de Deus (Universal Church of the Kingdom of God) |
| MDB: | Movimento Democrático Brasileiro |
| MPF: | Ministério Público Federal (Federal Public Prosecutor's Office, Brazil) |
| PAD: | Processo Administrativo Disciplinar (Administrative Disciplinary Process) |
| PL: | Partido Liberal (Liberal Party) |
| (P)MDB: | Partido do Movimento Democrático Brasileiro (Brazilian Democratic Movement) |
| PRF: | Polícia Rodoviária Federal (Federal Highway Police) |
| PSDB: | Partido da Social Democracia Brasileira (Brazilian Social Democracy Party) |
| PT: | Partido dos Trabalhadores (Workers' Party) |
| SDG: | Sustainable Development Goals |
| SUS: | Sistema Único de Saúde (Unified Health System) |
| TRE-PE: | Tribunal Regional Eleitoral de Pernambuco (Regional Electoral Court of Pernambuco) |
| TSE: | Tribunal Superior Eleitoral (Superior Electoral Court) |

# 1
# The faces of authoritarianism: an introduction

Katerina Hatzikidi and Andreza Aruska de Souza Santos

This book draws inspiration from historiographical and anthropological approaches that examine structural conditions together with circumstantial elements in an attempt better to situate and understand the 2020s. In so doing, it seeks to contribute to ongoing debates on Brazil's manifold and recurring expressions of authoritarianism by taking the discussion a step further: rather than looking back to the country's authoritarian past, we are interested in exploring the ways in which authoritarianism most recently emerged and was confronted. Taking the Bolsonaro administration (2019–2022) as a case in point, we analyse in tandem forms of repression and dissent: efforts to dismantle democratic foundations alongside forms of contestation and resistance to authoritarianism. In this way our broader aim is to explore the varied ways (and spaces) in which struggles over the meaning and practice of democracy took place during that period. The ten chapters that comprise this edited volume offer valuable theoretical and ethnographic insights, from interdisciplinary perspectives, into the complex realities that Brazilians experienced over the four years of Jair Bolsonaro's presidency.

The book is organised around four sections. Each addresses a core area in which democracy, both as meaning and practice, was contested, attacked and defended. The first section, titled 'National myth, international pariah?', places the former president Jair Bolsonaro in a domestic and international political context. The chapters by Marcos Nobre and Ariel Goldstein that comprise this section consider some of the key issues at stake, including fragile parliamentary coalitions and global far right alliances, and sketch a horizon of future political possibilities following the 2022 electoral result. The second section, titled 'Small actions, great impacts', delves into the varied institutional struggles that have occurred, especially over the management of the Covid-19 pandemic. The chapters by Katherine Bersch, Gabriela Lotta and Daniel Thomas; Katerina Hatzikidi; and Lorena Barberia, Natália de Paula Moreira and Isabel Seelaender Costa Rosa in this section explore a variety of contentious situations involving state and non-state actors, private sector initiatives that endorsed – and were buttressed by – government actions and segments of the broader civil society.

The third section, titled 'God above all', brings together the chapters by Manoela Carpenedo and David Lehmann that both reflect upon how anti-democratic subjectivities are constructed among evangelical Christians. Their discussions diligently explore how perceptions of the political are informed by religious imaginaries steeped in theological and pastoral narratives that project dualisms between light and darkness, the visible and the invisible, and speculate about the forces behind them. Such religious imaginaries shape in turn followers' vision of the world; many become mobilised around notions of spiritual warfare, according to which elections are no longer a dispute between political opponents in a pluralist democratic society, but a battle between good and evil. In such a contest, nuance, context and disagreement are abandoned in favour of fervent adherence to the (one and only) 'truth'. The fourth and final section, titled 'Political peripheries at the centre', includes two chapters by Aaron Ansell and Flávio Eiró that shed much needed light into how disputes and tensions around democratic and authoritarian practices play out in the ambiguous relationships between local politicians and their constituencies.

Overall, this book is about changing and lasting perceptions and manifestations of authoritarianism and acts of resistance. In this sense, it is essentially concerned with struggles over what democracy – and its opposite – is and how it manifests: not only between Jair Bolsonaro's government and those who resisted it from within and outside the state, but also between state and non-state actors, public and private sectors, considering the country's polarised political landscape and the impact such struggles have had on civil society. The discussions within individual chapters move from exploring specific and situated forms of repression and dissent to contributing to the book's broader scope, which addresses recent struggles around democracy and against authoritarianism. Such discussions thus provide a framework that better encompasses the varied ways and spaces in which these struggles played out.

## Authoritarian and democratic pasts and presents

Towards the end of the 1970s and throughout the 1980s in Brazil, there was a boom of studies, particularly in historiography, that sought to uncover and explore 'the foundations of Brazilian authoritarianism' (Gomes 2010, 49, cited in Müller and Iegelski 2018, 17). Understood as a painful but necessary inward-looking process of historical reckoning as the country was nearing the end of a military dictatorship (1964–1985), searching for authoritarianism's roots led many social scientists to the study of the Estado Novo (1937–1945), (among them Carone 1976; Souza 1976; Medeiros 1978; Camargo et al. 1982). Although better construed as ambiguous than uniform as regards its ideological underpinnings and policies implemented, the impact of this period on the country's political culture was seen as long-lasting (Gomes 2014, 12–13) and one that, in certain ways, profoundly shaped its future.

Looking back to the country's authoritarian past also marked the period following the election of Jair Bolsonaro in 2018. Once again, social scientists sought to make sense of the avalanche of social and political changes that shook the country over just a few years. Some of these changes were seen as disruptive to the process of re-democratisation that was initiated in 1985. The watershed moment that set forth a gradual process of 'de-democratisation' began for some with the street protests of June 2013 (Solano et al. 2017; Payne and de Souza Santos 2020). For others the moment that triggered an all-encompassing crisis of democracy came a year later, when the Brazilian Social Democratic Party officially questioned the 2014 electoral result after the Workers' Party (PT) candidate, Dilma Rousseff, secured a narrow win in the second round of the presidential elections (see Nobre 2020, 60–5; Bianchi et al. 2021).

In dissecting the conditions that gave Jair Bolsonaro his 'meteoric rise' to the presidency (Hunter and Power 2019, 70), analysts focused on the different components involved. For some, it was the result of an 'illiberal backlash' reacting against everything the 1988 Constitution guaranteed and represented (Rocha et al. 2021). With its attacks on gender and equal democratic participation (Biroli 2019), its intolerance towards religious and ethno-racial minorities (Arruti and Held 2021), its anti-intellectualism (Souza Lima and Gonçalves Dias 2020) and its exaltation of the military regime, many saw the political project that evolved in the aftermath of the 2018 presidential elections as consolidating a 'progressivist shock' (Rocha 2021), which had in fact emerged in the early 2000s but gained traction only in the second decade of the twenty-first century.

However, the escalating polarisation after 2013 (Dullo 2021), which largely split Brazilian society into opposing moral and political camps, was far greater than political disenchantment, or a reaction to progressive politics. As Rosana Pinheiro-Machado and Lucia Scalco (2020, 26) put it, 'the rise of conservatism in Brazil is not merely a backlash'. It is also the expression of deep-seated political legacies and structural phenomena that had been sidelined for many years but never stopped working behind the scenes, remaining relevant to several segments of the population.

In this vein, and beyond pointing to comparable changes across the world, in a sort of authoritarian or illiberal wave that was sweeping through democracies from the USA to Turkey and from Poland to the Philippines, scholars emphasised the need to look at Brazil's own history of authoritarianism and its enduring influence on its present (Avritzer 2018; Ferreira and Neves Delgado 2018; Neiburg and Ribeiro Thomaz 2020; Hatzikidi and Dullo 2021). The dictatorship of the Estado Novo period, the foundation of modern Brazil and also its imperial and colonial histories were all explored, to a greater or lesser extent, as instances of a long-standing authoritarianism – a phenomenon which, although it might share characteristics with authoritarianisms elsewhere, was unmistakably national.

For Lilia Moritz Schwarcz (2019), for example, Brazil's long history of slavery, together with enduring structures of violence, paternalism, fiefdoms, public insecurity and unequal access to education, are the roots of its authoritarianism, constantly bringing the country's past into the present (see also Moritz Schwarcz 2021). With tensions arising from dissenting and contradictory claims to democracy and accusations of authoritarianism, the discussions in this book seek not only to encompass the complex and varied ways in which such tensions played out nationally, but also to provide a point of comparison between the Brazilian case and contemporary authoritarian transformations and forms of democratic resistance around the world.

## Authoritarianism and/in the Bolsonaro administration

If a process of de-democratisation was already underway during the highly controversial impeachment process of President Dilma Rousseff in 2016, Michel Temer's administration implemented a series of policies that certainly accelerated it. Saad-Filho (2020) described his term as one of 'authoritarian neoliberalism':

Under the pretence of fighting corruption, Temer undermined the constitution, normalised a state of exception, brought the armed forces back into politics, protected gangster-politicians and imposed an accumulation strategy based on an unprecedentedly exclusionary, authoritarian and internationalised variety of neoliberalism. (Saad-Filho 2020, 21)

After taking over in January 2019, Bolsonaro continued and deepened a process that had been initiated in previous years.

Despite his well-known views on the 1964–85 civil-military dictatorship, human rights and majority rule, Bolsonaro insists that he is a democrat. During the pandemic, for instance, he repeatedly claimed to defend democracy and individual liberties against the 'dictatorial' social distancing measures imposed by municipal and state governments (de Souza Santos et al. 2021). Yet, in an address to young cadets in February 2021, he admitted, 'If it was up to me, this would not be the regime we would be living under. And, in spite of everything, I represent democracy in Brazil' (Arias 2021).

Bolsonaro's views of democracy sometimes invert common-sense knowledge, as when he commemorated the anniversary of the 1964 coup d'état in 2020 by saying that 'today is the day of freedom' (Della Coletta 2020). His vice-president and former army general, Hamilton Mourão, similarly celebrated the 'election' of General Castello Branco, which he understands to have 'initiated the reforms which developed Brazil' (Mourão 2020). On the same day, the former Minister of Defence, General Fernando Azevedo e Silva, lauded the military regime as a 'landmark for democracy' (Gielow 2020).

Indeed, for Bolsonaro and members of his cabinet, a 'democratic' military regime does not appear to be a contradiction in terms. As Marcos Nobre argues in his chapter, unpacking this paradox is crucial to an understanding of Bolsonaro and his political project. For Nobre (this volume), the election of Jair Bolsonaro breaks with the democratic conservatism of *pemedemismo*; that is to say, the peculiar yet democratic mode of the political system in place since 1985. If this democratic conservatism slowed down social forces of transformation that aimed to combat inequalities, Bolsonaro's administration marks the beginning of an era in which the far right dominates the political field of the right and begins to operate outside the rules of the democratic game. The political project itself is to provoke an institutional collapse, with institutions forced to work beyond their capacity or 'functioning in a dysfunctional way', as Nobre describes it. This collapse is, for the author, an essential component of the authoritarian agenda. For him the main challenge – one that remains even after Bolsonaro's electoral defeat – is to isolate the currently dominant far right from the political field.

In their chapter Katherine Bersch, Gabriela Lotta and Daniel Thomas also explore operations that occurred outside of democratic rules during the Bolsonaro administration. Here they discuss tactics of control and intimidation used against public servants, and the latter's strategies of dissent and resistance. Like Nobre and other contributors to this volume, the authors examine both continuities and breaks in the ways that democratic institutions functioned during recent administrations. They note that the institutional weakening did not begin with Bolsonaro, but was rather intensified under his time in office. In conditions of increased political control over bureaucratic autonomy, the pro-democratic technocracy adopted different strategies of resistance.

Bersch, Lotta and Thomas refer to Albert Hirschman's (1970) famous work *Exit, Voice and Loyalty* as options available to public servants at odds with their superiors. However, they also explore another possibility that lies somewhere between these options: active resistance from within that seeks to advance dissent within organisations. The authors then describe four strategies employed by civil servants to resist these encroachments: subversive action, resistance, survival and abandonment. As much as such strategies importantly claim autonomy against authoritarian repression, the authors argue that the space for reaction decreases with time, discouraging further acts of dissent and eventually enabling the consolidation of political control.

On the other hand, in analysing the human cost of corporate decisions made by Prevent Senior, a health insurance and healthcare provider, during the Covid-19 pandemic, Katerina Hatzikidi shows that while the space for reaction may indeed decrease with time when authoritarian practices are continuously working against autonomy, the relation between the two is far from linear. Prevent Senior's logo, 'loyalty and obedience', as well as its financial ambitions, were some of the key elements for the company's convergence with the Bolsonaro administration, in what former employees described as common ideological and economic ground. The company offered a health protocol which the government began broadly to implement irrespective of its inefficiency, and the government offered Prevent Senior ample space for experimentation unobstructed by accountability. Physicians working under tight supervision in a corporate culture of intimidation, coercion and fear initially found a narrow space for disobedience. One of the forms of dissent was confidentially to recommend patients *not* to take the drugs included in the (ready-made) prescriptions they were handing to them. Other physicians, who chose to voice their dissent more openly, were summarily discharged. Yet as soon as some of them made their criticisms and accusations public, the space for reaction opened up for more former employees to join. As a result, and building on Castoriadis's theorisation of autonomy, Hatzikidi construes dissent as a negotiated and gradational practice that may oscillate with time and increase or decrease, in relation to its dynamic relationship with the broader context in which it is situated.

The discussion by Lorena Barberia, Natália de Paula Moreira and Isabel Seelaender Costa Rosa also grapples with the human cost of strategic decisions during the pandemic. In their chapter the authors analyse Bolsonaro's official and unofficial presidential speeches, tweets from @jairbolsonaro and press interviews from 10 January to 31 December 2020, discovering that, in contrast to the common impression that the former president was against Covid-19 vaccination, his discourse was rather contradictory. It in fact yielded a mixed record, sometimes in favour of vaccines and vaccination and sometimes against. What the authors' findings show is that the president's discourse was informed less by public health recommendations and medical developments and more by political rivalries which ultimately determined whether – and of which vaccines – he would speak favourably. At the same time, this oscillation is even more nuanced by Barberia, Moreira and Costa Rosa. Their analysis reveals that even during the same period the president would often make contradictory statements, depending on the medium through which his message was communicated and the degree of formality it represented – for example, an official presidential speech as opposed to an unofficial statement in front of his supporters. Evidence brought to light by this chapter shows that Bolsonaro's rhetorical strategy against vaccines increased vaccination hesitancy, more pronounced among those who approved of the president's job performance.

Bolsonaro received international criticism not only for his administration's handling of the global health emergency, but also his foreign policy. In his chapter Ariel Goldstein discusses the connections forged between Itamaraty, Brazil's Ministry of Foreign Affairs, and far-right administrations elsewhere in the world. This sort of 'authoritarian international', as Nobre calls it in his chapter, is formed on the basis of elective affinities among their respective political projects. Especially during the time that Ernesto Araújo, an admirer of conspiracy theorist and self-proclaimed philosopher Olavo de Carvalho, was heading the Ministry,

Brazil's foreign policy involved seeking to establish alliances based on ideological proximities, dismantling previous policies and jeopardising diplomatic relations when such proximities were not evident (Hatzikidi 2023a). In the past few years, argues Goldstein, Brazil formed part of the 'global family of the radical right'. This membership, which included a series of meetings with politicians and state officials from such parties as the Republican Party (USA), Fidesz (Hungary), AfD (Germany), La Libertad Avanza (Argentina), Partido Republicano (Chile) and Vox (Spain), weighted on decision-making and on drafting future strategies. The consequences of these meetings, and how Brazil's case dialogues with others worldwide, are discussed in the chapter.

An important component of the Bolsonaro administration's authoritarian practices was the militarisation of government and bureaucracy, prioritising discipline and hierarchy over autonomy and equality. The militarisation of his government is symptomatic of how the former president views 'democracy' – not unlike Ernesto Geisel's attempt to 'institutionalise the revolution'. In the words of historian Maud Chirio, Geisel's 'old authoritarian project of conciliation with the liberal reforms' in fact involved 'the development of a hybrid security-based, elitist political system, which borrowed a few elements of legitimisation and effective functioning from representative democracy' (Chirio 2018, 180).

Casually referring to the armed forces as 'my army' (*meu exército*) and threatening to act against the 'democratic excesses' of the judiciary, Bolsonaro's actions strived to strengthen the entanglements between his government and sectors of the armed forces, decidedly displacing them from their non-partisan place outside the political realm.

According to a survey by the Tribunal de Contas da União, more than 6,000 members of the armed forces were occupying civil positions by July 2020 – an increase of more than 100 per cent since the previous record high of 2018 (*O Globo* 2021). A recent report published by the Institute of Applied Economic Research shows an increase of 193 per cent in the presence of members of the armed forces in civil posts over the period 2013–2021 (Schmidt 2022; see also Bersch, Lotta and Thomas, this volume).

Besides the overwhelming presence of the armed forces in the government, and in strategic civil positions more broadly, the Bolsonaro administration also endeavoured to intensify and amplify the presence and scope of action of police forces in Brazil. The case of the Federal Highway Police (Polícia Rodoviária Federal: PRF) is illustrative. While the federal constitution and the Brazilian traffic code clearly affirm its purpose to patrol federal highways, subsequent decrees have sought to modify the scope of the PRF's jurisdiction. In the first month of Bolsonaro's term, a modification authorised the PRF's Direction of Operations to enable participation in operations together with other municipal, state and federal institutions of public safety in the prevention of and fight against crime. Yet at the same time a lack of training – for instance, on human rights education (*Jornal Nacional* 2022) – opens up the question of whether the force is sufficiently prepared for its expanded duties. In May 2022 the joint operation between the PRF and the Military Police in Vila Cruzeiro, a favela in Rio de Janeiro, in which 26 people were killed, was a blatant case of excessive violence that disproportionally affects non-white and economically vulnerable Brazilians. As Didier Fassin put it:

> Law enforcement agents target certain territories and certain populations and this focus has less to do with the incidence of crime than with logics of control and performance that determine practices that would hardly be imaginable in other places and with other categories: in disadvantaged neighbourhoods, stop-and-frisks mostly serve to impose and manifest a social order; they are meant to 'remind these people of their place' in society and more specifically to remind them that they are 'police properties'. (Fassin 2018, 106)

While police violence in Brazil's poorest neighbourhoods is by no means a new phenomenon, it has taken a new turn in recent years. As president, Bolsonaro publicly congratulated law enforcement agents involved in killings, even when the conditions under which they operated remained unclear. The Bolsonaro administration also made concerted efforts to increase tolerance of, and reduce accountability for, police violence even further. In March 2022, for example, the president sent a bill to the National Congress that expanded the so-called 'illegality excluder' (*excludente de ilicitude*), thus making it even easier to exempt law enforcement agents involved in deadly operations from any liability. Among other things, and in what often appeared as gestures of appeasement for a key electoral base, Bolsonaro's administration fought to raise salaries for the different law enforcement units and asked lawmakers to increase punishment for crimes committed against police officers during the exercise of their duties.

Similar preferential treatment has been given to the armed forces. With both the police and the armed forces increasingly being integrated into executive and legislative bodies, as well as occupying other civil positions in recent years, fears arose that the government was attempting to co-opt members of these forces and use them to defend anti-democratic and authoritarian acts. Although for some Bolsonaro's election had posed a clear threat to the country's democracy from the very beginning (Abranches et al. 2019), many only saw a potential or imminent threat during his term in office. And while the former president had frequently threatened – directly or indirectly – military intervention, the mob invasion in Brasília on 8 January 2022 was a startling attempt to concretise what was for some a long-awaited coup d'état. Bolsonaro's direct involvement in these efforts remains to be clarified, but the Brasília attacks against democracy were not the only ones in recent years. In May 2020 the former president appeared close to actually ordering the shutdown of the National Congress and the Supreme Court (Gugliano 2020).

## Regimes of truth

When Jair Bolsonaro won the 2018 presidential election, he accepted the result with reservations: he claimed that had it not been for fraud, he would have been elected in the first round. Already, in a televised interview a month ahead of the election, he had declared that he would only accept the result if he was elected (*G1* 2018). He repeatedly declared that he would present evidence of the alleged fraud, but never did. Nonetheless, he continued to attack the credibility of the electoral system – among the most well-acclaimed in the world for its safety and efficiency (*Conectas* 2022) – throughout his time in office. After persistently fanning the flames of doubt for months, in July 2021 the president made a livestreamed address in which he said he would present evidence of the vulnerability of the electronic ballot system. However, instead of evidence Bolsonaro simply recited conspiracy rumours and false allegations that had been circulating on- and off-line and that had already been debunked. Against his push for printed voting receipts (*voto impresso*), which would supposedly counteract the vulnerability of the electronic ballots, the Congress rejected a constitutional amendment to adopt them.

Yet, despite failing to translate Bolsonaro's allegations into policy, distrust had been seeded. Indeed, instilling doubt and distrust are fundamental practices in the authoritarian playbook. 'Truth', argues Foucault (1984, 74), 'is linked in a circular relation with systems of power which produce and sustain it, and to effects of power which it induces and which extend it. A "regime" of truth'. By 'regime of truth', Foucault designates a 'set of processes and institutions by which, under certain conditions and with certain effects, individuals are bound and obliged to make well-defined truth acts' (Foucault 2014, 94). Importantly, however, these obligations 'are indifferent to the fact of whether or not it is a matter of truth, of true or false' (94). Indeed, 'when it is a question of truth itself there is no need for a regime of truth' (96). Drawing from this formulation of truth regime, we understand truth as part of mechanisms and decisions, connected to juridico-political regimes and moral dispositions more than to ideology, that determine what counts as true and how truth operates at a given conjuncture.

Constantly nourishing alternative spheres of 'the real' in a struggle for hegemony over truth, authoritarian leaders revel in vagueness and disinformation. Some of their statements may be 'half-truths': a combination of facts and fictive content in which the former are purposefully exaggerated, distorted or placed in a misleading context (Gess 2022, 164). Very often, however, the statements are entirely fabricated. Alfred Moore (2018) discusses the case of a re-tweet by Donald Trump: in 2012, during Barack Obama's presidency, the US Bureau of Labour Statistics released a report on unemployment, showing a low level of 7.8 per cent. Jack Welch, the former CEO of General Electric, reacted to the report by tweeting: 'Unbelievable jobs [*sic*] numbers ... these Chicago guys will do anything ... can't debate so change numbers'. Although this tweet provides no evidence to support its claim that the numbers are 'cooked', nor does it elaborate on a conspiracy theory, it does question the validity of the report. Trump endorsed and repeated the message which circulated widely (Moore 2018, 112).

Rumours, rather than fully fledged conspiracy theories, have become ever more numerous in the digital era (Butter 2020, 137). What is more important than evidence, for a rumour to resonate, is its repetition. For rumours have 'a self-validating quality. The more a story is told, and the more often people hear it, the more likely they are to believe it' (Barkun 2013, 13). Indeed, what Muirhead and Rosenblum (2019, 3) termed the 'new conspiracism' in effect 'dispenses with the burden of explanation'; it is conspiracy without the theory, and its main consequence is delegitimation. When Bolsonaro, as president, casts doubt on the legitimacy and reliability of the national electronic voting system, referring to a 'secret room' where electoral results are decided by 'half a dozen technicians' (Motta 2022), his statements do not only '*express* distrust; they clearly also have the potential – and are possibly even designed to – *generate* distrust' (Moore 2018, 113; original emphasis). As such, conspiracy rumours can be detrimental to democratic institutions. For some, indeed, conspiracism gains traction 'as leaders [take] their countries in authoritarian directions' (Radnitz 2018, 356).

In his chapter in the present volume, David Lehmann explores possible connections between distrust that favours authoritarian dispositions and the role of religious beliefs and practices concerning the supernatural. Drawing on multi-sited fieldwork with the Universal Church of the Kingdom of God (Igreja Universal do Reino de Deus; IURD) across different countries, Lehmann's contribution to the volume revolves around the relationship between evangelicals and authoritarianism through an examination of the former's understanding of transparency and opacity beyond the realm of the supernatural. Followers, argues Lehmann, are told by pastors that the forces of evil have ever-changing manifestations; appearances cannot be trusted or taken at face value. This language, the author discusses, not only seeds distrust, but also encourages a level of receptivity to conspiracy theories that extends well beyond the church; it influences the ways in which followers perceive democratic politics, as well as 'the opaque formalisms of the bureaucratic apparatus' or 'the impersonal professional and judicial expertise'. However, instead of asking whether neo-Pentecostal evangelical churches encourage political authoritarianism, Lehmann provokes us to entertain the possibility that these churches tend to attract people of an authoritarian disposition.

Manoela Carpenedo directly engages with the questions opened up by Lehmann in her chapter on evangelicals and moral politics. She defends the argument that, in order to understand the current political scenario in Brazil, one needs to appreciate the role of religious imaginaries and theological narratives in providing 'a corpus of discourses and practices [that] mobilise conservative masses'. For a considerable segment of the evangelical population, the 2022 elections were a 'spiritual warfare' in which God was confronted by evil forces, argues Carpenedo. For the author, religious imagination structured around spiritual warfare discourses serves not only to shape the political realities of many Pentecostal believers, but also to inform specifically authoritarian political modalities.

Jair Bolsonaro, who had ascended to power performing a leadership characterised by nationalist rhetoric combined with an aggressive political style to defend traditional values of the 'good citizen', as Ansell also discusses in his chapter, tapped into this good versus evil dualistic narrative throughout his campaign. This politicisation of the realms of good and evil helped to animate 'a Crusade of purification to liberate the nation and politics from the influence of Satan' (Carpenedo, this volume). As discussed by Carpenedo and Lehmann, the forces of evil can take different forms. One therefore needs to tread cautiously in navigating the visible and the invisible, the true and the false. Carpenedo also highlights how Christian values were mobilised by Bolsonaro before the 2022 political campaign, and even before his victory in 2018. As congressman, he was already opposing politicians such as Jean Wyllys and as such becoming a sort of moral defender in Brazil's Congress (de Souza Santos 2023). What Carpenedo's chapter in this volume elucidates is the 'strategic level spiritual warfare' that took shape in the narratives of Pentecostal believers:

> By identifying Jair Bolsonaro as the candidate aligned with biblical values and Lula as the representative of evil forces, evangelical Pentecostal pastors, influencers and politicians understood the 2022 Brazil elections as a spiritual battlefield.

These narratives are put together by the author when she analyses a corpus of discourses and practices, including speeches by Michelle Bolsonaro, Jair Bolsonaro's wife.

Responding to the rumours spread about the electronic voting system, the Superior Electoral Court (Tribunal Superior Eleitoral, or TSE) decided to take measures to amplify the transparency of the voting and counting process. Among other things they created, in 2021, an external committee consisting of members of various state and civil organisations, including lawmakers, academics, law enforcement agents and members of the armed forces. In inviting them to this collegiate body, the judges made a gesture of goodwill in the hope that the participation of external observers – especially members of the armed forces – would appease rumours and restore trust in the electoral system. In reality, the rumours not only continued but increased.

Indeed, in what was generally seen as a partisan approach in favour of President Bolsonaro, members of the armed forces intentionally and publicly attempted to discredit the voting system further and to question its reliability. Their position even raised concerns and generated disagreement within the armed forces themselves. For example, General Francisco Mamede de Brito Filho spoke of a 'mistake' which began with the TSE's invitation and was extended by its acceptance: 'It is not the Armed Forces' role to overview the electoral process', he affirmed (Godoy 2022). Whether or not the invitation was a mistake is hard to establish – if only because the role of members of the armed forces in destabilising democratic institutions was but one of many authoritarian expressions that (re)surfaced in recent years. What is understood, however, is that the intentional spread of baseless rumours that delegitimise democratic norms and institutions is unlikely to recede or to lose its appeal because of actions taken to debunk them.

In his chapter, Aaron Ansell explores the ways in which the logic of municipal politics shapes Piauienses's perceptions of national scale politicians. Drawing on some 36 months of ethnographic fieldwork in rural Piauí state since 2003, he analyses how a local patronal model of self-governance and its authoritarian aspects, which rely on principles of (patriarchal) family hierarchy, shapes how corruption is understood in rural Piauí. In the context Ansell discusses, ideology is far less important than morality. A perception of being 'present' and providing for 'the people' can make or break a politician's popularity. Indeed, the idea of 'abandonment' by a politician is more likely to direct voters towards a different candidate – perceived as more caring – than is their involvement in a kickback scheme. This folk model of corruption explains the ambivalence felt by rural Piauienses towards former president Jair Bolsonaro amid their overwhelmingly positive regard for President Lula. While Lula appears among Ansell's interlocutors as a morally upright patronal leader, the case of Bolsonaro is more complex: depending on how Piauienses apply local ideas of corruption and moral governance, Bolsonaro appears to epitomise either corruption or its opposite. Moral values supported by Bolsonaro, the idea of 'functional' heteronormative families, made him a 'good citizen'. At the same time Lula was viewed as a caring, 'present father' whose policies put food on the table. Ansell's findings importantly complexify notions of what being a 'good' politician means, bringing moral politics to the forefront.

Conducting research with politicians in urban Pernambuco state during the pandemic, Flávio Eiró also explores moral dimensions of municipal and state-level political interactions. His chapter shows how his interlocutors – municipal and state-level candidates and their staff – navigated the tension between being idealists who work towards collective benefits and being *prestadores de serviço*, providers of direct favours to individual voters. Looking at politicians' narratives, the author demonstrates how the image of the state as a provider of services is central to their perceptions of low-income voters' engagement with electoral politics. In doing so, Eiró sheds light on morally charged perceptions against such voters, often viewed as apolitical, self-interested, naive or and even as ignorant. In an open dialogue with

Ansell's findings in this volume, Eiró's chapter contributes to the understanding of the 2022 elections, marked by the contest between a 'good citizen Bolsonaro' and a 'good citizen Lula', which in the case of Bolsonaro meant branding himself as a traditional – read heteronormative, Christian, with an 'uncompromising and heavy-handed moralism', as Ansell put it – man and 'good citizen' Lula, who provided something to those who need most: food and the fight against hunger, which were strongly associated with Lula's image. While many see the 2018 election of Bolsonaro as a radical break from past elections, Eiró shows that it was actually not that novel, at least not in terms of municipal and state elections – with the exception that poor voters were seen as increasingly turning away from established forms of trust building.

## Democracy, authoritarianism, exceptionalism

Many Brazilians who voted for Bolsonaro expected that his pre-electoral radicalism would not be reflected in his government – or at least not to the same degree. This supports the findings of Almeida and Guarnieri (2020), who observed that the vast majority of their interviewees had a shared respect for democracy and that their vote for Bolsonaro was rather exceptional – justified, in their view – during periods of perceived generalised crises. Their findings are also in line with the 2020 Latinobarómetro survey: 35.2 per cent of Brazilians interviewed agreed that democracy is the best system of government, while 58.9 per cent said that under no circumstances would they support a military government. Nonetheless, 52.5 per cent agreed or strongly agreed with the statement that they would not mind if a non-democratic government came to power if it were able 'to solve the problems', while 37.9 per cent agreed or strongly agreed that the president could control the media 'in case of difficulties'. So while radical populist electoral promises may not always be taken at face value by voters, expecting further moderation after the election, segments of the population believe that authoritarianism may be justified if understood as able to bring about solutions, or if it serves a specific purpose which they consider important.

Recent publications bringing insights from different parts of the world have stressed the key influence leaders have in shifting public opinion on democratic institutions and norms, and even on perceptions of democracy as a whole. Comparatively analysing public opinion survey data from European countries, for instance, Larry M. Bartels (2023) argues that it is political elites – not citizens – who are the major moving force in democratic politics. Discussing country-specific examples, Bartels shows that social factors and political leadership (and the degree to which they adhere to democratic norms) played a far more central role than the actual existence of given crises in influencing public opinion, one way or another. To put it another way, if democratically elected leaders chose to implement authoritarian agendas and bring about anti-democratic shifts, as happened paradigmatically in Hungary and Poland, these were usually gradual changes of which citizens typically did not directly approve but were prepared to tolerate when their subjective perception of wellbeing – especially vis-à-vis the economy – was rather positive.

Once instituted in power, a would-be authoritarian leader has many opportunities to set in motion a process of democratic erosion. As Steven Levitsky and Daniel Ziblatt (2018) have argued, this process begins by ignoring a series of 'soft' and 'informal norms' of democracy, which necessarily yet tacitly accompany laws and constitutions, inflicting potentially long-lasting blows to a country's democratic institutions (Hatzikidi and Dullo 2021, 4–10). This process of 'mining' democracy from within may include attacking and delegitimating independent press and branches of state power, such as legislative and judicial authorities, or the appointment of loyalists at key positions of state bureaucracy. Besides directly attacking and undermining democratic institutions, another way their gradual erosion can be achieved is by creating 'parallel' institutions that have a similar function to the existing ones, but are created separately to function under strict control by the government.

Pérez Hernáiz (2008, 973) describes how during the Chávez administrations, an 'alternative "revolutionary" parallel system' was created that the government could 'closely control economically and ideologically' in order to bypass 'the hurdles of bureaucratic and institutional controls'. This practice bears resemblance to the 'parallel cabinet' (*gabinete paralelo*) which, as a congressional panel investigation showed, was informally created and stuffed with advisors sympathetic to the government's alt-scientific approach to the pandemic who were working parallel to, and at some points against, the Ministry of Health (Senado Federal 2021).

Such practices create conditions where authoritarianism can prosper and consolidate itself. Authors in this volume have used different terms to describe such phenomena: Bersch, Lotta and Thomas, for example, speak of 'the aegis of authoritarian practices' under which the tension between bureaucratic autonomy and political control becomes a conflict which takes place outside the democratic rules. Also grappling with the notion of autonomy, Hatzikidi speaks of 'an infrastructure of authoritarian affordances', where loyalty and obedience took precedence over reflectiveness and resistance, conflating freedom with unregulated personal licence in the case of Prevent Senior. Carpenedo and Lehmann, on the other hand, speak of 'authoritarian political modalities' and 'authoritarian dispositions' respectively in their discussions of the ways religious beliefs and a conspiratorial imagination may influence the ways political phenomena are interpreted. With distinct foci of analysis, these four chapters understand nonetheless that specific dispositions produced propitious conditions for the emergence and strengthening of authoritarian attitudes, with direct social implications.

Much has been said, in recent years, of how authoritarian political expressions around the world have often taken a particularly populist direction. It is therefore appropriate to add here a brief reflection on 'populist authoritarianism'. To begin with, it is important to say that the two are distinct phenomena. In paying attention to both structural conditions and conjunctural opportunities, as this book does, it is also salient to consider that much like authoritarianism, which can be found in either end of the political spectrum, populism too does not have a predetermined ideological orientation.

Although the term is still debated among scholars of populism, there is relative consensus around a minimal definition that understands the phenomenon as a discursive and performative logic of political articulation, centring around the antagonistic frontier between 'the people' on the one hand and 'the elites', 'the system' or 'the establishment' on the other (see, for example, Laclau 2005; Ostiguy et al. 2021). The minimal definition argues that 'a populist politics is never exhausted by its populist dimension' (de Cleen and Stavrakakis 2019, 318) and encourages us to shift our attention instead to the articulation between populism and other dimensions of that politics (authoritarian, nationalist, and so on) without imposing theory-driven assumptions upon distinct and context-specific case studies (Katsambekis 2022; Hatzikidi 2023b). Moreover, it is important to recognise that populism is a gradational phenomenon and not one that simply is, or is not, present.

In sum, while populism may provide a discursive and performative mechanism of political articulation, it is not there where we should look for the ideological drives that inform specific political programmes, policies and actions. These are usually guided by ideas and political projects that precede their populist discursive articulation. As Molyneux and Osborne (2017, 17) have suggested, 'they key is not what populisms have in common … but how they play out at a political level'. At that level, they argue, 'there is more difference than commonality' between the different populist manifestations and if we can draw any broader assumptions, these have to do with a 'narrowed and curtailed' trust in liberal democracies (2017, 17). This is particularly the case when populism and authoritarianism meet. Purposefully inculcating distrust in democratic norms and institutions, as discussed already, and reducing the social and political world to two radically opposed camps, split between 'us' and 'them', 'good' and 'evil', authoritarian populism erodes trust in liberal democracies.

The case on which this book focuses is paradigmatic of this unhappy encounter: although Bolsonaro's populist politics were arguably circumstantial and opportunistic, his authoritarian inclinations were of long duration (Ichimaru and Cardoso 2020; Nobre 2020). While a populist performative and discursive style offers an appealing form of political articulation through the innovative uses of digital media and technologies, old core ideological components, with deep roots in Brazil's authoritarianism and militarism, are the key tenets of Bolsonaro's populism. It is to these that he repeatedly resorts in an effort to reinforce his understanding of democracy and popular rule.

As discussed already, and as some chapters in this volume explore in more detail, the spread of different conspiracy theories is another important part of Bolsonarismo's truth regime. Both conspiracy theories and populism offer simpler and sometimes redemptive solutions to complex social problems. Some of these problems may even be fictitious (Nunes 2020), but conspiratorial and populist narratives tap into pre-existing anxieties, which are often latent: 'present but not central, mundane but still worrisome, publicised but not politicised' (Curato 2016, 99). What such narratives do is call attention and lend urgency to those anxieties, bringing them to the forefront. However, because they are structured around an 'us' versus 'them' polarity, effectively erasing nuances and subtleties, the kinds of solutions they propose also tend to reduce the complexity of the problems they wish to tackle. Rodrigo Nunes has identified this feature as characteristic of the far right; the 'violent picture' it paints:

> at once recognis[es] that yes, we are facing an abyss, and fabulat[es] an abyss that is less traumatic than the one we actually face, as its causes and fixes, though painful, are comparatively simple. (Nunes 2020)

Or, as Michael Barkun had phrased it some years earlier:

> The conspiracy theorist's view is both frightening and reassuring. It is frightening because it magnifies the power of evil ... [yet] it is

reassuring, for it promises a world that is meaningful rather than arbitrary. Not only are events non-random, but the clear identification of evil gives the conspiracist a definable enemy against which to struggle. (Barkun 2013, 4)

## Dissent and resistance to authoritarianism

Political indignation marked the years prior to Bolsonaro's ascension to power. As discussed above, June 2013 is for some the foundation of Bolsonaro's march to the presidency. This month also saw the birth of a street movement that enabled Brazilians from different cities to claim better transportation – an agenda that soon became much more complex and all-encompassing, but which had in common a manifestation of political indignation. During Bolsonaro's administration the grievance agenda was no less intense; it started with mismanagement of the Covid-19 pandemic (discussed in this volume by Barberia, Moreira and Costa Rosa, and Hatzikidi), but also encompassed corruption scandals and deforestation, among other things. Rather than indignation being taken to the streets, however, a system of intimidation imposed by Bolsonaro's government was in place, as described by Bersch, Lotta and Thomas in this volume. In addition, amid a health crisis, street protests were far from materialising.

Social movement theory (Dahlum et al. 2019, 1495) states that political grievance is not enough for mobilisation, and what may lead to indignation (poverty, inequality, poor public service delivery, corruption) may also undermine the capacity and duration of any mobilisation that is achieved. Revolt is thus a fine balance between deprivation, as catalyst for social turmoil, and availability of opportunities to enable organisation. 'Protests of abundance' is how Mangonnet and Murillo (2020) refer to social movements in Argentina during the commodity cycle. De Souza Santos (2021) also unpacks social protests in the Brazilian city of Mariana by looking at the social and economic upturn of marginalised groups. Although June 2013 has not been referred to as a 'protest of abundance', it did happen when Brazil was just beginning to experience economic setbacks after a decade of growth. While economic losses were occurring, the expectations and possibilities brought on by the previous decade of fighting against poverty made social mobilisation possible. In addition, and despite a violent police force, famous for repressing protests with disproportional force, the PT party then in power was closely associated with its social movements' foundation and democratic vision.

When Bolsonaro won the election, however, the rise of the armed forces within the corridors of power, as well as positive messaging around the years of military dictatorship, sent out a clear note of repression.

Intimidation also took the form of political scrutiny. Bersch, Lotta and Thomas discuss in this volume how public servants had their social media as well as daily activities monitored. Simply doing their job was seen as a betrayal if not carried out in line with the ideological agenda of Bolsonaro's administration. No other example is as clear as the dismissal of Ricardo Galvão from the National Institute for Space Research (Instituto Nacional de Pesquisas Espaciais) when he released data on Amazon fires. Galvão was sacked from his job literally for doing his job (Phillips 2019).

When indignation faces intimidation, resistance must be seen through different lenses. Brazilian diplomats wrote an anonymous letter, published by the *Folha de São Paulo* newspaper, when Bolsonaro and the then Foreign Affairs Minister Ernesto Araújo declared their admiration for the country's last military dictatorship (*Folha de São Paulo* 2019). Diplomats, as public servants in Brazil, have a stable career. They enjoy tenured job security in a well-paid position. These economic advantages allow for political exposure (Cornwall and Shankland 2013), and yet diplomats were nonetheless among the groups that resisted with means other than exposure or verbal confrontation. When James Scott (1985) famously wrote about the weapons of the weak, his was a study about rural workers in Southeast Asia, not diplomats in Brazil. When we see Brazil's intellectual and economic elite resisting by using so-called weapons of the weak, such as non-verbal confrontation, procrastination and civil disobedience, what forms of resistance are available for those in the lowest income strata?

Avoiding dispute over social and economic boundaries – well-known in Brazil as 'knowing one's place' – is both a mechanism of defence against discrimination (Sheriff 2001; Schofield et al. 2016, 3057) and of shunning conflict, especially when people are in positions of economic vulnerability (de Souza Santos 2019). Political intimidation was a common feature of Bolsonaro's administration (Bersch, Lotta and Thomas, this volume). In addition, poverty is a recognised form of political oppression (Scott 1985; Goldstein 2003), and Brazil's population lost purchasing power between 2018 and 2022 (Ferrari Filho and Terra 2023). Publicly voicing misgivings against the state, for those who rely on it, is not a resource always available. Such a situation is acknowledged in Brazilian political anthropology by the saying 'those who command do so because they can, those who obey do so because they are sensible' (Goldman 2013; de Souza Santos 2019). The saying implies the degree of reservation that comes when making enemies can have a strong impact on economic survival (Rebhun 1999).

The mechanisms of claiming rights often happen in silence, such as quietly voting, rather than through open confrontation. This is what happened in October 2022. What Bolsonaro called 'DataPovo', alluding to the famous survey company called DataFolha, referred to Brazilians who dressed in green and yellow to vote. According to his visual survey, he was leading the electoral race. However, many Brazilians did not feel comfortable publicly expressing their vote against those in power, preferring instead to wear neutral colours on election days. Lula went on to win the election, albeit by a slim margin, despite the strong predominance of green and yellow (the colours of the Brazilian flag, used almost exclusively by Bolsonaro's followers) on election days.

This is not to say there was no visual resistance or protest (such as people wearing red shirts on election days or during street protests) during Bolsonaro's administration. However, in a country famous for social mobilisations, the degree of intimidation – whether through political scrutiny, police violence or the limitations brought about by the health crisis – halted the ability to mobilise and sustain mobilisation despite the shared grievances. A general sense of loss in Brazil included a high number of deaths due to mismanagement of the Covid-19 pandemic, freezes or cuts to social programmes and loss of consumption power, to name but a few. But a grievance agenda alone is not enough to mobilise publicly.

For good historical reasons, the poor expect less from the ruling classes. In addition, they often lack the conditions (permanent employment, self-sufficient income, a degree of anonymity) to mobilise. Emotions such as indignation or resignation are thus not purely individual, but a response to social, demographic and political arrangements. Indignation, fear, hope and nostalgia are all collective sentiments that may be exploited politically. Writing on participatory politics in Porto Alegre, Junge (2014) discussed how envy demotivated community leaders who felt over-exposed to the energy of others when taking prominent roles in the community. Their material goods were disclosed in the vicinity, attracting the evil eye and affecting their willingness to remain in politics. Such exposure in the public eye also puts individuals in danger of violence in situations where criminal incidence is high (Silva 2007). However, resources that provide 'strategic leverage and that enable sustained collective action' (Dahlum et al. 2019, 1495) among the poor do exist to an extent. Secret voting is one of these resources.

Economic barriers, such as a lack of formal contracts or unions that historically enabled workers to mobilise (Holland 2018), have not yet disrupted democracy – at least not when that is understood as electoral competition. What requires further examination, to be dissected by the chapters that follow, is how on a day-to-day basis Brazilians encounter and resist a pervasive authoritarianism that has taken shape in virtual scrutiny, daily interactions and economic intimidation, among other forms.

Confronting those in power during Bolsonaro's administration was thus chiefly a privilege often connected to cultural and economic capital (Cornwall and Shankland 2013), and was especially seen among ministers of the Supreme Court. During the Covid-19 pandemic many of the arbitrary initiatives set up by the president's discretionary actions – a president who himself denied the severity of the pandemic and the need to curb social interactions – were quickly overruled by the Supreme Court, which empowered mayors and governors to pass lockdown decrees despite the president's denialism.

As well as the Supreme Court, Congress and local and regional administrations also curbed the president's discretionary powers. For example, in addition to the Supreme Court's decision that local governments have the autonomy to determine non-pharmaceutical interventions during the pandemic, Congress overruled Bolsonaro's veto against the compulsory use of masks in schools, churches and shops, pressuring him instead to pass a decision in favour of an emergency aid payment for members of certain socio-economic groups. Furthermore, the majority of mayors and governors ignored a presidential decree which stated that hair salons, barber's shops, gyms and churches should be among the 'essential services' able to remain open during the pandemic. The president was also repeatedly fined for flouting local health regulations and encountered staunch resistance from national health agencies and research institutes, such as Butantan and Anvisa.

Such efforts attest to the assertion frequently repeated by Supreme Court Justices that, despite the serious challenges faced, Brazilian institutions continued to function properly (*as instituições funcionam*). What requires further examination is whether the functioning of these institutions is sufficient to sustain democracy when public servants, and society at large, remain intimidated.

Finally, the moment at which we write this book matters: this is the end of Bolsonaro's administration, but it is not the end of authoritarian disruptions in Brazil. The composition of Brazil's Congress in the aftermath of the 2022 national elections, with its conservative majority, has showed the degree of continuation, not disruption, of democratic fissures in the country following Bolsonaro's electoral defeat. That said, Lula is famous for forming governing majorities through coalitions. His power to bring political adversaries together was evident not only in the formation of his cabinet – which included Marina Silva as Minister of the Environment and Climate Change, who had departed from the PT party and was Dilma's contender in 2010 – but also in what took place when the fateful 8 January storming of Brasília's Three Powers Plaza occurred. On that day, when Bolsonaro supporters vandalised Brazil's Houses of Congress, the Supreme Court and the Presidential Palace, Lula, in response, brought together governors from across Brazil and the political spectrum in support of democracy and institutions.

Democracy, threats to it and resistance to authoritarianism remain on the frontline in Brazil's long route to democratic consolidation. Looking beyond political disputes and into civil society at large, the role of authoritarianism needs to gain sophistication when examining the consequences and results of Bolsonaro in power, together with a regime of misinformation and health crisis. One example of what this combination can create in civil society is the rise in popularity of military careers in Brazil (de Souza Santos et al. 2025). What we see is that both conservative attitudes and views, as well as the search for better economic opportunities (scarcer among young people since the pandemic and cuts on education), have led to a favourable attitude towards military careers. Occupational socialisation may also make young people in the armed forces and the police more inclined to support authoritarian tendencies, structured as these organisations are around the values of hierarchy and discipline.

Authoritarianism may thus resist not only through electoral disputes, policies and regimes of misinformation, but also in the form of economic precarity. This in turn can lead to reduced possibilities for contestation, or a greater likelihood for young people to embark on military careers, which are still abundant in the country and were on the rise during Bolsonaro's administration. This book is thus an invitation to study democracy and its contestations from both above and below, from the perspective of its global networks and political elites, as well the everyday struggles in ordinary society.

The chapter contributions that follow highlight case studies in Brazil during Bolsonaro's administration (2018–2022) and the period immediately preceding it to engage with the social, economic and political changes in Brazil's recent history. From the perspective of the State, the voters or the politicians, the book shows how conservative, religious, internationally networked forces were catalysts for a right-wing authoritarian government in 2018–2022, and illustrates the strategies of resistance that co-existed during those years leading up to Lula's election in 2022.

## References

Abranches, S. et al. 2019. *Democracia em risco? 22 ensaios sobre o Brasil hoje*. São Paulo: Companhia das Letras.
Almeida, M. H. T. and F. H. Guarnieri. 2020. 'The unlikely president: The populist captain and his voter', *Revista Euro Latinoamericana de Análisis Social y Político* 1(1): 139–59.
Arias, J. 2021. 'Bolsonaro tira a mascara e diz que não gosta da democracia', *El País*. 21 February 2021. Available at https://brasil.elpais.com/brasil/2021-02-22/bolsonaro-tira-a-mascara-e-diz-que-nao-gosta-da-democracia.html. Accessed: 28 June 2024.
Arruti, J. M. and T. Held. 2021. 'Denied recognition: Threats against the rights of quilombola communities'. In *A Horizon of (Im)possibilities: A chronicle of Brazil's conservative turn*, edited by K. Hatzikidi and E. Dullo, 57–80. London: University of London Press.
Avritzer, L. 2018. 'O pêndulo da democracia no Brasil: Uma análise da crise 2013–2018', *Novos Estudos Cebrap* 37(2): 273–89. https://doi.org/10.25091/S01013300201800020006.
Barkun, M. 2013. *A Culture of Conspiracy: Apocalyptic visions in contemporary America*. Berkeley, CA: University of California Press.
Bartels, L. M. 2023. *Democracy Erodes from the Top: Leaders, citizens and the challenge of populism in Europe*. Princeton, NJ and Oxford: Princeton University Press.
Bianchi, B., J. Chaloub, P. Rangel and O. Wolf (eds). 2021. *Democracy and Brazil: Collapse and regression*. New York: Routledge.
Biroli, F. 2019. 'A reação contra o gênero e a democracia', *Nueva Sociedad*, December issue, 76–87.
Butter, M. 2020. *The Nature of Conspiracy Theories*, translated by Sharon Howe. Cambridge and Medford: Polity Press.
Camargo, A. et al. 1982. *A revolução de 30*. Seminário internacional realizado pelo Centro de Pesquisa e Documentação de História Contemporânea da Fundação Getúlio Vargas. Brasília: Editora UnB.
Carone, E. 1976. *O Estado Novo (1937–1945)*. Rio de Janeiro: Difel.
Chirio, M. 2018. *Politics in Uniform: Military officers and dictatorship in Brazil, 1960–1980*. Pittsburgh, PA: University of Pittsburgh Press.
Conectas. 2022. 'What international observers said about the first round of elections in Brazil', 20 October 2022. Available at www.conectas.org/en/noticias/what-international-observers-said-about-the-first-round-of-elections-in-brazil/. Accessed: 28 June 2024.
Cornwall, A. and A. Shankland. 2013. 'Cultures of politics, spaces of power: Contextualizing Brazilian experiences of participation', *Journal of Political Power* 6(2): 309–33. https://doi.org/10.1080/2158379X.2013.811859.
Curato, N. 2016. 'Politics of anxiety, politics of hope: Penal populism and Duterte's rise to power', *Journal of Current Southeast Asian Affairs* 35(3): 91–109. https://doi.org/10.1177/186810341603500305.
Dahlum, S., C. H. Knutsen and T. Wig. 2019. 'Who revolts? Empirically revisiting the Social origins of democracy', *The Journal of Politics* 81(4): 1494–9. https://doi.org/10.1086/704699.
de Cleen, B. and Stavrakakis, Y. 2019. 'How should we analyse the connections between populism and nationalism: A response to Rogers Brubaker', *Nations and Nationalism* 26(2): 314–22. https://doi.org/10.1111/nana.12575.
de Souza Santos, A. A. 2019. *The Politics of Memory: Urban cultural heritage in Brazil*. New York and London: Rowman & Littlefield Publishers.
de Souza Santos, A. A. 2021. 'From participation to silence: Grassroots politics in contemporary Brazil'. In *A Horizon of (Im)possibilities: A chronicle of Brazil's conservative turn*, edited by K. Hatzikidi and E. Dullo, 141–58. London: University of London Press.

de Souza Santos, A. A. 2023. '"In the name of the family": The evangelical caucus and rights rollbacks in Brazil'. In *The Right against Rights in Latin America*, edited by L. A. Payne et al., 112–28. Oxford: Oxford University Press.

de Souza Santos, A. A., et al. 2021. 'Dataset on SARS-CoV-2 non-pharmaceutical interventions in Brazilian municipalities', *Scientific Data* 8(73): 1–6. https://doi.org/10.1038/s41597-021-00 859-1.

de Souza Santos, A. A. et al. 2025. '"Becoming or getting by": Youths' inclination to join a military career in times of crisis in Brazil'. Forthcoming.

Della Coletta, R. 2020. 'Bolsonaro se refere a aniversário do golpe de 64 como "dia da liberdade"', *Folha de São Paulo*, 31 March 2020. Available at www1.folha.uol.com.br/poder/2020/03/ bolsonaro-se-refere-a-aniversario-do-golpe-de-64-como-dia-da-liberdade.shtml. Accessed: 28 June 2024.

Dullo, E. 2021. 'A political ritual without closure: Serial liminality and the escalation of conflict in Brazil's street demonstrations', *Bulletin of Latin American Research* 41(5): 695–709. https:// doi.org/10.1111/blar.13236.

Fassin, D. 2018. *The Will to Punish*. Oxford: Oxford University Press.

Ferrari Filho, F. and F. H. B. Terra. 2023. 'The political economy of Bolsonaro's government (2019–2022) and Lula da Silva's third term (2023–2026)', *Investigación Económica* 82(324): 27–50. https://doi.org/10.22201/fe.01851667p.2023.324.84246.

Ferreira, J. and Neves Delgado, L. d. A. 2018. 'Apresentação'. In *O tempo da Nova República: Da transição democrática à crise política de 2016. Quinta República (1985–2016)*, edited by J. Ferreira and L. d. A. Neves Delgado. Rio de Janeiro: Civilização Brasileira.

Folha de Sao Paulo. 2019. 'Carta apócrifa de diplomatas critica posição de Bolsonaro sobre ditadura'. Available at www1.folha.uol.com.br/mundo/2019/04/diplomatas-divulgam-carta-apocrifa-com-critica-a-posicao-de-bolsonaro-sobre-ditadura.shtml. Accessed: 28 June 2024.

Foucault, M. 1984. 'Truth and power'. In *The Foucault Reader*, edited by P. Rabinow, 51–75. New York: Pantheon Books.

Foucault, M. 2014. 'Lecture five: 6 February 1980'. In *On the Government of the Living: Lectures at the Collège De France 1979–1980*, edited by M. Senellart, F. Ewald and A. Fontana. Translated from the French by G. Burchell and edited by A. I. Davidson, 93–113. New York: Palgrave Macmillan.

G1. 2018. 'Bolsonaro diz: "Não aceito resultado das eleições diferente da minha eleição"', *O Globo*, 28 September 2018. Available at https://g1.globo.com/sp/sao-paulo/eleicoes/2018/noti cia/2018/09/28/bolsonaro-diz-que-nao-aceitara-resultado-diferente-do-que-seja-a-minha-el eicao.ghtml. Accessed: 28 June 2024.

Gess, N. 2022. 'Half-truths: On an instrument of post-truth politics (and conspiracy narratives)'. In *Plots: Literary form and conspiracy culture*, edited by B. Carver, D. Cracium and T. Hristov, 164–78. London and New York: Routledge.

Gielow, I. 2020. 'Golpe de 64 é "marco para a democracia brasileira", diz Defesa', *Folha de São Paulo*, 30 March 2020.

Godoy, M. 2022. 'Urnas eletrônicas: Ministério da Defesa prepara novo documento para rebater TSE', *O Estado de São Paulo*, 6 June 2022. Available at www.estadao.com.br/politica/marcelo-godoy/urnas-eletronicas-ministerio-da-defesa-prepara-novo-documento-para-rebater-tse/. Accessed: 28 June 2024.

Goldman, M. 2013. *How Democracy Works: An ethnographic theory of politics*. Canon Pyon, Herefordshire: Sean Kingston Publishing.

Goldstein, D. M. 2003. *Laughter out of Place*: Race, clase, violence and sexuality in a Rio shantytown. Berkeley, CA: University of California Press.

Gomes, A. d. C. 2010. 'Estado Novo: Ambiguidades e heranças do autoritarismo no Brasil'. In *A construção social dos regimes autoritários* [2], edited by D. Rollemberg and S. Quadrat, 38–45. Rio de Janeiro: Civilização Brasileira.

Gomes, A. d. C. 2014. 'O Estado Novo e o debate sobre o populismo no Brasil', *Sinais Sociais* 9(25): 9–37.

Gugliano, M. 2020. 'Vou intervir! O dia em que Bolsonaro decidiu mandar tropas para o Supremo', *Revista Piauí*. Available at https://piaui.folha.uol.com.br/materia/vou-intervir/. Accessed: 28 June 2024.

Hatzikidi, K. 2023a. '"The communavirus is here": Anti-communist conspiracy theories in Brazil's response to the Covid-19 pandemic'. In *Covid Conspiracy Theories in Global Perspectives*, edited by M. Butter and P. Knight, 366–78. London and New York: Routledge.

Hatzikidi, K. 2023b. 'Populisms in power: Plural and ambiguous'. In *Right Wing Populism in Latin America and Beyond*, edited by A. Pereira, 50–67. London and New York: Routledge.

Hatzikidi, K. and E. Dullo. 2021. 'Introduction: Brazil's conservative return'. In *A Horizon of (Im)possibilities: A chronicle of Brazil's conservative turn*, edited by K. Hatzikidi and E. Dullo, 1–33. London: University of London Press.

Holland, A. C. 2018. 'Diminished expectations: Redistributive preferences in truncated welfare states', *World Politics* 70(4): 555–94. https://doi.org/10.1017/S0043887118000096.

Hunter, W. and Power, T. 2019. 'Bolsonaro and Brazil's illiberal backlash', *Journal of Democracy* 30(1): 68–82. https://doi.org/10.1353/jod.2019.0005.

Ichimaru, M. and S. Cardoso. 2020. 'O bolsonarismo e o populismo: Bolsonaro populista?', *Revista Rosa* 2. Available at https://revistarosa.com/2/o-populismo-e-o-bolsonarismo. Accessed: 28 June 2024.

*Jornal Nacional*. 2022. 'PRF não tem mais aulas de direitos humanos no curso de formação', *O Globo*, 27 May 2022. Available at https://g1.globo.com/jornal-nacional/noticia/2022/05/27/prf-nao-tem-mais-aulas-de-direitos-humanos-no-curso-de-formacao.ghtml. Accessed: 28 June 2024.

Junge, B. 2014. '"The energy of others": Narratives of envy and purification among former grassroots community leaders in Porto Alegre, Brazil', *Latin American Research Review* 49(S1): 81–98. https://doi.org/10.1353/lar.2014.0058.

Katsambekis, G. 2022. 'Constructing "the people" of populism: A critique of the ideational approach from a discursive perspective', *Journal of Political Ideologies* 27(1): 53–74. https://doi.org/10.1080/13569317.2020.1844372.

Laclau, E. 2005. *On Populist Reason*. London: Verso.

Levitsky, S. and D. Ziblatt. 2018. *How Democracies Die*. New York: Crown.

Mangonnet, J. and M. V. Murillo. 2020. 'Protests of abundance: Distributive conflict over agricultural rents during the commodities boom in Argentina, 2003–2013', *Comparative Political Studies* 53(8): 1223–58. https://doi.org/10.1177/0010414019897417.

Medeiros, J. 1978. *Ideologia autoritária brasileira: 1930–1945*. Rio de Janeiro: FGV.

Molyneux, M. and T. Osborne. 2017. 'Populism: A deflationary view', *Economy and Society* 46(1): 1–19. https://doi.org/10.1080/03085147.2017.1308059.

Moore, A. 2018. 'On the democratic problem of conspiracy politics'. In *Conspiracy Theories and the People Who Believe in Them*, edited by J. E. Uscinski, 111–21. Oxford: Oxford University Press.

Moritz Schwarcz, L. 2019. *Sobre o autoritarismo brasileiro*. São Paulo: Companhia das Letras.

Moritz Schwarcz, L. 2021. 'The past of the present'. In *A Horizon of (Im)possibilities: A chronicle of Brazil's conservative turn*, edited by K. Hatzikidi and E. Dullo, 37–55. London: University of London Press.

Motta, R. 2022. 'PGR diz ao Supremo que não vê crime de Bolsonaro ao afirmar que TSE tem "sala secreta" para contar votos', *O Estado de São Paulo*, 6 June 2022. Available at: https://www.estadao.com.br/politica/blog-do-fausto-macedo/pgr-supremo-nao-ve-crime-bolsonaro-tse-sala-secreta-contagem-votos/. Accessed: 28 June 2024.

Muirhead, R. and N. Rosenblum. 2019. *A Lot of People Are Saying: The new conspiracism and the assault on democracy*. Princeton, NJ: Princeton University Press.

Müller, A. and F. Iegelski. 2018. 'O Brasil e o tempo presente'. In *O tempo da Nova República: Da transição democrática à crise política em 2016*. Quinta República (1985–2016), edited by J. Ferreira and L. d. A. Neves Delgado, 13–25. Rio de Janeiro: Civilização Brasileira.

Neiburg, F. and O. Ribeiro Thomaz. 2020. 'Ethnographic views of Brazil's (new) authoritarian turn', *HAU: Journal of Ethnographic Theory* 10(1): 7–11. https://doi.org/10.1086/708670.

Nobre, M. 2020. *Ponto final: A guerra de Bolsonaro contra a democracia*. São Paulo: Todavia.

Nunes, R. 2020. 'Are we in denial about denial?' *Public Books*, 25 November 2020. Available at www.publicbooks.org/are-we-in-denial-about-denial/. Accessed: 28 June 2024.

*O Globo*. 2021. 'Presença de militares em cargos civis mais que dobrou no governo Bolsonaro', *O Globo*, 27 June 2021. Available at https://oglobo.globo.com/politica/presenca-de-militares-em-cargos-civis-mais-que-dobrou-no-governo-bolsonaro-25079165. Accessed: 28 June 2024.

Ostiguy, P., F. Panizza and B. Moffitt. 2021. 'Introduction'. In *Populism in Global Perspective: A performative and discursive approach*, edited by P. Ostiguy, F. Panizza and B. Moffit, 1–18. London and New York: Routledge.

Payne, L. A. and de Souza Santos, A. A. 2020. 'The right-wing backlash in Brazil and beyond', *Politics & Gender* 16(1): 32–8. https://doi.org/10.1017/S1743923X20000057.

Pérez Hernáiz, H. A. 2008. 'The uses of conspiracy theories for the construction of a political religion in Venezuela', *International Journal of Humanities and Social Sciences* 2(8): 970–81.

Phillips, D. 2019. 'Brazil space institution director sacked in Amazon deforestation row', *The Guardian*, 2 August 2019. Available at https://www.theguardian.com/world/2019/aug/02/brazil-space-institute-director-sacked-in-amazon-deforestation-row. Accessed: 28 June 2024.

Pinheiro-Machado, R. and L. Scalco. 2020. 'From hope to hate: The rise of conservative subjectivity in Brazil', *HAU: Journal of Ethnographic Theory* 10(1): 21–31. https://doi.org/10.1086/708627.

Radnitz, S. 2018. 'Why the powerful (in weak states) prefer conspiracy theories'. In *Conspiracy Theories and the People Who Believe in Them*, edited by J. E. Uscinski, 347–59. Oxford: Oxford University Press.

Rebhun, L. A. 1999. *The Heart is Unknown Country: Love in the changing economy of northeast Brazil*. Stanford, CA: Stanford University Press.

Rocha, C. 2021. 'From Orkut to Brasília: The origins of the New Brazilian Right'. In *A Horizon of (Im)possibilities: A chronicle of Brazil's conservative turn*, edited by K. Hatzikidi and E. Dullo, 81–101. London: University of London Press.

Rocha, C., E. Solano and J. Medeiros. 2021. *The Bolsonaro Paradox: The public sphere and right-wing counterpublicity in contemporary Brazil*. Cham, Switzerland: Springer.

Saad-Filho, A. 2020. 'Varieties of neoliberalism in Brazil (2003–2019)', *Latin American Perspectives* 47(1): 9–27. https://doi.org/10.1177/0094582X19881968.

Schmidt, F. d. H. 2022. 'Presença de militares em cargos e funções comissionados do executivo federal', *Instituto de Pesquisa Econômica Aplicada (IPEA)*. Available at www.ipea.gov.br/portal/images/stories/PDFs/pubpreliminar/220530_publicacao_preliminar_presenca_de_militares_em_cargos.pdf. Accessed: 28 June 2024.

Schofield, P., J. Das-Munshi, L. Bécares, C. Morgan, V. Bhavsar, M. Hotopf and S. L. Hatch. 2016. 'Minority status and mental distress: A comparison of group density effects', *Psychological Medicine* 46(14): 3051–9. https://doi.org/10.1017/S0033291716001835.

Scott, J. C. 1985. *Weapons of the Weak: Everyday forms of peasant resistance*. New Haven, CT: Yale University Press.

Senado Federal [Federal Senate]. 2021. *Comissão Parlamentar de Inquérito (CPI) da Pandemia, Relatório Final*. Available at https://legis.senado.leg.br/comissoes/mnas?codcol=2441&tp=4. Accessed: 28 June 2024.

Sheriff, R. E. 2001. *Dreaming Equality: Color, race and racism in urban Brazil*. New Brunswick, NJ: Rutgers University Press.

Silva, R. A. C. D. 2007. 'Sobre lotes, lares e sonhos: estudo antropológico sobre cotidiano, trajetória social e ação política de moradores da Vila Batista Flores em Porto Alegre-RS'. Master's thesis. Porto Alegre: Universidade Federal do Rio Grande do Sul.

Solano, E. G., P. Ortellado and M. Moretto. 2017. '"Guerras culturais" e "populismo anti-petista" nas ruas de 2017', *Notas N.10*. Brasil: Friedrich Ebert Stiftung Brasil.

Souza, M. d. C. C. d. 1976. *Estado e partidos políticos no Brasil (2930–1964)*. São Paulo: Alfa-Omega.

Souza Lima, A. and C. Gonçalves Dias. 2020. 'Anthropology and the state in Brazil: Questions concerning a complex relationship', *Vibrant* 17: 1–21. https://doi.org/10.1590/1809-43412020v17d454.

Tribunal de Contas da União. 2020. *Memorando nº57/2020*. Available at www.conjur.com.br/dl/levantamento-tcu.pdf. Accessed: 28 June 2024.

# Part I
# National myth, international pariah?

# 2
# From Bolsonaro to Lula: theoretical and practical challenges in Brazilian politics

Marcos Nobre

Like many other countries which have experienced recent processes of democratisation or re-democratisation, Brazil requires the consideration of particular historical features typical of such a condition. First of all, Brazilian re-democratisation came about after 21 years of military dictatorship, which ended in 1985. The military regime left a legacy of hyperinflation and an external debt crisis. Hyperinflation has been controlled since 1994 on, using the so-called Plano Real of economic and political stabilisation. The debt crisis was overcome in the mid-2000s – a point at which Brazil passed from the position of debtor to that of creditor vis-à-vis the International Monetary Fund and accumulated a significant number of external reserves, denominated in US dollars.

The military regime also left at least two generations of authoritarians who did not disappear simply because democracy was restored. As we know all too well, dictatorships die hard. After the end of the military dictatorship, however, the authoritarian forces and impulses were scattered; they did not have a public face, much less a public organisation. Jair Bolsonaro not only brought a public face and a public organisation to authoritarian voters; he also won the presidency in 2018.

The second, and very important, historical feature is the coinciding of Brazilian re-democratisation with the rise of neoliberalism – a condition that the country only fully adapted to from the mid-1990s, by which time hyperinflation had been overcome. Such an adaptation in the middle of a transition to democracy has been extremely turbulent and difficult. The generation that led this transition has been formed under the country's previous development model, known as national-developmentalism. Initially the dominant line of thought was that it would be possible to return to this model, now in democratic conditions, and so to reconnect with the project interrupted by the military coup of 1964. This idea was abandoned in the late 1980s by some of these leading political figures, a move that eventually led to the adjustment of the mid-1990s.

Such major moves were possible because of a peculiar institutionalisation of democracy in Brazil, which was itself shaped by such moves. This constituted what eventually was understood as 'the system', in the terms that Bolsonaro won the 2018 presidential election, so to speak, as an 'anti-system' candidate. It is thus important to consider in more depth what 'system' means in Brazilian politics. This is the object of the first part of this chapter. It includes addressing the characterisation of the Brazilian political system both as a 'coalition presidentialism' and as an alternative characterisation, that of the *'pemedebismo'*, as well as analysing the significance of such an arrangement in the rise of Bolsonaro and *Bolsonarismo* more generally.

The second part of the chapter will address the question of the future of authoritarianism in Brazil – effectively the question of the future of *Bolsonarismo*, following the president's defeat in a bid for re-election in 2022 and his ineligibility until the 2030 elections, declared in June 2023. This means examining the differences between the 2018 and 2022 elections and analysing their consequences for the present landscape of Brazilian politics in comparison to other countries. It also means considering the requirements and conditions for isolating the far right in Brazil.

Some final remarks will follow, in which the argument will be summarised within the more general theme of the 'crisis of democracy'.

## Brazil's political system, 1994–2014

In the 'system', as it functioned in Brazil between 1994 and 2014, the vast majority of the parties formed a relatively indistinct mass of political machines – enclosed in the state in which they reproduce themselves and functioning as companies selling parliamentary support. With rare exceptions, all parties were always in the government, whatever its political complexion and whoever's candidacy they had supported in the presidential election.

For most of the time during these 20 years what was in place was a political management model, based on the formation of congressional supermajorities and, correspondingly, of super coalitions of government. One of the many consequences of this arrangement is that government and opposition had their roles respectively inflated and shrunk. On the one hand, there is a flagrant disproportion between the vote received by the presidential candidates and the total number of congressional and opposition parties in Congress. On the other hand, a 'swollen' government support base stimulated dissensions and fractures within the government itself.

During the years of the Plano Real arrangement, from 1994 to 2013, ministries, agencies and state agencies were at risk of fracturing government action. They had to cope with the explosive combination of party fragmentation and the establishment of congressional supermajorities and super coalitions of government noted above. The fragmentation of the political system tended not only to be inefficient; it also threatened to block the creation of a 'brand' of government to be used at the times of elections.

It was up to the condominium manager to confer a possible homogeneity on to this archipelago of interests, establishing cross-cutting agendas of government. This function of a manager of the government condominium was performed in this period by the Brazilian Social Democracy Party (PSDB) and the Workers' Party (PT), which served as opposing poles of agglutination and coordination. As most of their resources were placed in the cross-sectional organisation of the governments they led, these two leading parties had to 'outsource' the search for votes to other parties. Neither PT and PSDB were able to make congressional benches significantly larger each time and, at the same time, produce a functional government.

Since there were no cadres available to perform the two tasks at the same time, it was necessary to balance the two objectives. While this ensured that whoever ran the government could not impose themselves on all the other parties in the electoral dispute, using all the weight of the federal government for the benefit of their own party, the growing partisan fragmentation made the task of government coordination increasingly difficult.

## *'Pemedebismo'*: a form of democratic conservatism

I have proposed characterising this way of operating, which dominated the political system during Brazilian re-democratisation, as '*pemedebismo*' (Nobre 2013 and 2022). *Pemedebismo* proposes a critical appropriation of the results of empirical research guided by the dominant paradigm of 'coalition presidentialism',[1] in which some of the elements ignored by such a model nevertheless rise to the centre of the analysis. In so doing they allow us to ask questions that are usually absent, such as why are parliamentary supermajorities necessary for the functioning of democracy in Brazil? Why do the vast majority of the parties adhere to the government, whatever it is, and whoever the candidate they have supported in the presidential election may be?

*Pemedebismo* is a name derived from the Brazilian Democratic Movement Party (PMDB, currently MDB) because this party was an exemplary case of a governist party – independent of the government and independent of the presidential candidacy supported during the elections. Such a model is characterised by the formation of parliamentary supermajorities in support of the current government, whatever government this may be. Although driven by the broader social objective of understanding Brazilian conservatism, *pemedebismo* as a notion is limited to how the political system operates.

Such a mode of operation, democratic since 1985, may well be explained as a peculiar way of adapting to neoliberal requirements, as a means of democratically fighting social forces of transformation that seek to combat inequalities at a far more intense pace. At the same time it is a mode of operation of the political system that works in favour of an extremely slow pace of democratisation. These two characteristics constitute the core of the democratic conservatism represented by the *pemedebista* functioning of the political system, the specificity of Brazilian democratic conservatism.

This emphasis is necessary because democratic periods were effectively an exception in the republican history of the country. One should not be surprised, therefore, that this accent is not that of the classical interpretations of Brazil, mainly produced in an environment of more or less open authoritarianism. However, it is still symptomatic to note that the more general thread of conservatism present in these classical studies was not taken up in considerations of Brazilian democracy.

In my view, only such a characterisation of the functioning of the political system may account for what 'the system' effectively stood for in recent electoral disputes in Brazil, against which the 'anti-system' candidates presented themselves. The accurate characterisation of 'the system' becomes more decisive when it comes to explaining the specificity of Bolsonaro's election in 2018. More than a simple 'anti-system' leader, Bolsonaro considers himself to be the leader of a conservative revolt with authoritarian goals. He does not seek assimilation at the institutional level. For Bolsonaro, everyone who accepted the rules of the 1988 Constitution is 'left-wing'. The Constitution itself is 'left-wing', it is part of 'false democracy'. For Bolsonaro, re-democratisation is responsible for all the ills in the country. The 'true democracy' is the one that existed during the military dictatorship. Anyone who can understand the expression 'the democracy of the dictatorship was the true democracy' will be able to understand Bolsonaro.

In this context, it is important to emphasise that Bolsonaro's government from 2019 to 2022 cannot, and should not, be understood as comparable to all those who preceded it. *Pemedebismo* was occupied both from the right – with the Cardoso government (1995–2002) and with Michel Temer (2016–18), after a parliamentary coup that ousted President Dilma Rousseff – and from the left – with the governments led by PT (2003–16). Since Bolsonaro's government was the first since re-democratisation directly and concretely to threaten democracy as such, it represents *pemedebismo* taken to its limits.

*Pemedebismo* is certainly a form of conservatism, but it is crucially a *democratic* form of conservatism. Brazilian history in the twentieth century is largely marked by authoritarian governments and/or *coronelismo* – that is, by repressive regimes that block collective organisation and the struggles for rights. *Pemedebista* conservatism occurs, on the contrary, in a democratic environment, so that it is impossible to block the implementation of rights by force. The only way that remains is to control the speed of their effective implementation, carried out according to highly selective criteria. That is to say, to produce a slow pace of fighting inequalities and of the deepening of democracy itself (Nobre 2015). Since the Bolsonaro government represents the project of destroying democracy and implementing an authoritarian regime, it cannot be compared to the previously mentioned governments and regarded as 'just' another configuration of *pemedebismo*. This is why Bolsonaro's regime represents *pemedebismo* taken to its limits.

## The context of Bolsonaro's election

Be that as it may, the role played by the *pemedebista* logic of the political system in producing the conditions that led to the election of Jair Bolsonaro should not be underestimated. It is true that the Bolsonaro government represents an occupation of *pemedebismo* by the far right, *pemedebismo* taken to its limits. But what truly matters here is that the identification between the 'system' and the mode in which the political system organised itself between 1994 and 2014 was, in Bolsonaro's case, aimed at the destruction of democracy.

To understand the strategy and the tactics of Bolsonaro, it is necessary to take as a starting point the fact that in order for the conservative uprisings of the last decade – and the authoritarian strains they contain –to take over state power, they had to draw on real deficits. They deem any concept of a democracy that can effectively presuppose a shared set of rules of justice to be an outright falsity. According to this discourse, it is hypocritical to believe it possible to find a common basis for democratic dissent. This scheme of thought and action concludes that democracy is necessarily the neutralisation of those who do not belong to the winning social and political conservative electoral coalitions.

Democracy therefore becomes a weapon that an alliance of particular strata of the electorate openly points at the rest of the electorate, with no subterfuges. Conservative uprisings point to no possible reconstruction of shared rules of justice in internal connection with institutionalised democratic forms. Nor do they set their sights on a horizon based on the construction of an institution that has a universal character. They highlight the gap between the 'popular will' and the established mechanisms of political representation, but do not believe it is possible to overcome such a gap[2] – nor do they intend to attempt it.

Yet such conservative uprisings are based on social coalitions of convenience. They can only win elections and remain mobilised by making the institutional collapse that brought them together a long-lasting one. They use the same profound nature of democratic forms and their obsolescence to attain power, and employ the same exclusionary mechanisms they denounce to produce new models of exclusion. It is not by chance that the recent discussion on the 'crises of democracy' is full of references to the informal and implicit rules of formal-institutional functioning that had until very recently been pretty much ignored.[3]

Understanding Bolsonaro's general strategy requires an assumption that the foundations of the functioning of the political system in Brazil from 1994 to 2014 have collapsed, and that they have not been replaced by new ones. There has been no real reorganisation of the political system on a new basis, although some important changes have been ongoing in the last few years, as will be revealed in the second part of this chapter. The result was a permanent state of institutional collapse that, in the case of Brazil, emerged on the streets, both digital and physical, with the June 2013 uprisings.

By 'institutional collapse' I do not mean here the frequent topic of discussion in Brazil on whether the 'institutions are or are not working/functioning'. When, during the Covid-19 pandemic, comments such as the 'health system collapsed' were made, this did not mean that it was not 'working/functioning'. It meant rather that the health system was working beyond its capacity, so it was unable to perform as one would expect. It means that it continuing to function, but only in a dysfunctional way.

It is because of such a permanent state of institutional collapse that Bolsonaro was elected in the first place. His victory was the result of the collapse of Brazilian democratic institutions as established from 1985 on, most particularly after 1994. Bolsonaro thus needed institutional collapse to endure. That is why his way of doing politics is one of a permanent production of chaos. There is method in chaos. Or rather: chaos is the method.

Anyone or anything that opposes Bolsonaro's rule is labelled part of the 'system', of belonging to 'old politics'. Despite his known ties with figures from the organised crime in Rio de Janeiro, militias that recruit former police officers, Bolsonaro still convinces a large portion of the electorate that his far-right positions are in line with the defence of everything ethical and decent. The rest – the entire political system – is identified with 'the left', that is to say, with everything corrupt and corrupting of social life in general. Bolsonaro's strategy is to force whoever wants to oppose him to defend 'politics', to defend the existing institutions, even the 'system' itself.

## Governing against the system

Bolsonaro was an anti-system candidate in 2018 and he was an anti-system president from 2019 to 2022. This is despite the fact of him having reached an agreement with 'the system' when he thought that he would need protection against an impeachment, after the arrival in March 2020 of the Covid-19 pandemic in Brazil. One of the most impressive political operations Bolsonaro made was to convince his electorate that such an agreement with the *pemedebismo* of the political system was necessary for him to continue his war *against* the system. He just gave up governing in favour of congressional forces, negotiating not only his survival against impeachment but also his electoral survival for the 2022 election, when he lost to Lula by less than two per cent of the vote.

From 2020 on the Bolsonaro government actively cooperated with Congress to create a parallel, opaque budget controlled by Representatives and Senators that came to be called a 'secret budget'. In return, Congress not only did not impeach Bolsonaro, despite the many requests in this direction that were presented. It also approved items and programmes that allowed his candidacy to reach 2022 alive, in good enough shape to achieve a spot in the second round ballot of the presidential election. In addition, Congress guaranteed that no investigatory committees of government activities would be created. Nor would any interference be made with trusted men of the Attorney General's Office, the Federal Police and the Judiciary in a broader way, not only for Bolsonaro's own defence against charges, but in defence of members of his family.

In the logic of the new authoritarianism that arose in the 2010s, the first stage of an anti-democratic project through elections is mainly a destructive one: it is about ruining confidence in democratic institutions and transforming them from within, redefining their function to operate against their original purpose. It is only in the second stage – after re-election, after radical constitutional and institutional changes – that authoritarian projects are definitively established, gradually suppressing democratic institutions. Only then is the 'system' is declared 'defeated', with the new authoritarian government being instituted as 'an authentic representation of the true people'.

Unlike established electoral authoritarian regimes such as those of Hungary or Turkey, Bolsonaro's proto-authoritarian government from 2019 to 2022 was still in its infancy. It was indeed still seeking to establish its bases when it was hit by the pandemic crisis. When the Covid-19 pandemic arrived in Brazil, Bolsonaro's authoritarian plan, even if still very vague, was only in its first phase: that of dismantling democratic institutions. He counted on re-election in 2022 to move on to the next phase, the construction of the new Brazilian authoritarianism, whatever face it might assume.

However, he lost his bid for re-election in 2022. Furthermore, Bolsonaro has been declared ineligible to stand by Brazilian Electoral Justice in June 2023. The questions are now twofold. What will become of Bolsonaro and his authoritarian project? What are the challenges confronting the democratic field in Brazil?

## From 2018 to 2022

If we compare the present situation to the one of the 2018 election, there are some relevant differences to be highlighted. The first is that something now exists that may be called '*Bolsonarismo*'. In Brazil, the far right had been dispersed for more than 30 years after the end of the military dictatorship in 1985. It only gained face, organicity and federal power itself with Bolsonaro.

In countries such as France, Spain, Greece and Germany, after democracy was established or restored, the far right took decades to become relevant, to normalise itself and to learn how to maintain democratic appearances. In Brazil, however, all it took was a few years of political self-destruction since 2014. In one fell swoop Bolsonaro organised and normalised the far right and won the presidential election. With this, he also gained hegemony for the far right in the broader field of the right in Brazil.

The 2018 and 2022 elections produced a real division – beyond mere polarisation, as had been the case between 1994 and 2014. Polarisation means that the forces occupy the same magnetic field – but here we are referring to two different fields, political forces that are not disputing on the same ground. This type of division, effectively between two worlds, means that the same rules of the democratic game are no longer shared when conflicts need to be resolved. Those who lose elections do not recognise the legitimacy of new rulers, which is nevertheless an essential condition of democracy.

It is true that since Lula's electoral victory in October 2022, many internal divisions among the far right showed up. They are mainly of tactical nature, since the shared strategy continues to be that of establishing an authoritarian rule. The putschist ruck that hoped to start a coup on 8 January 2023 was in favour of an immediate break of the constitutional order. Other strands in the far right want to go for the impeachment of Lula. Other groups want to wait for the next presidential election.

It is also true that the 8 January ruck has been isolated and defeated. But this does not mean at all that authoritarianism has been isolated, much less defeated. Furthermore, Lula's government did not seize that opportunity to isolate the far right, which allowed them to rally and reorganise. Bolsonaro intends to remain the point of convergence of these different strands within the far right, even as he continues to look for maintaining the hegemony of the authoritarian project in the broader field of the right.

To achieve this, an important novelty of the general 2022 electoral strategy will be maintained – that of a mixture of digital and traditional political strategies used by the candidacies of *Bolsonarismo*. I would further suggest that this kind of arrangement will prevail from now on, not only in Brazil. In my view, the future of political organisations lies in the combination of traditional and digital players. It is with this combination that Bolsonaro will seek to maintain his hegemony over the broader right-wing camp, presenting himself both as the leader of the opposition and yet still hand-in-hand with traditional party organisations, in particular his current party, the Liberal Party (PL).

However, such a combination of digital and traditional players in politics does not mean that both strategies are always perfectly coordinated and in line with one another. This in turn means that Bolsonaro and *Bolsonarismo* do not intend fully to institutionalise, integrating themselves in traditional politics. In the 2022 campaign there were many places where these two lines of action conflicted – resulting in the victory of one or the other of the campaign strategies, of either digital or traditional politics. However, these conflicts only happened where at least two Bolsonarista candidacies were the best-placed in the electoral races.

More generally, the electoral results have improved considerably through such a combination of strategies. This was the case of important Brazilian states, for example, in which *Bolsonarista* candidates won something close to 60 per cent of the electorate at the level of State governments – especially the states that weigh the most in Brazil's economic and political life. *Bolsonarismo* also succeeded in securing an impressive number of congressional seats.

On the other hand, Lula won in an essentially traditional scheme, even if a decisive part of the electoral battles took place in the digital universe. This is a sign of the difference in scale regarding *Bolsonarismo* when we compare the elections of 2018 and 2022. Such a difference lies both in the fact that the presence and the mobilisation and organisational capacities of *Bolsonarismo* are incomparably greater today than in 2018, and in the fact that there is now a real *Bolsonarista* digital ecosystem. The latter has diversified a lot and is now financially self-sufficient – and this goes far beyond any illegal financing of electoral campaigns.

## Digital battles and the new configuration of the political system

Generally speaking, the 2022 election represented a consolidation of the hegemony of the far right over the broader field of the right. That is to say that Bolsonaro not only managed to maintain this hegemony when he was in the presidency, but that he also controls it even when removed from power. The major symbol of such consolidation is the very successful amalgam operated by *Bolsonarismo* between 'conservatism' and 'far-right'. On the other hand, everything seems to indicate that Lula will continue to operate mainly in a traditional analogue environment in which he won the election; this is the field that he knows how to play.

However, such a situation means that the dispute in the digital field tends to remain very unequal, strongly favouring the far right. As a result, although Lula's victory is certainly a huge relief for the democratic camp, this electoral victory is not yet social and political in the broadest sense of the word. Far from it. The central issue is not even whether or not *Bolsonarismo* will remain institutionalised in partisan terms as it is today. It rather involves the link between what I call the *Bolsonarista* Digital Party – not an official, institutionalised party – and institutions in the broad sense of the term. The *Bolsonarista* Digital Party, as well as the government team formed under Bolsonaro's tenure, have been hosted in states across the country ruled by *Bolsonaristas*.

Another relevant difference of the present situation vis-à-vis 2018 regards the logic of coalition building. The configuration of the political system in Brazil is quite different today from the one that prevailed from 1994 to 2014. I will briefly explore just two aspects of these changes here. Since 2017 there have been efforts to diminish one of *pemedebismo*'s most characteristic features, that of party fragmentation. With comings and goings, the discussion on electoral reforms dragged on until the Temer government when, in 2017, coalitions in proportional elections were banned, campaigning time was reduced and a barrier clause was introduced, due to increase with each election until 2030. By 2030 the minimum threshold shall be three per cent of the votes, with a minimum of two per cent in each federate entity, or with the election of 15 deputies over a minimum of nine different federate entities.

This electoral reform came along with another important change in party and election legislation. In 2015, in the course of the crisis of Dilma Rousseff's second term as president, the so-called 'imposable budget provisions' for individual parliamentary amendments were approved. From then on, two extensions of this practice were implemented. First, in June 2019, they were extended also to amendments made by state caucuses. In 2021 the extension was based on an unusual and original use of the long-existing practice of amendments made by the chairman of the budget committee to create what has been called a 'secret budget', amendments without a clear author and a known destination. Lula's government is committed to abolishing this practice. The move conferred a great deal of power to the *pemedebismo* of the political system, enabling it to negotiate with the Executive branch in far better conditions than ever before. This new bargaining structure has been reinforced by the 2015 Supreme Court's decision against the corporate financing of political campaigns – in that it allowed parties to pass a bill that skyrocketed the public financing of parties and electoral campaigns.

All this has already changed the dynamics of politics in Brazil, which will change much more over the coming years. Party fragmentation continues to be high despite the aforementioned electoral and party legislation reforms. But any government now faces new forms of coordination difficulty beyond party fragmentation. The power of both the Speaker of the House (Câmara dos Deputados) and the Federal Senate have increased enormously, for instance; both now negotiate the support of an important part of individual congressmen and congressional groups directly with the government (Testa 2023). The central conditions for the functioning of coalition presidentialism were undermined, a model previously characterised by the undisputed predominance of the Executive over the available resources.

The other complementary movement that undermined the foundations of coalition presidentialism, carried out during the Temer government, was the decline of the logic of the two organising poles of the political system. Temer's right-wing government was no longer subjected to the leadership of the right-wing pole of the system, the PSDB, nor did it take on the task for the president's own party, PMDB. This was the first experience of *pemedebismo* as a government – and not just in the government. It was during the Temer government that for the first time, or since 1994 at least, *pemedebismo* governed directly, with no intermediaries or transversal coordinators. It was also the first time Temer refused to be guided and decided to guide.

However, the programme implemented by the Temer government did not find resonance in the new social, economic and political alliance already being formed at that time. This grouping became the electoral alliance through which Bolsonaro ended up being elected in 2018. The Temer government was unable to suppress this movement of tectonic plates in Brazilian politics. The PSDB also failed in this task, which explains its decline as the pole party of the right.

The experiment of *pemedebismo* as a government continued during Bolsonaro's mandate. At first the Speaker of the House of Representatives, Rodrigo Maia, who also had this position during the Temer government, managed to operate as a kind of supplementary parliamentarism: in everything that was not of interest to the Bolsonaro government (almost everything), the Legislature continued as if it were still under the Temer government. With the arrival of the Covid-19 pandemic in the country, at the beginning of 2020, a new pattern of relationship between the Executive and Legislative branches was established.

## The new pattern of Brazilian politics

The new pattern was consolidated following the election of Arthur Lira to the presidency of the Chamber in February 2021. It was a matter of maintaining the functioning of the *pemedebismo* as a joint body that had already existed since the Temer government, but of adding even more power over the budget to it, as well as further concentrating legislative power in the Speakership of the House. In this model, the coalition contract is not negotiated on a party-by-party basis. There is a prior agreement by the Legislature on what will be the share and the responsibility of each political force, followed by a subsequent negotiation with the Executive as if the bargaining involved a single party.

In Lula's current third term, despite a government coalition that reaches 16 parties, not all of them govern, as they did under Temer or Bolsonaro. Many parties belong formally to the coalition, with correspondent appointments and funds, but aim at an alternative coalition to that of the current government for the 2026 elections. In particular, a triad of parties – Progressistas, União Brasil and Republicanos – intends to be the focal point of this alternative coalition to that of the Lula government, of whose coalition they currently form part.

This alternative coalition intends to represent the correlation of forces of the 2018 election, the model election for the new congressional political elite. The same social, economic and political coalition that the PSDB was unable to represent, the same coalition that came to power with Bolsonaro. It is a coalition whose social base is constituted by large shares of the agribusiness and extractivism, the evangelical electorate, the Armed Forces and police forces and segments of the financial market unhappy with the type of accommodation usually sought by large institutions in the sector.

It is in this larger context that the major political challenge of Brazil should be addressed. That is to say, the search for a method of isolating the far right, which currently dominates the camp of the right and therefore threatens Brazilian democracy permanently. That is why Lula's victory was not only important from a strictly Brazilian point of view – if such a thing exists, since the globalisation of politics has become an inescapable fact. Several countries have already carved out the path to authoritarianism through elections; many more may do so shortly.

It is true that the electoral success of the 'authoritarian international' that took shape in the 2010s, to which the victory of Bolsonaro in 2018 also belongs, coincided with an economic crisis paralleled only by the one that began in 1929. However, this should not underestimate the fact that such a wave of authoritarian victories mobilised real deficits in the way in which existing democracies worked. As William Scheuerman correctly stresses, there are important differences between those who stormed the Capitol in Washington DC on 6 January 2021 and previous authoritarians and authoritarianists. As he observes:

> Unlike many previous authoritarians, they remain committed to some measure of political competition, even as they work to destroy some of democracy's core traits. This crucial difference complicates the question of how best to respond to the challenges they pose. (Scheuerman 2023, 44)

## Final remarks

With the transformation of parties into parastatal entities, in hands of the state used to control society, the divorce between mobilisation and organisation was gradually established as a new, lasting characteristic of political systems. It is no coincidence that so many attempts to reform political institutions go through the reconstruction of parties as movements. As David Runciman (2018, 158) notes, 'the political parties that have been most successful in recent years are those that have become social movements'. In Brazil only the far right, under the leadership of Bolsonaro, has managed to make this move also in the digital arena. Runciman rightly remarks:

> [D]emocracy is not working well – if it were, there would be no populist backlash. But attempts to make it work better focus on what we feel we have lost rather than on what we have never even tried. Political arguments revolve around ideas of recovery and rescue – of the welfare state, the constitution, the economy, our security and our freedom. Each side wants to recapture something that has been taken away. (Runciman 2018, 56)

This makes us look the wrong way, no doubt. Runciman is correct. The whole issue today should be to focus 'on what we have never even tried' rather than around a return to models of democracy that have lost their social ballast, whatever such ballast may be thought to be.

In my view, this is why we should focus on digital parties and their re-shaping of political systems, for instance. That is why we should go back to thinking about the actual internal life of parties and engage with party theory, something that has been left behind for quite a while now (Gerbaudo 2019). This will be not achieved if some fundamental assumptions of much of the literature on the crisis of democracy are maintained – the same assumptions that also underlie the 'coalition presidentialism' paradigm in the case of Brazilian politics.

These assumptions may be also found in Runciman himself, in formulations such as 'Representative democracy longs for what it can't have' or 'Representative democracy cannot close the circle'.[4] The 'circle' cannot be closed because the fundamental theoretical premise already establishes that it cannot be closed. Such a mixing up between the crisis of democracy and certain theories of democracy is largely responsible for the consequence of putting the terms of the discussion as the alternative to returning to the previous mode of operation of institutional politics (even with some corrections), or of simply watching democracy die. Yet one of the aspects of greatest interest in Runciman's book is precisely that of showing the infeasibility of the democratic position in an alternative put in these terms.

This does not mean that Runciman is not right on many fronts. Party systems, now obsolete, see new forms of political organisation as competitors to be slaughtered, rather than as signs of a necessary and inevitable re-organisation. The survival tactic of these obsolete party systems is to try to reduce the problem to a choice between survival of the establishment or authoritarianism. In their struggle for survival, political systems built a solid strategy of blackmail: they merged with democratic rule. They operate according to the motto: if existing political systems go down, democracy goes down with them.

Much of what was seen in the 2011–13 cycle of global uprisings was a return to national states in search of solutions (Gerbaudo 2017). Political systems have so far taken advantage of this return of the state to the centre of the arena to ensure that only they can make the state itself continue to function democratically. And yet, with the widespread rejection of political systems as they used to work and as they still do, this perverse symbiosis has so far only resulted in creating the ideal fuel for far-right-led revolts. It is this state of affairs that needs to be overcome – and not only in Brazil.

## Acknowledgements

This chapter draws on the arguments of my 2022 book *Limits of Democracy: From the June 2013 uprisings in Brazil to the Bolsonaro government*. Cham, Switzerland: Springer.

## Notes

1 I have in view here seminal works such as the following: Abranches 1988, Limongi and Figueiredo 1998, Santos 2003, Melo e Pereira 2013.
2 Bernard Manin (2012 [1995]) famously showed that, in its genesis and historical development, representative government's antipode was not 'direct democracy', but rather 'democracy' *tout court*. The eventual compatibilisation between representative government and democratic rule should not obscure the fact that what appears today as a gap between popular will and representation should be thought of in far more complex terms.
3 Although present in the literature since at least the 1990s, the idea of informal rules gained momentum in the context of the current 'crisis of democracy' literature with *How Democracies Die* by Steven Levitsky and Daniel Ziblatt (2018).
4 Runciman (2018, 107). Müller (2016, 76) also starts from a very similar premise: 'the success of populism can be connected to what can be called unfulfilled promises of democracy and, in a sense, simply cannot be fulfilled in our societies'.

## References

Abranches, S. 1988. 'Presidencialismo de coalizão: O dilema institucional brasileiro', *Dados: Revista de Ciências Sociais* 31(1): 5–32.
Gerbaudo, P. 2017. *The Mask and the Flag: Populism, citizenism and global protest*. Oxford and New York: Oxford University Press.
Gerbaudo, P. 2019. *The Digital Party: Political organisation and online democracy*. London: Pluto Press.
Levitsky, S. and Ziblatt, D. 2018. *How Democracies Die*. New York: Crown.
Limongi, F. and A. Figueiredo. 1998. 'Bases institucionais do presidencialismo de coalizão', *Lua Nova: Revista de cultura e política* 44: 8–106. https://doi.org/10.1590/S0102-64451998000200005.
Manin, B. 2012 [1995]. *Principes du gouvernement représentatif*. Paris: Flammarion.
Melo, M. A. and Pereira, C. 2013. *Making Brazil Work: Checking the President in a multiparty system*. New York: Palgrave Macmillan.
Müller, J.-W. 2016. *What is Populism?* Philadelphia, PA: University of Pennsylvania Press.
Nobre, M. 2013. *Imobilismo em movimento. Da redemocratização ao governo Dilma*. São Paulo: Companhia das Letras.
Nobre, M. 2015. 'Conservadorismo em chave democrática. A redemocratização brasileira, 1979–2013'. In *1964: do golpe à democracia*, edited by A. Alonso and M. Dolhnikoff, 247–66. São Paulo: Hedra.
Nobre, M. 2022. *Limits of Democracy: From the June 2013 uprisings in Brazil to the Bolsonaro government*. Cham, Switzerland: Springer.
Przeworski, A. 2019. *Crises of Democracy*. Cambridge: Cambridge University Press.
Runciman, D. 2018. *How Democracy Ends*. New York: Basic Books.
Santos, F. 2003. *O poder legislativo no presidencialismo de coalizão*. Belo Horizonte: Editora UFMG.
Scheuerman, W. E. 2023. 'A not-very-new structural transformation of the public sphere', *Constellations* 30(1): 42–7. https://doi.org/10.1111/1467-8675.12665.
Testa, G. 2023. 'Fortalecimento do Legislativo ou centralização do poder? Governabilidade e a formação de base no Congresso Nacional (2019–2023)'. In *Governabilidade: instituições, atores e estratégias*, edited by H. Dantas, M. Fernandez and G. Testa, 57–81 [second edition]. Rio de Janeiro: Konrad Adenauer.

# 3
# The radical right in Brazil: part of a global family
Ariel Goldstein

## Introduction: the radical right in Latin America as part of a global family

In the last years, empowered by the connections that social media allowed, radical right manifestations around the world have morphed into a sort of 'global family' (Forti 2021). Such groups have developed an agenda that shares common issues and values. Some key points of this agenda encompass the defence of traditions and national identities against globalisation, advocating 'pro-life' policies that oppose abortion and emphasising the role of religion as a guiding force in the public sphere, in collaboration with conservative evangelical, Jewish and Catholic leaders. While there are indeed distinctions between the radical right movements in the Americas and Europe, certain points are shared, though not necessarily as formal agreements among various political factions. However, in recent years international gatherings such as the Foro Madrid and CPAC have broadened in scope, indicating a more cohesive and organised agenda among these parties.

Yet the internationalism of the far right is not a novelty. During the dictatorships of the Southern Cone in Latin America, Italian fascists such as Stefano Delle Chiaie, CIA agents like Michael Townley or Nazi war criminals such as Klaus Barbie participated in operations of repression and murder of political opponents throughout the region. The dictatorships were allied with the United States and the Condor operation for the persecution and killing of political opponents. This context was conducive to the strengthening of ties between far-right groups, formed from European fascist experiences that found in Latin America a place where they could continue their tasks and where their terrorist knowledge was valued. What is new is that the current far-right international meetings are openly endorsed, in contrast to past clandestine operations, such as Operation Condor, which were conducted in the shadows. Mudde (2019) has stated that the extreme right is anti-democratic and the radical right is democratic but not liberal. The most important characteristic of the radical right would be 'nativism', a combination of nationalism and xenophobia. It is an ideology that declares that states must be inhabited by their native members, believing that non-natives threaten the homogeneous constitution of the national state. Castelli Gattinara (2020) considers the distinction established by Mudde between 'radical right' and 'extreme right' to be important. The radical right exists within democracy, but in tension with liberalism. In contrast, the extreme right is outside of democracy, for example the Ku Klux Klan and other groups. However, in more recent years this distinction has been blurred. We have seen violent actions in the United States (2021) and Brazil (2023) organised and carried out against democratic institutions by radicalised right-wing groups.

Zanotti and Roberts (2021) consider Brazil and Chile, with Jair Bolsonaro and José Antonio Kast, to be the clearest manifestations of radical right leaders in Latin America. A key distinction between radical right groups in Latin America and Europe is the place of nativism. Although nativism is central in European radical right parties, in Latin America radical right ideas appear to be channelled more through the defence of colonialism, traditional family and neoliberalism (Raygada 2021). In Europe a 'welfare chauvinist' defence of the state role appears in cases such as the National Front (now National Rally) in France or the Law and Justice incumbent party in Poland, while radical right-wing options in Latin America are clearly aligned with neoliberal reforms and privatisation programmes. Where the Latin American right is limited in their offers of economic incentives to popular sectors, churches often provide a mass right-wing nucleus, aligned with conservative values and the defence of the 'traditional family'. There is an elective affinity (Weber 2012) between the conservative vision of the evangelical churches and the emerging forces of the radical right.

This chapter will explore the significance and consequences of Brazil's integration into the global family of the radical right under Jair Bolsonaro's administration (2019–22). It examines the networks established with radical right leaders and parties worldwide, including figures from the Republican Party in the United States, Fidesz in Hungary, Alternative for Germany, La Libertad Avanza in Argentina, Partido Republicano in Chile and Vox in Spain. Bolsonaro's controversial stance during the Covid-19 pandemic, particularly his opposition to scientific recommendations, also fostered closer ties with leaders such as Donald Trump.

The chapter will address key questions: How did these connections influence Brazil's traditional foreign policy? What contributions did the global radical right gain from Brazil's involvement? And who were the most significant allies of Bolsonaro's government within these networks? This chapter has two main aspects. The first analyses the influence of philosopher Olavo de Carvalho and his conspiracy theories on Bolsonaro's government. The second considers the links between the Brazilian radical right, in power during Bolsonaro's administration, in the context of their relationship with other leaders who shared similar views, notably Javier Milei, Santiago Abascal and José Antonio Kast.[1] An important factor in solidifying these links has been the 2021 meeting Brasil Profundo, which we explore at this section. Later in this chapter we reflect on possible outcomes after the end of Bolsonaro's government and the arrival of Lula's administration with a different political orientation. In particular we consider how the latter may act in a context marked by the definitions of the previous radical right administration.

## Olavo de Carvalho and the influence on foreign policy of *Brazilian Trumpers*

When the Bolsonaro administration began in 2019, it received the support of different leaders from the radical right. Prime Minister Benjamin Netanyahu, making the first visit of an Israeli premier to Brazil, and the Hungarian Prime Minister Viktor Orbán were among those present at Bolsonaro's inauguration. Both presences were unusual, but Netanyahu and Orbán were also representative of radical right positions in those countries. There was also a big convoy from the US, with the presence of Republican congressman Mark Green[2] and Trump's Secretary of State Mike Pompeo. The Republican Party under Trump's leadership has been a place where *Bolsonarismo* obtained partnerships.

When Bolsonaro arrived in government, the context offered great opportunities for the development of a radical right foreign policy, with Trump in the US and Netanyahu in Israel. There were strong relations between evangelical right-wing groups in Brazil and religious groups in Israel. Evangelical groups have been influential on foreign policy under Bolsonaro's government. Also enjoying great influence in that context was Yossy Shelley, a military and political ambassador sent to Israel by Netanyahu who participated on the Marcha para Jesus in 2019, the most important evangelical meeting in Brazil. In recent years Israel has been one of the most important allies of radical right governments in the world.

In addition, the Brazilian government was the last in Latin America to recognise Trump's defeat in 2020, one month after Biden's victory (Struck 2020).

During his visit to Washington in 2019, accompanied at a dinner by former Trump adviser Steve Bannon, Bolsonaro commented:

> What I always dreamed of was freeing Brazil from the nefarious ideology of the left. One of my great inspirers is sitting to my right, Professor Olavo de Carvalho. Great inspirer of many young people in Brazil. To a great extent we owe the revolution we are experiencing to him. (Poder 360, 2019)

On 24 January 2022 Olavo de Carvalho, the Brazilian self-proclaimed philosopher and former astrologer, passed away in Virginia in the United States. This former communist had turned into a famous visceral anti-communist, captivating students with his online philosophy courses. An admirer of Donald Trump, he predicted the decline of the West and was recognised by the radical right across the world. During the governments of the Workers' Party (PT) he decided to live in the United States, considering that his country had been invaded by 'communists'. The former Atlas Network president, Alejandro Chafuen, an Argentine-American resident, called him a philosopher with a following exceeding any Brazilian think tank.

An important part of Olavo's political activity was to spread conspiracy theories about the dominance of 'communism' at universities and in the media. Those ideas strengthened the ideological positions of the Brazilian radical right. According to those theories, a hegemony of the left exists on the main fronts of cultural ideas, propagated especially by universities and the media. These conspiracy theories started to gain traction from 2013 onwards, when journalists and right-wing politicians in Brazil started to share them. After the impeachment of Dilma Rousseff and the pro-market period of the right-wing government of Michel Temer came the arrival of Bolsonaro. During Bolsonaro's presidency Olavo proved an influential disseminator who managed to appoint important officials on Education and Foreign Affairs.

In his first live on Facebook as president-elect, Bolsonaro had shown himself with a copy of the Constitution, a Bible and Olavo's bestseller entitled *The Least You Need to Know not to be an Idiot*. After Olavo's death Bolsonaro decreed a day of national mourning to honour his memory with the message:

> Today one of the greatest thinkers in the history of our country leaves us ... A giant in the fight for freedom and a beacon for millions of Brazilians. His example and his teachings will mark us forever.

However, there was more. The influential X (formerly Twitter) account *Visegrad 24*, which defends the conservative European governments of the Visegrad Group – made up of Poland, Hungary, the Czech Republic and Slovakia – also celebrated Olavo after his death by quoting his phrases:

> Communism is not a great ideal that has been perverted. It is a perversion that has been sold as a great ideal. ... When a communist wants to slander someone, he does not have to invent crimes: he assigns him one of his own, and that's it.

Hermann Tertsch, one of the leaders in foreign policy of the radical right-wing Vox party in Spain, echoed this tribute, observing: 'How many truths Olavo de Carvalho has said in his life! He will be missed'. The global right, until a few years ago a space of heterogeneous and culturally divergent trajectories, seems suddenly to be finding common ground.

Filipe Martins, advisor of Bolsonaro in foreign policy, is a former student of the philosophy courses that Olavo de Carvalho gave. He sustained a vision against those he calls 'globalists' that represents a worldwide conspiracy theory. The diplomat Ernesto Araújo was part of this environment of ideas, the reason why he was designated as Minister of Foreign Policy.

In an article from 2017 Araújo praised Trump as a representative of God in defence of Western civilisation and Christianity, which caught the interest of Bolsonaro's sons, influential at the beginning of their father's administration. In this article Araújo said that 'only Trump can still save the West', and that 'the alliance of the United States with Russia as the two great Christian powers will perhaps be the dream of Trump and Putin' (Araujo 2017). This article received the admiration of Olavo, who shared it with the Bolsonaro family. Olavo's gesture of approval allegedly prompted Bolsonaro subsequently to appoint Araújo as Minister of Foreign Policy. While holding this position,

Araújo wrote an article for the American conservative magazine *The New Criterion*, in which he argued that 'God united the ideas of Olavo de Carvalho with the determination and patriotism of Jair Bolsonaro' (Della Coletta 2018).

In his first speech as Foreign Minister, Ernesto Araújo declared:

> We admire the Latin American countries that freed themselves from the regimes of the São Paulo Forum. ... That is why we admire the new Italy, that is why we admire Hungary and Poland. (Araujo 2019)

He praised those countries where radical right administrations prevail as models to follow. Furthermore, Araújo echoed one of the most important conspiracy theories from the Latin American right: the overwhelming power of the Sao Paulo Forum.[3] The radical right uses that figure to explain any danger posed by the left in Latin America as a communist and terrorist organisation that obtains money from drug trafficking.

Itamaraty, Brazil's Ministry of Foreign Affairs, has historically been a place where the country could show a continuity on foreign policy and a trained bureaucracy. Ernesto Araújo belonged to Itamaraty as a career official, but he had no experience as ambassador – an issue that, in the structured world of Itamaraty, constituted a heresy. His occupation of the top diplomatic position despite his lack of experience consequently displeased some of his colleagues. However, in April 2021, a little more than two years later, he was replaced by a career diplomat with more experience, Carlos França, due to an increasingly tense relationship with China.

Days before assuming the presidency, Bolsonaro received a visit from Orlando Gutierrez Boronat, a Cuban anti-Castro activist from the United States. Boronat told me that the conversation concerned:

> Bolsonaro's interest in the lack of freedom in Cuba and Lula's complicity with the Communist regime in Cuba. We talked about the Castro-Communist penetration in Brazil, which is remarkable, and is reflected in the Cuban Institute of Friendship with the Peoples in Brazil. This institute had a remarkable growth in Brazil under the presidency of Lula.[4]

The Cold War language that Bolsonaro brought to government made him closely aligned with people and leaders opposed to the political regimes in Cuba and Venezuela, among others. Bolsonaro also received the visit of José Antonio Kast, the Republicano Party leader in Chile, whose political vision is close to that of Bolsonaro.

Bolsonaro was also praised in his victory by Mary O'Grady, the Latin American editor of *The Wall Street Journal*, the only newspaper that celebrated Bolsonaro in the international press. O'Grady presented him as a 'swamp drainer', adopting the terminology of Donald Trump in the US, who postulated his candidacy in 2016 as a battle against the 'swamp' in Washington. O'Grady was also present at the dinner at the Brazilian Embassy in Washington in honour of Bolsonaro which took place at the beginning of 2019. She has been described as the most influential person in the North American conservative world on Latin America.[5] At that dinner, in an emblematic speech about his radical right strategy to confront the status quo and the perceived left-wing hegemony in his country, Bolsonaro observed that in Brazil 'to construct, first we have to destroy many things'.

In January 2022, at the meeting in Bogota of the Madrid Forum, organised by the Spanish radical right party Vox, Araújo developed a vision in which he accused Bolsonaro of treason for allowing the possibility of the return of 'communism' to Brazil if the Workers' Party (PT) returned to power; he also denounced the 'communist' influence of China on Brazil. In fact, the final declaration of the Madrid Forum expressed a clear rejection of the probable return of 'communism' to Brazil.

## Eduardo Bolsonaro, the Brasil Profundo meeting and the approach with the radical right

At the end of 2021 Bolsonaro established an approach with the leadership of Vox, the Spanish radical right party. Euro-parliamentarian Hermann Tertsch and Santiago Abascal, Vox's main leader, travelled to Brazil to participate in a meeting called Deep Brazil (*Brasil Profundo*) in Mato Grosso. It was organised by Eduardo Bolsonaro, Federal Deputy, son of Jair Bolsonaro and former President of the Foreign Policy Commission at the Brazilian Congress.[6]

Mato Grosso, one of Brazil's leading agribusiness hubs, was one of the federal states that most strongly supported Bolsonaro's government. As also happens in Poland, Hungary, the United States and Chile, areas of the countryside where traditions and the agribusiness sector prevail are the most important for the support of the radical right. Mato Grosso is one of the Brazilian states in which Bolsonaro obtained his best backing during the 2018 elections, achieving 66 per cent in the second round against 33 per cent for Fernando Haddad, the main contender from the Workers Party (PT) (*Gazeta do Povo* 2018). In 2022 Bolsonaro obtained 65 per cent of the vote, against 35 per cent for Lula on the second round.

'In Mato Grosso we are all Bolsonaro,' declared his followers in the 2018 presidential campaign.[7] '[H]ere the people support this government. We never want the left in power again, we will do everything in our power to make sure that this never happens again,' affirmed a rural unionist from the area in 2019 (Zanini 2019). Another rural landowner said that 99 per cent of the 620 rural owners in his union backed Bolsonaro in 2018. In addition, the measures for unrestricted carrying of weapons on rural properties announced by the government were received there with great support (Zanini 2019b).

During the Brasil Profundo meeting, rural farmers carrying weapons presented themselves as 'good people' and 'good citizens who love their family'.[8] In this way they emphasised the theme of the 'traditional family', one of the ideological cores not only of *Bolsonarismo*, but of the radical right internationally.

That meeting, in a state that may be considered the heart of *Bolsonarismo*, was organised by the Liberal Conservative Institute. The Liberal Conservative Institute (Brazil), created by Eduardo Bolsonaro, was also one of the organisers of the conservative CPAC conference in Brazil in 2021. The Institute was launched in December 2020 in defence of 'family, faith and freedom'. For the former Foreign Affairs Minister, Ernesto Araújo, this Institute:

> is liberal because it proposes a market economy, capitalist in nature, and because one of its goals is to defend freedoms. But it is also conservative, because it favours the values of the family, religion and the country. (Pérez Osuna 2020)

Eduardo, citing examples such as the right-wing Heritage Foundation or the Jaime Guzmán Foundation of Chile, pointed out that his purpose in establishing the Institute was to form a climate of discussion of ideas related to conservatism, in the style of the Conservative Political Action Conference of the United States, since in his country the 'problem was that we elected a conservative president without a conservative infrastructure'. In response to this, Eduardo created what he denominates as a 'conservative university' called Prepara Brasil. Formed by important figures of *Bolsonarismo* in order to 'organise and structure the right wing', it promotes a nationalistic and conservative vision of Brazil against the left.⁹ Abascal himself declared on the occasion of the Brasil Profundo meeting that:

> Spain and Brazil have a past and a present in common. Neither the separatist movements nor the globalist oligarchies have been able to defeat our countries. We are part of a community of 700 million speakers of two sister languages, a community that has never looked at the colour of the skin and that now has to become a decisive pole for the world to come.¹⁰

Abascal later defined Bolsonaro as 'the leader who has fought most frontally and effectively against communism and the extreme left in the entire *Iberosfera*'.¹¹ During his visit to Brazil in December 2021, Abascal also pointed out that he had come to learn how to turn from left to right, which had also happened in Brazil.

In addition, Eduardo Bolsonaro was at the CPAC Orlando in 2022 with Hermann Tertsch, Euro parliamentarian of Vox, and with the Mexican far right Catholic leader Eduardo Verástegui.¹² In Orlando 2022 he joined Eduardo Bolsonaro's radical right deputy Carla Zambelli from the movement *Nas Ruas*.

Eduardo Bolsonaro was at the forefront of international relations with the radical right in government. A signatory of the Vox *Carta de Madrid*, Eduardo has travelled to Hungary ruled by Victor Orbán, from whom he claims to take his model. Eduardo Bolsonaro organised the CPAC in Brazil in 2019 and 2021, in which the former president Bolsonaro also participated. In February 2022, during his visit to Budapest, President Bolsonaro had a meeting with Victor Orbán, the first visit of a Brazilian president to Hungary, in response to Orbán's presence at the inauguration of Bolsonaro in Brasilia in 2019:

> It is a great satisfaction for us to be in Hungary. I consider your country our little big brother. Small if we consider our differences by territorial extensions. And great for the values we represent, which can be summed up in four words: God, country, family and freedom. We also share the defence of the family with great emphasis. A well-structured family makes its respective society healthy. And we must not lose that focus. (de Souza 2022)

That relationship includes the visit to Budapest in May 2022 of Angela Gandra Martins, former Secretary of the Family of the Brazilian Government. Martins used to work with the conservative Minister of the

Family and Human Rights, evangelical pastor Damares Alves. Gandra travelled to Budapest to assist a conference in defence of the 'traditional family' organised by the Political Network for Values, a conservative and anti-abortion platform presided over by the radical right Chilean politician José Antonio Kast. In addition, this conference featured the presence of officials from the Hungarian government.

Bolsonaro also had a meeting in 2021 with Beatriz Von Storch from the party Alternative to Germany (Alternative fur Deutschland). Both she and her German Chilean husband Sven Von Storch come from aristocratic families in northern Germany who lost their land. They held a meeting in July 2021 in Brasilia with Bia Kicis, signatory of the *Carta de Madrid*,[13] and former President of the Constitution and Justice Commission of the Brazilian Congress, Eduardo and Jair Bolsonaro. There Beatrix praised the president of Brazil in glowing terms.

> Unlike what is portrayed by the main media, he is humble, funny and loveable in his personal treatment. The President is without a doubt a man of deep convictions, of Christian faith and deep love for his country.

At the same event she also emphasised:

> His clear understanding of the problems in Europe and the political challenges of our time. At a time when the left promotes its ideology globally through its international networks and organisations, we conservatives must also network more closely and defend our conservative values internationally.[14]

Bolsonaro also travelled days before the start of the war in Ukraine to Russia, where he held discussions with Vladimir Putin. It appears that the two men found some common ground in their defence of a 'traditional family' vision. That position is coherent with the relations that Putin has with others in the European radical right, for example Vox, Fidesz and other parties. The French leader of the radical right, Marine Le Pen, sees Putin as a defender of the family and Christianity against irreligious cultural decay (Cohen 2022). That alignment was expressed through Brazil's neutrality or abstention during the April 2022 United Nations vote to expel Russia from the Human Rights Council. Another aspect to consider is Brazil's relationship with China. Bolsonaro started his government with an open questioning of China's 'communist' role in the Brazilian economy. As his administration progressed, however, he started to adopt a more conciliatory position reflecting the importance of Brazilian exportations to that country – especially in the south, where agrobusiness is one of the main sources of livelihood. In fact, Bolsonaro did allow China to install 5G technology in Brazilian territory. Tensions with China did not stop at the beginning of his term, however. During the Covid-19 pandemic Bolsonaro publicly attacked China several times, including calling Covid-19 the 'Chinese virus' and insinuating that China deliberately created the virus to create a market for its vaccines.

One more relationship has to do with the Argentinian party La Libertad Avanza, led by the libertarian and radical right economist Javier Milei. Eduardo Bolsonaro expressed many times his admiration for Milei's leadership, and for his growth at the polls for the 2023 presidential elections in Argentina. During the centre right-wing administration of Mauricio Macri, Bolsonaro had a close alignment with him, but following the victory of Alberto Fernández with a Peronist coalition in Argentina, Bolsonaro started a verbal struggle against his neighbour. In addition, his son started to claim that with this Peronist government Argentina, due to the economic problems and high inflation, would in time become a 'Venezuela of South America'.

Bolsonaro and his son Eduardo prefer to establish relationships with radical right politicians. In this sense, Milei best represents that political vision. Deputy Eduardo Bolsonaro has told Milei that:

> I see Bolsonaro as a conservative who walked towards classical liberalism. And in you I see an economic liberal who is taking steps in accordance with conservative flags, such as the issue of abortion.[15]

Jason Miller, communication strategist of Donald Trump and founder of the social media GETTR, was present at the CPAC meeting organised in Brazil.[16] His attendance was not casual, as GETTR was the social media founded after Trump's account was closed by Twitter following the attack on the Capitol on 6 January 2021. Furthermore, another friend of Eduardo Bolsonaro, Eduardo Bittar from anti-Chavist Rumbo Libertad, the CEO of GETTR in Spanish; the Brazilian directors of GETTR are also linked to Eduardo Bolsonaro. Elon Musk, the technology billionaire, was another invited recently to Brazil by President Bolsonaro. Musk highlighted his narrative of buying the social media Twitter supposedly to defend the 'freedom of speech' of conservatives.

Thus the issue of defending the traditional family becomes a common core for governments very different in their geographical location, but united by a common agenda of the radical right. They include Law and Justice in Poland, Fidesz in Hungary and the Republican Party under Trump leadership in the US (Korolczuk and Graff 2018). This allows us to think of today's radical right as one big global family, united by technology.

## The radical right in Brazil: what comes next?

We saw that Bolsonaro and his family, especially the federal lawmaker Eduardo Bolsonaro, have established links with radical right figures around the world. Their closest alliances are represented by Vox in Spain, Orbán in Hungary and Trumpist forces in the US.

The ideas of Olavo de Carvalho were influential in defining the most important officials' foreign affairs and allowing the Brazilian radical right to connect with similar movements in other parts of the world. Olavo's thoughts were related to the perspective of creating a defence of what he designated 'patriotism' against what is called 'globalism'. He also promoted the conspiracy theory of a left-wing cultural hegemony in the media and universities that has to be destroyed to secure the prosperity of conservative ideas. Such a situation would justify the idea of a government confronting the status quo. This perception of a radical right daring to confront the establishment is shared by most of the radical right allies of Brazil in Europe and Latin America. It becomes clear in the speech delivered by Bolsonaro in 2019 at the Brazilian embassy in the US, in which he stated that:

> Brazil is not an open terrain where we intend to build things for our people. We have to deconstruct a lot of things. Undo a lot. Then we can start doing. (*Valor Econômico* 2019)

This radical right can be together because they a share a common perspective on the 'others', defined as "leftist" or "communist" enemies that represent a threat to their own existence. This quasi-religious vision constitutes their type of exercise of politics. In the case of the Latin American right, the Spanish party Vox provides a narrative that associates the left with the Sao Paulo Forum, seeking to identify left-wing politics with criminals who have to be eradicated. This finds common ground with *Bolsonarismo* in Brazil and its strong anti-left agenda.

Lula may have won the 2022 elections, but Bolsonaro and his movement continue to retain a certain impact on Brazilian political and social life. That was clear with the coup attempt that took place in Brasilia in January 2023 – very similar to what happened at the Capitol in Washington DC in January 2021. These events serve to illustrate the deep intertwined strategies between the US and the Brazilian far-right.

Foreign policy is changing, however. Lula has established some alliances with centre-left governments such as Gustavo Petro in Colombia and Andrés Manuel López Obrador in Mexico, trying to consolidate a progressive pole. Yet the situation will not be as it was at the beginning of the twenty-first century, with the strongest alliance being that of leftist and progressive governments. The situation is rather of uncertainty and economic crisis. The strength of the radical right in the region represents a significant challenge for progressive movements and the president alike.

## Acknowledgements

I would like to thank Rafael Rezende for his comments on this chapter.

## Notes

1. Javier Milei is the President of Argentina since 2023, representing the far-right libertarian movement. Santiago Abascal leads Spain's far-right party, Vox, known for its nationalist and anti-immigration stance. José Antonio Kast is a Chilean politician and leader of the far-right Republican Party, who narrowly lost the presidential election in 2021.
2. Mark Green was joined by Eduardo Bolsonaro at the CPAC Conference 'Can CPAC save Latin America?' in 2022.
3. The São Paulo Forum is an organisation that emerged in the 1990s, bringing together left-wing parties from across Latin America. Led by Brazil's Workers Party (PT) and maintaining close ties with Cuba, it has played a significant role in regional politics. Notably Valter Pomar, a prominent figure from the left wing of the Workers Party, has served as one of its key secretaries. However, in recent years the organisation has faced challenges due to the broader decline of left-wing movements in the region. Despite this decline, some radical right-wing parties, such as Spain's Vox, have propagated various conspiracy theories. These suggest that the São Paulo Forum still wields disproportionate power, often associating it with unfounded claims of involvement in drug trafficking.
4. Personal interview with Orlando Gutierrez Boronat, 31 January 2022.
5. Interview with Alejandro Chafuen, former CEO of Atlas Network, 9 March 2022.
6. Eduardo Bolsonaro also established relations with Donald Trump's guru Steve Bannon. He wanted to give greater support to 'The Movement', an organisation of far-right politicians across the world, but in the end that did not work out.
7. Pro-Bolsonaro campaign act on Avenida Paulista, 21 October 2018. Live stream, Carla Zambelli on Facebook.
8. *Brasil Profundo* meeting, YouTube, 10 December 2021.
9. Preparabrasil.info. The course includes the figures of Onyx Lorenzoni, Augusto Nunes, Ana Campagnolo, Damares Alves and Ricardo Salles.
10. *Brasil Profundo* meeting, YouTube, 10 December 2021.
11. The concept of Iberosfera by Vox pretends to unite a far-right movement of the Portuguese-speaking and Spanish-speaking world, while also considering the Hispanic community in

the US. An alliance appears to exist between Vox and the Republican Party as they seek to take Hispanic communities to conservatism in the US.
12   Verástegui is a former actor who promotes conservative traditions through his Catholic movement in Mexico called Viva México. He also organised a version of CPAC in Mexico 2022.
13   The Madrid letter is a document signed by the most important leaders from the Latin American radical right. It was promoted by the *Fundación Disenso*, from the Spanish party of the radical right Vox. For more details see my 2022 book: *La Reconquista Autoritaria. Cómo la derecha global amenaza la democracia en América Latina*. Buenos Aires: Marea Editorial.
14   Beatrix von Storch, Instagram, 26 July 2021.
15   'Vivo Javier Milei con Eduardo Bolsonaro', Javier Milei's YouTube channel, 3 May 2022.
16   In his speech at the United Nations, President Bolsonaro spoke against climate change and denounced what he defined as 'Christophobia'. The prosperity gospel, important for the evangelical churches in the United States, has also influenced evangelical churches in Brazil, another reason for close connections between the two countries. Evangelical pastors in Brazil, such as Marco Feliciano, obtained the direction of the groups in Congress that conduct the policies towards Africa. This is important, considering that evangelical churches such as Universal Church of the Kingdom of God (Igreja Universal do Reino de Deus – IURD) have expanded their model to Angola and other countries. However, Bolsonaro has also been strategic in the construction of alliances with pastors from different churches, such as Silas Malafaia, Magno Malta and Valdemiro Santiago, a former IURD but now leader of the World Church Power of God (Igreja Mundial Poder de Deus).

# References

Araujo, E. 2017. 'Trump e o Ocidente, in Cadernos de Política Exterior'. Instituto de Pesquisa de Relações Internacionais, 3(6): 323–58.
Araujo, E. 2019. 'Chanceler Ernesto Araújo – Discurso de Posse no Itamaraty', *Defesanet*, 4 January.
Castelli Gattinara, P. 2020. 'The study of the far right and its three E's: Why scholarship must go beyond Eurocentrism, electoralism and externalism', *French Politics* 18(3): 314–33. https://doi.org/10.1057/s41253-020-00124-8.
Cohen, R. 2022. 'Le Pen closer than ever to the French Presidency (and to Putin)', *New York Times*, 22 April 2022.
Della Coletta, R. 2018. 'Chanceler de Bolsonaro: "Deus uniu ideias de Olavo de Carvalho ao patriotismo do presidente"', *El País*, 28 December 2018. Available at: https://brasil.elpais.com/brasil/2018/12/27/politica/1545925083_475905.html#. Accessed 28 June 2024.
de Souza, A. 2022. 'Na Hungria, Bolsonaro nega destruição da Amazônia e chama país de Orbán de "pequeno grande irmão"', *O Globo*, 17 February 2022.
Forti, S. 2021. *Extrema derecha 2.0. Qué es y cómo combatirla*. Madrid: Siglo XXI de España.
*Gazeta do Povo*. 2018. 'Resultado da eleição para Presidente no Mato Grosso no 2º turno', 28 March 2018.
Korolczuk, E. and A. Graff. 2018. 'Gender as "Ebola from Brussels": The anticolonial frame and the rise of illiberal populism', *Signs: Journal of Women in Culture and Society* 43(4): 797–821. https://doi.org/10.1086/696691.
Mudde, C. 2019. *The Far Right Today*. Hoboken, NJ: John Wiley & Sons.
Pérez Osuna, N. 2020. 'El Instituto Conservador-Liberal de Brasil, una gran noticia', *La Gaceta de la Iberosfera*, 24 December 2020.
Poder 360. 2019. 'Jantar de Bolsonaro em Washington teve Olavo de Carvalho e Steve Bannon', 18 March 2019.
Raygada, J. C. Ubilluz. 2021. 'Sobre la especificidad de la derecha radical en América Latina y Perú. De Hitler y Mussolini a Rafael López Aliaga', *Discursos del Sur. Revista de Teoría Crítica en Ciencias Sociales* 7, 85–116. https://doi.org/10.15381/dds.n7.20903.
Struck, J. P. 2020. 'Bolsonaro finalmente reconhece vitória de Biden', *Deutsche Welle*, 15 December 2020.
*Valor Econômico*. 2019. 'Nós temos é que desconstruir muita coisa, diz Bolsonaro durante jantar', 18 March 2019.

Weber, M. 2012. *La ética protestante y el espíritu del capitalismo*. Buenos Aires: Fondo de Cultura Económica.
Zanini, F. 2019. 'Atos abrem fissura na aliança liberal-conservadora que elegeu Bolsonaro', *Folha de São Paulo*, 21 May 2019.
Zanini, F. (2019b) 'No circuito da soja de MT, fazendeiros aplaudem decreto pró-armas', *Folha de São Paulo*, 10 May 2019.
Zanotti, L. and M. Roberts. 2021. '(Aún) la excepción y no la regla: La derecha populista radical en América Latina', *Revista Uruguaya de Ciencia Política* 30(1): 23–48. https://doi.org/10.26851/rucp.30.1.2.

# Part II
# Small actions, great impacts

# 4
# Bureaucratic resistance and its limits in Bolsonaro's Brazil

Katherine Bersch, Gabriela Lotta and Daniel Thomas

## Introduction

The conflict between politicians and bureaucrats has long been analysed in social science literature. Weber has emphasised that democracy requires bureaucracy, as bureaucrats guarantee the legality and continuity of democratic institutions (1978). However, bureaucrats can also pose a risk to democracy if they corrupt processes or use institutions to their own advantage. This delicate balance between political control and bureaucratic autonomy is crucial for understanding modern democracies. Most social science literature considers these conflicts within the democratic rules of the game and institutions, observing how both politicians and bureaucrats use the democratic process and institutions to their advantage. However, in recent years a new type of conflict between bureaucracy and populist leaders has emerged, pushing back the boundaries of democratic norms.

Brazil presents an interesting case through which to understand this phenomenon. Under Bolsonaro the country exhibited anti-democratic tendencies, as the president attacked democratic institutions, policies, practices and bureaucrats. Yet at the same time we witnessed heroic attempts by Brazilian bureaucrats to resist these efforts. Such empirical realities are at odds with much of the literature on the relationship between political actors and bureaucrats, which has traditionally focused on political actors as principals (often assuming it is the principal who wants what is in the public interest) and bureaucrats (who are self-interested and seek to avoid work). The Brazilian case provides a powerful rejoinder to such a conceptualisation. It reveals that political actors often do not want what is in the public interest, and that instead it is public servants who are often more responsive to the public interest.

Albert Hirschman famously argued that dissatisfied individuals within states, organisations and firms have three choices, expressed in the title of his book *Exit, voice and loyalty* (Hirschman 1970). These are indeed options for public servants at odds with their superiors. They can either leave the organisation, voice their complaints or remain loyal (i.e. put up with it and do what they are told). However, there is another possibility that lies somewhere between these options: active resistance from within, which seeks to advance dissent within organisations. The focus on dissent is often overlooked entirely by social science literature. Indeed, the strong focus of political science on principle-agent relationships or patronage-client exchanges has served to obscure important – even heroic – actors.

This chapter highlights the tension between 'unprincipled' (Brierley 2020) political principals and a bureaucratic technocracy's resistance to Bolsonaro's political project and control. We analyse the strategies developed by bureaucrats to defend democracy, and argue that understanding bureaucratic resistance (and appreciating its limits) requires comprehension of the dynamic that develops between bureaucratic resistance and political control. Drawing on over 200 interviews with bureaucrats of the Brazilian federal government conducted during 2021 and 2022, we show not only the success of strategies of resistance, but also when, and why, the pro-democracy technocracy reaches the limits of resistance. In doing so, we demonstrate how the insertion of military expertise throughout the ranks of bureaucracy has reduced the bureaucracy's ability to react. Appreciating public sector workers' efforts to resist – their active subterfuge and efforts to take matters into their own hands, and their limits – is an important step forward in understanding democratic governance, especially under populist administrations.

## Research design

This study focuses on the Brazilian federal bureaucracy, specifically national civil servants, during the Bolsonaro administration, which has been considered a case of democratic backsliding. We selected this case because Brazilian federal-level civil servants are considered to be the best-case scenario for bureaucratic resistance due to their high levels of expertise, meritocratic recruitment, high salaries and strong tenure protections. Despite this, the Bolsonaro administration was able to assert political control over many areas of the bureaucracy (Milhorance 2022; Lotta et al. 2023; Story, Lotta and Tavares 2023; Bersch and Lotta 2024).

The data were collected through 200 semi-structured interviews with bureaucrats from 15 different federal organisations. This is a convenience sample, constructed through snowball sampling. Based on the previous contact one of the authors had with civil servants, we approached them and asked for an interview. After that, the interviewees indicated other people, based on the criteria that the interviewee should firstly be available to talk and secondly have faced conflicts with Bolsonaro's government and experienced political control. Despite the potential limitations of the snowball method, it is considered a good strategy for dealing with sensitive topics and contexts (Cohen and Arieli 2011).

To ensure diversity, interviewees were from different ages, professions, levels of expertise and organisational affiliations, covering 15 different federal organisations. We concluded the interviews when we reached saturation point, meaning that the interviews yielded consistent information from a diverse range of subjects. In addition, despite the critical situation, all interviewees agreed to tell their cases, believing that the interviews were anonymous and confidential. These decisions were also due to their confidence in the interviewer and in the person who recommended them as potential subjects, who was also interviewed.

The interview guide included questions about profile, career trajectory and recent experience in Bolsonaro's government. We asked interviewees to detail cases in which they experienced (or witnessed) political control and resisted (or witnessed those who did resist) such control. We considered resistance as cases in which a civil servant acted against a measure of political control, but did that in order to defend the rule of law, legality of decisions, constitutional rights and democratic rules; resistance based on individual or corporate agendas was excluded. All interviews were conducted online using different platforms (recommended by the interviewee to guarantee their protection). The interviews lasted between 30 and 150 minutes; they were not recorded, but the interviewer took notes. As discussed above, the analyses draw upon an understanding of the dynamics of control and resistance in Brazil, but took account of the variation within state agencies to identify causal mechanisms and processes.

## The Brazilian case

Brazil is an interesting case to use in analysing tensions between politicians and bureaucrats. On one hand, the country has developed high levels of bureaucratic capabilities; its bureaucracy is recruited by strong meritocratic mechanisms and contains tenure protections that ensure stability at the federal level. With comparatively high salaries, public sector jobs attract many talented individuals, most of whom were recruited in the last 20 years in democratic Brazil, where public participation and democratic principles were emphasised. Nevertheless, since the impeachment of Dilma Rousseff (2016), there has been a growth in the processes of institutional weakening, intensified by Bolsonaro's government in 2019. Since then scholars have noted considerable democratic regression, including diverse forms of political attack on bureaucrats (Peci 2021; Lotta and Costa 2021; Lotta and Silveira 2021; Lotta et al. 2024).

The pro-democratic technocracy that emerged during the impeachment of Dilma Rousseff was not a new group of bureaucrats, but rather a more visible and organised effort. It is likely that pro-democratic bureaucrats had already existed prior to the impeachment proceedings. Rousseff's political inability to negotiate with parties and aversion to politics are often cited in explanations of her impeachment. As she lost political support, particularly during the last year of her first term and immediately after her re-election, essential changes occurred in the government's conduct. Many bureaucrats have characterised Rousseff's administration as 'the beginning of the end,' meaning that policies were slowly dismantled, especially in the wake of budget cuts (Jacobs 2016). At the same time Rousseff's loss of political support induced her to distribute positions in many ministries, resulting in the political occupation of previously technical positions. She was also pressured to appoint officials from parties not previously aligned with the government, thus creating a regime characterised by a lack of policy alignment and high fragmentation.[1,2]

The ongoing loss of political support and the financial crisis led to an impeachment process in 2016. This was supported by a large part of the legislature and led by Vice-President Michel Temer, who became the new president when Rousseff was impeached. The process itself, which lasted for almost eight months, created a significant split in society that was reproduced within the federal bureaucracy. Some bureaucrats created fronts of 'pro-democracy civil servants' and organised demonstrations during this period. In addition, several became personally involved in an active mobilisation on social media against impeachment. Another group of bureaucrats, mainly those who resented the centralising attitudes of the president and the bureaucracies in the realm of economics, mobilised in support of impeachment.

Here one sees that, in the context of Brazil, public statements by civil servants regarding politically charged events, such as the impeachment of Dilma Rousseff, may not necessarily indicate a breach of non-partisanship. This is because impeachment is a constitutional and legal procedure rather than a purely partisan one. Civil servants, as citizens, can express their opinions on matters of public interest, including significant political events, without necessarily aligning themselves with partisan agendas. Moreover, civil servants may have professional expertise or insights relevant to such events, making their perspectives valuable contributions to public discourse. However, the challenge lies in ensuring that these opinions do not compromise public institutions' perceived impartiality and integrity. While civil servants may engage in political discussions or express personal views, they are expected to do so in a manner that upholds the principles of neutrality and professionalism in their official capacities.

When President Temer took over in August 2016, he introduced a new agenda focused on economic issues aligned with liberal pro-market and agribusiness policies. During this period it was well known that the government compiled a 'red list' of bureaucrats who were aligned against the impeachment and who consequently should not be given important positions. During Temer's government the main positions were filled by political appointees aligned with Temer's agenda, especially people from political parties or the private sector, increasing the process of politicisation (Bersch and Lotta 2024). Many bureaucrats decided deliberately to resist political orders, seeking in doing so to try to protect democratic institutions and processes, as well as policies in the public interest (Bersch and Lotta 2024, 34). As they had more expertise and knowledge than many political appointees, not to mention the legal authority, bureaucrats were often able to oppose orders and defend ideas on many policy issues.

However, after the elections in 2018, Bolsonaro took a more aggressive approach to dismantling democratic institutions and processes. As he insisted in one of his official agendas as a president, 'First we have to destroy everything, have razed land, and then build the new country we want' (*Valor Econômico* 2019). To deliver this agenda of change, Bolsonaro politicised the state using loyal appointees – especially those from his ideological group and, most importantly, members of the armed forces.[3] However, other areas, especially economic and agribusiness ministries, continued to be occupied by interest groups already installed at the end of the previous administrations with a more liberal agenda (da Silva and Cardoso Jr. 2022).

One of the findings from the interviews we conducted was that initially bureaucrats thought they would be able to impose barriers to limit these changes. First, they believed that democratic institutions would check Bolsonaro's ability to act unilaterally. Second, they believed that their expertise – much greater than that of the new appointees – would be sufficient to save the policies and agendas. At first this was indeed true. They resisted by voicing complaints, attending demonstrations and writing letters, while also avoiding some duties and threatening the government, using their knowledge about the law.

After acquiring experience, however, the government also learned how to gain control over resources, how to reinterpret the law and, most significantly of all, how to impose costs and constrain reluctant bureaucrats. Over time, this dynamic of bureaucratic resistance and political attack became more systematic. We will explore this in the section below.

## Political control

On the part of the government, oppressive actions have sought to achieve two objectives. First, to induce bureaucrats to carry out the administration's changes, such as dismantling institutional processes and procedures. Second, if the government is unable to convince or coerce bureaucrats to comply, the Bolsonaro administration has sought to remove these individuals as a barrier to change. The administration has sought to compel and purge problematic bureaucrats using a toolbox of enforcement strategies.

### Physical oppression

Physical oppression is one of the most evident strategies that the Bolsonaro administration has employed to control bureaucrats. We conceptualise this form of oppression as changes in the workplace environment that restrict bureaucrats' movements and subject them to intense surveillance and censorship. As a result, these intimidation strategies give politicians greater control over bureaucrats' actions and behaviour. For example, Bolsonaro's political appointees across agencies have used various methods to quell resistance. One official (I36) explained:

> They changed the layout of the rooms; they opened everything, everybody together, no walls, glass. So everyone is looking at each other. And then they put all the political appointees in another room where they can see us, but we don't know what they're doing.[4] (I36)

Here we see how this example of physical oppression decreases privacy, increases surveillance and creates an atmosphere of fear and distrust.

In addition, the Bolsonaro administration sought to restrict the level of knowledge that civil servants have about his administration's actions, inhibiting their resistance. In 2019 the administration took steps to weaken transparency laws by allowing a greater number of political appointees to designate government information as 'secret' and 'ultra-secret' (Marcello 2019). Because these classifications can be made by political appointees, heads of agencies and public companies' head executives, it restricts access to public records from lower-ranked civil servants, thus restricting their ability to act on government misconduct.

Furthermore, the high percentage of political appointees from the military exemplifies the administration's attempt to solidify oppressive tactics. Given the military's hierarchical power structures, appointing individuals adept at these military tactics of control proved helpful in suppressing bureaucratic resistance. The Bolsonaro administration's reliance on political appointees from the military highlights their strategy of reinforcing oppressive measures. Military officials, steeped in the culture of command and obedience, are instrumental in suppressing bureaucratic resistance and ensuring compliance with the administration's policies. Their presence emphasises the administration's commitment to hierarchical control and serves as a deterrent to dissent, their allegiance to the chain of command often overriding concern for bureaucratic norms. The appointment of military personnel to political positions reflected an effort to institutionalise control mechanisms within the government.

## Control over routine administrative processes

Another strategy that the Bolsonaro administration has used was the repurposing of routine administrative processes. Increasing political appointments served to prohibit the use of systems, erase institutional memory and change administrative procedures. Unlike physical oppression, which sought to control the actions and behaviour of bureaucrats informally, the manipulation of administrative processes helped to codify coercive tactics. Moreover, it ensured that legal and routine procedures were altered to benefit Bolsonaro's political agenda. Michener (2023), for example, highlights how Bolsonaro subverted transparency by weakening institutions, erasing and suppressing transparency and promoting the corruption of transparency through misinformation and misuse.

The volume of politically appointed positions was unprecedented in comparison with Temer's tenure. Unlike Temer, Bolsonaro had many political goals across all aspects of the government and he used these appointments to meet his objectives. The transition from administrative to political appointments is an example of how the Bolsonaro administration manipulated administrative processes to further his agenda.

We can see this transformation from administrative to political appointments in Bolsonaro's 2019 appointment of the Chief for the Public Prosecutor's Office. Historically the Associação Nacional dos Procuradores da República (the prosecutors' national association) recommends highly qualified candidates to serve as the office's Chief. However, despite the association's high credibility and commitment to selecting the most talented individuals, Bolsonaro rejected their recommendations. Instead he chose Augusto Aras, a fervent political ally to Bolsonaro (J. Guedes-Neto and Peters 2021, 223).

As expected, Aras took a number of actions to further Bolsonaro's political objectives. For example, he led a lobbying campaign targeting an anti-corruption effort, called Operação Lava Jato, to weaken oversight of government officials (J. Guedes-Neto and Peters 2021, 223). This example of the change from administrative to political appointments in an agency significantly impacted the Bolsonaro administration's ability to meet its political goals.

The Bolsonaro administration's ability to use legal and administrative procedures to weaken bureaucrats was a gradual one. It occurred over time as the administration became increasingly adept at learning how to manipulate policies and laws to further their goals (Bersch and Lotta 2024). For example, one interviewee explains that at first:

> The law was in our favour. They didn't know the procedures, and it was easy for us to say: 'You cannot do this; the rules do not allow you to'. They used to be afraid.[5] (I49)

Given the administration's initial lack of knowledge regarding the bureaucratic system and civil servants' negative view of the administration's actions, there was a concern that these factors could hinder Bolsonaro's political goals. However, over time the administration learned how to navigate the complexities of the legal and administrative system effectively; this served to dilute bureaucratic resistance and further increase political control over civil servants. As a result, the administration pushed aggressively to implement its preferred policies without fear of potential resistance.

## Psychological dominance

Psychological dominance is distinct from physical domination and domination in routine administrative processes because it directly affects bureaucrats on a personal, emotional and interpersonal level. Examples include verbal harassment, public humiliation, the targeting of individuals based on their personal attributes or convictions and the creation of a toxic work atmosphere that strains relationships and trust among colleagues. Psychological dominance is characterised by an intense monitoring of bureaucrats; the constant threats directed at these civil servants ensure obedience even as they damage interpersonal connections. Furthermore, it serves to restrict interactions with external and internal parties through strategies of humiliation, harassment and the invalidation of technical knowledge.

As a result of these tactics of oppression, we see a breakdown of relationships between workers and managers. A policy report organised by Barbosa da Silva and Cardoso Jr. (2022) exposes dozens of cases of psychological domination in different federal organisations. Bolsonaro also mobilised a 'digital militia' to oppress and intimidate scientists (Escobar 2021). Scientists have reported severe personal attacks and online threats that have even led to physical altercations. As a result there are reports that researchers have been 'afraid' about publishing their work and worry about their safety if they do (Escobar 2021).

The Bolsonaro administration's use of psychological dominance was particularly evident in the Chico Mendes Institute for Biodiversity Conservation (ICMBio), located within the Ministry of the Environment. As Bersch and Lotta (2024) document, the administration implemented a restrictive rule requiring ICMBio executives to inspect scientists' work prior to publication, which undermined their autonomy and created an atmosphere of fear. Minister Salles employed further intimidation tactics, threatening civil servants with disciplinary proceedings for their absence at an event in Rio Grande do Sul in April 2019 to which they had not been invited. This incident prompted the resignation of ICMBio's president and all directors, who were promptly replaced by officers in the military police (Éboli 2019). These resignations, along with the strategic replacement of career civil servants with military officials loyal to Bolsonaro, intensified the psychological pressure on the remaining staff. The tactics of psychological dominance effectively silenced dissenting voices and weakened resistance within ICMBio. This allowed the administration to pursue its anti-environmental agenda with minimal internal opposition.

## Silencing or erasing

Tactics of silencing and 'erasing' bureaucrats include laws forbidding publications, exclusion from decision-making processes and censorship of work and other activities. For example, we see evidence of silencing and erasure tactics in March 2019, when the administration formally prohibited civil servants in the Ministry of the Environment (Ministério do Meio Ambiente) and the Brazilian Institute of the Environment and Renewable Natural Resources (Instituto Brasileiro do Meio Ambiente e dos Recursos Naturais Renováveis, IBAMA) from giving interviews or publishing documents. In 2020 the administration further increased censorship measures by restricting civil servants from the Ministry of the Environment and IBAMA from posting on their social media sites.

Over time these tactics of silencing and erasure moved from collective and workplace censorship to individual and private surveillance. Isolated attacks were often used to send warnings about consequences to civil servants; these reduced the likelihood of a coordinated response, making it an effective strategy of coercion. One official (I38) stated that once 'they started taking individual action, acting on each of us individually, we lost the control and the capacity to react'.[6] The erosion of collective agency and the imposition of individualised pressures led to a loss of control, reducing civil servants' capacity to mount effective resistance.

The reference to 'individual action' suggests a deliberate strategy, employed by those in power to target and isolate dissenting voices within the bureaucracy and so undermine collective opposition. This targeted approach rendered individuals vulnerable and isolated; it impeded their ability to organise and respond collectively to authoritarian measures. This official's account underscores the detrimental impact of such tactics on organisational cohesion and the ability to challenge oppressive regimes effectively.

These strategies provide a menu of different options, but they all rely on two fundamental aspects: the politicisation of appointees and the creation of a fearful work environment. In both the militarisation of public organisations plays a fundamental role. It allows politicisation of the bureaucratic hierarchy (the appointment of loyal individuals) and the creation of an environment driven by fear, oppression and control. Ultimately, these various forms of oppression aim to decrease the bureaucrats' autonomy and to dehumanise them, which facilitates the implementation of changes desired by the government. More than 6,000 positions across government were occupied by individuals affiliated with the military, many of whom were either on active duty or in the reserves (Stuenkel 2020, 2024). These included roles in strategic areas such as human resources, ethical committees, Comptroller General and the environmental ministry, where members of the military occupied more than 90 per cent of the positions.

## Bureaucratic reaction

Throughout this period bureaucrats sought to resist in a variety of ways. We identify four key strategies they employed.

### Subversive action

We define subversive action as secret activities conducted by civil servants, such as sabotaging politicians or undermining proposed changes. This strategy includes avoiding certain tasks, using established agency systems when prohibited and following laws strictly to impede a potential change. Strict adherence to laws and statutes, as well as the use of technical language, could be used to remove politically motivated supervisors by triggering external reviews into an appointee's transgression of a regulation. Furthermore, sending information to external entities, such as the press, judicial bodies and non-governmental organisations, are instances of subversive acts.

Other examples include using technical language to get rid of bosses. This tactic refers to the use of bureaucratic or procedural mechanisms to remove superiors from their positions. The process might involve citing specific regulations, rules or policies to justify the removal of a superior, often in cases where there are disputes or conflicts within the organisation. By framing the action in technical terms, individuals seek to navigate organisational structures or legal frameworks in order to challenge their superiors' authority or tenure. This type of action can be seen as a strategic manoeuvre to assert influence or control within the hierarchy of an organisation.

In Brazil, civil servants both engaged in sabotage and actively sought to undermine the Bolsonaro administration's unethical actions. For example, bureaucrats sent reports to non-governmental organisations (NGOs) that could sue the government, wrote anonymous articles describing the adverse conditions and sought support from external actors to apply pressure on the administration. Others participated in covert meetings to hinder the administration's undemocratic plans. One official (I86) disclosed an involvement in covert meetings to circumvent the government's prohibition on international agreements (e.g., meetings that discuss the SDGs and other agendas), stating that they 'continued to participate in secret meetings of international agreements that the government banned'.[7] Despite the explicit ban imposed by the authorities, the official persisted in attending these clandestine gatherings, driven by a sense of duty to uphold democratic principles and resist authoritarian measures. This covert opposition highlights the lengths to which individuals were willing to go to counteract oppressive government policies, demonstrating a deep-rooted commitment to preserving democratic norms.

Oppugning political decisions and using established agency systems to report information is an example of subversive action. For example, one interviewee (I22) recounts:

> Once a colleague was forbidden by our chief to put any information in the system, as they didn't want any decision to be formalised. The chief threatened her if she included any new information.

Here the civil servants' chief explicitly instructed their colleague not to input any data or information into the established agency informational system. This deliberate act aimed to prevent the formalisation of decisions, thereby maintaining ambiguity and evading accountability. The chief's warning, coupled with the implicit threat of consequences, underscored the extent to which certain individuals within the bureaucratic hierarchy sought to control the flow of information and decision-making processes, potentially undermining transparency and the proper functioning of government protocols. The interviewee then explained the reaction from other civil servants:

The other day, we all decided to do the same and included her information all together. So now, if they wanted to punish someone, they had to punish all of us together. This is how we gave them the message that we were not alone'.[8] (I22)

As described above, bureaucrats coordinated their efforts to resist political decisions by strictly following protocols.

## Collective resistance

Resistance, in this context, refers to overt, public actions that openly express the challenges faced by civil servants. These strategies often involve collective efforts, such as actions organised by unions, speaking to the media, initiating legal proceedings and organising protests. By engaging in these visible forms of resistance, civil servants actively voiced their concerns and drew attention to the issues they encountered, seeking to bring about change and hold those in power accountable.

The concept of resistance is seen within Brazil's Ministry of Foreign Affairs (Ministério das Relações Exteriores). In 2018 Bolsonaro selected Ernesto Araújo to be Brazil's foreign minister. As previously discussed, Bolsonaro made political appointments of individuals across various agencies, with Araújo being another ideological supporter of the President. Under his tenure, the Ministry of Foreign Affairs adopted ideologically extreme positions on the environment, reproductive rights and other pressing issues (Phillips 2021). Additionally, Araújo's ideological positions and antagonistic behaviour toward countries such as China and the United States were factors in the government's inability to secure vaccines and other equipment to manage the Covid-19 pandemic (Phillips 2021).

As a result, Brazilian diplomats made a coordinated effort to publish a letter condemning Araújo. In it they described the 'serious harm' that Araújo was doing to the country and the ministry's credibility (Phillips 2021). Placed under extreme pressure, Araújo resigned from his position. Here we see how diplomats at the Ministry of Foreign Affairs effectively resisted and forced the resignation of Bolsonaro's political appointee. While Araújo and the administration sought to quell dissent, the coordinated action among diplomats – against the backdrop of its foreign minister inhibiting Brazil's response to the Covid-19 pandemic – proved highly effective. The Ministry of Foreign Affairs' policy stances were unlikely to change during Bolsonaro's presidency. However, diplomats were able to remove an erratic and 'nefarious' individual from office (Phillips 2021).

Bureaucrats have also taken action against Bolsonaro's political appointees publicly. For example, in the case of Aras, as previously described, prosecutors signed a public petition condemning the appointment of Aras; they also supported a letter that rebuked the policies and discourse of Aras (Oliveira 2020; J. Guedes-Neto and Peters 2021). Furthermore, following the selection of Aras as the Prosecutor General, the National Association of Attorneys of the Republic (ANPR) organised protests throughout the country against Aras (Mota 2019). Prosecutors referred to his appointment as a regression on constitutional standards as 'he does not have any leadership to command an institution with the weight and importance of the [The Federal Public Ministry, Ministério Público Federal] MPF' (Mota 2019). The main goal of demonstrations is to fortify the need for 'career position[s] in defence of the democratic and institutional principles of the MPF' (Mota 2019).

## Survival

Survival in this context refers to taking the minimal steps required to preserve one's position, livelihood and personal wellbeing while refraining from actively supporting agendas perceived to be against the public interest or unlawful. For bureaucrats working under the Bolsonaro administration, survival frequently involved engaging in subtle forms of resistance, such as neglecting certain responsibilities or keeping a low profile. These enabled them to avoid participation in the government's undemocratic initiatives while also reducing the likelihood of facing workplace retaliation or job loss.

For instance, bureaucrats reported that shirking, or simply avoiding doing work, was a technique for keeping their jobs while not contributing to the government's agenda. One civil servant explains:

> Now I pretend I'm working, that I am reading stuff, attending meetings and webinars. But I just want to stay low profile.[9] (I21)

Another bureaucrat (I35) specifically referred to a desire 'to stay quiet' and 'not get engaged in the president's agenda'.[10] Here we see that shirking or neglecting to carry out particular tasks and duties was a valid strategy to avoid following undemocratic rules.

These acts should be understood as resistance rather than acquiescence. They reflect a deliberate effort to undermine or withhold support for the government's agenda, even if the opposition is not overt or confrontational. The civil servants' candid admissions shed light on the nuanced dynamics at play within bureaucratic structures operating under authoritarian regimes, in which outward compliance may mask internal dissent and resistance. Despite the challenges, individuals such as I21 and I35 demonstrate adaptability and resilience in safeguarding their livelihoods while continuing silently to resist. Their actions, although subtle, represent a form of resistance that allows them to maintain their moral integrity, and to avoid actively contributing to the erosion of democratic principles.

## Abandonment

Abandonment is a form of reaction that is a consequence of extreme oppression, as civil servants are 'exhausted with the suffered attacks' (Lotta and Silveira 2021). This is similar to the concept of 'Exit' proposed by Hirschman (1970). This strategy entails leaving the organisation or asking to go on leave. However, it is the only one that does not generate a new action by the government. It is as if the government has won the war.

The Bolsonaro administration, and specifically Ricardo Salles, Minister of the Environment from 2019 to 2021, were criticised by environmentalists – not only for their policy positions, but also for their disregard and tacit approval of illegal logging in the Amazon (Pearson 2021). Civil servants in particular took issue with the failure to enforce existing legislation, which many viewed as undermining the democratic rule of law. As a result the ministry saw 10 per cent of civil servants resign in the first two years of Bolsonaro's presidency (Shalders 2021).

Abandoning or leaving positions had different effects, depending on the context. In the case of the environment ministry, many civil servants left only after they realised that there was little they could do to resist. In other cases, their departures meant that civil servants significantly impeded the efforts of political appointees and the administration. For instance, in December 2021 more than 300 senior-level Receita Federal auditors resigned in protest over the Bolsonaro administration's decision to impose substantial budget cuts on the agency to accommodate pay raises for the police (Stargardter 2021), a core constituency of the President's political agenda (Peci 2021). These mass resignations resulted in tax and custom concerns during an overwrought holiday season.

Abandonment could also mean that bureaucracies simply became increasingly politicised and unprincipled. Indeed, as Schsuter et al. show, the bureaucrats inclined to resign were also those most willing to attempt to convince politicians to amend undemocratic policies, or to engage in subversive acts to hinder policy implementation, in contrast to those reluctant to leave their jobs (2022, 430).

## The dynamic of bureaucratic resistance and political control

The forms of bureaucratic resistance and political control in Brazil have changed over time. Initially, as noted above, civil servants were often able to resist the Bolsonaro administration's efforts at control by leveraging their expertise and the existing legal framework. Collective organising and action were also common strategies in the early period, with bureaucrats banding together to protest against disciplinary actions, to adopt joint work stoppages and to document and report malfeasance. However, as the Bolsonaro administration learned and adapted its approach, the space for resistance diminished.

The administration made sweeping infra-legal changes to institutional frameworks, rewriting regulations and eviscerating enforcement capabilities, particularly in the environmental arena. They instituted censorship laws that targeted both agencies and individual civil servants. Notably they shifted from collective punishments to attacking individuals, including a sharp rise in administrative disciplinary processes (PADs) against employees. Such targeted oppressive actions made open resistance increasingly untenable and perilous. Many bureaucrats turned to neglect of their duties or left the civil service entirely. Bersch and Lotta (2024) argue that isolating civil servants from collective support and institutionalising the intimidation of individuals proved seriously effective in suppressing resistance over time. Strategic appointment of military officials to human resource and leadership roles also played a key role.

By the end of Bolsonaro's term the space for resistance had greatly diminished, with fearful bureaucrats increasingly silenced and sidelined. The Brazilian bureaucracy became more vulnerable to politicisation under an authoritarian-leaning populist leader, despite its having started from a position of relative strength. As oppression grew, more and more civil servants were forced to abandon resistance in favour of passivity or exit.

While the administration succeeded in tightening control across many areas of government, others proved more resilient. The health ministries, for instance, drew on external support to resist Bolsonaro's control (Rich et al. 2024). Variation likely depended on factors such as the extent of Bolsonaro's focus on a given policy area, the number of military appointees and the degree of external and societal support. Indeed, checks and balances from other governmental branches played a significant role in constraining Bolsonaro's agenda, particularly through judicial decisions and congressional obstacles. Ultimately, these higher-level checks and balances, while important, are blunt tools; they can only be activated after considerable damage has already been inflicted.

## Conclusion

We used Brazil as a case study to illustrate strategies of political control and they ways in which bureaucrats react to these oppressive measures. To control civil servants in Brazil, we see four dominant strategies: physical oppression, oppression over routine administrative processes, psychological dominance and silencing and erasing. While these control mechanisms are unique, each strategy seeks to undermine and weaken the role of bureaucrats by politicising employees and constructing a fearful work environment.

However, Brazil's bureaucrats have reacted to these attempts at political control. We see four strategies employed by civil servants to resist these encroachments: subversive action, resistance, survival and abandonment. While we do not speak to the differing levels of effectiveness of these strategies, we cite numerous examples of how these approaches are employed by bureaucrats, highlighting the diversity of reactive measures.

Our research and findings present a unique insight often missing from the literature on bureaucratic actors and patron-client relationships. Instead of thinking of politicians as principals whose goal is to serve the public interest, we find that in Brazil it is often bureaucrats who act in the public interest. Moreover, unlike much of the patron-client literature, we do not assume that public servants have little or no autonomy or expertise. Our research on Brazil reveals that the interests of public sector workers often coincide with the public interest.

Furthermore, in many ways, public servants can act autonomously (at least to a certain degree). They work to safeguard the public interests and serve as defenders of the public good. Scholars such as Carpenter (2001) and Tummers and Bekkers (2014) have recognised the discretion and considerable autonomy afforded by some actors. Thus appreciating public sector workers' efforts to resist, their active subterfuge and their efforts to take matters into their own hands is an important step forward in understanding democratic governance, especially under populist administrations.

What allows civil servants to play this powerful role, and how long can it be sustained? Here it is helpful to put Brazil in context and revisit concepts introduced by Weber. Vis-à-vis so many countries in Latin America, or even across the world, Brazil, at the federal level, has strong mechanisms for meritocratic recruitment to the civil service and stability. Public sector wages, especially at the federal level, are quite high. As Weber has hypothesised, meritocratic recruitment and stability foster an *esprit de corps* among experts within the government, driven by a commitment to a common set of goals such as the scientific method or public health. Although such commitments are not a monolith, they stand in stark contrast to many political appointees, who respond to a greater degree to the political calculus.

We also know that political actors are limited in their ability to understand the details of the vast range of policy issues they face. Often, too, they have shorter time horizons. The limitations of political actors open space for experts who have a greater understanding of the details in a particular area and longer time horizons. They can use expertise and linkages with other areas of government, NGOs and the media quietly to resist political directives. Bureaucrats often leverage their knowledge and connections to shine a light on political directives at odds with the public interest. The case of Ricardo Galvão, a physicist and engineer who led the National Institute for Space Research, provides a good example of bureaucrats leveraging their knowledge to highlight directives that harm the public. He was removed as head of the Institute following his public statements and research explaining the contributions of Bolsonaro's policies to the Amazon's high rate of deforestation (Escobar 2019).

Of course, experts within the government cannot withstand prolonged attacks indefinitely. Political control and bureaucratic resistance are dynamic and relational processes that involve political learning by both sides (Bersch and Lotta 2024). Over time, Bolsonaro's politicians learned how to maximise individual and institutionalised repercussions and simultaneously to reduce areas of contestation. Political control and attacks have evolved, often relying on isolating individuals and formalising attacks. The Bolsonaro government improved its political control, using military management to guarantee obedience and control. In this regime individuals affiliated with the military occupied approximately one-third of the Brazilian government's positions. As previously noted, we see a concentration of these individuals appointed to strategic areas, such as human resources, ethical committees, Comptroller General and the environmental ministry. Military management is based on control over bodies, discipline and blind obedience to officers' requests, complemented by strong punishment for non-compliance (Andrade, Nogueira and Lotta 2021).

This new form of political control has proved very effective in generating fear and paralysis among bureaucrats, decreasing the capacity for reaction and resistance, as we have witnessed in the Brazilian federal government. The effectiveness of such tactics has fostered an increase in civil servants simply giving up and leaving. This learning process of political control effectively induces bureaucrats to remain silent or 'loyal', and to implement the president's preferences.

Moreover, when policymaking is increasingly centralised and experts are shifted into meaningless positions, the effects of resistance are attenuated. Resistance and 'voice' are second-best options – we would prefer strong leadership at the top. Given scientific denialism and an absence of leadership, individuals within the public sector have played an important role.

There may be longer-term advantages to resistance as well. When public sector workers resist orders from above and instead follow the norms of the scientific community, or principles of legality and public service, they not only may improve the quality of governance in the short term but also contribute to longer-term governance. Losing experienced public sector workers tears at the fabric of the state. While the Bolsonaro administration enacted what was described as an 'invisible administrative reform' (Carazza 2023), effectively halting the filling of public sector vacancies, restraining wage increases and weakening the bureaucracy, Lula's administration has taken steps to reverse this trend. By announcing plans to hire between 16,000 and 18,000 new federal workers (Audi 2023; Salomão 2023) and prioritising the recruitment of civil servants over political appointments, Lula's administration has sought to enhance the impartiality of the state.

Although these efforts seek to rebuild the state, the process of reconstructing institutions after the actions of Bolsonaro's administration, which reduced institutional memory and instigated a dynamic of polarisation, can be challenging. The road to rebuilding the state is long. Yet it is made less arduous thanks to the efforts of those committed bureaucrats who often resisted and sought to remain in their positions to defend democracy, legality and the impartiality of the state.

## Acknowledgements

We thank Mariana Costa Silveira for helping in data collection. We are grateful to Iana Alves, Olivia Guaranha, João Pedote and Michelle Fernandez for inspiring some of the ideas in this chapter, and to Daniel Thomas for research assistance.

## Notes

1. All interviews were numerated and quotes are presented with the number of the interviewee.
2. Interview with I18 in Zoom meeting, February–September 2021.
3. See especially Hunter and Vega 2022.
4. Interview with I36 in Zoom meeting, February–September 2021.
5. Interview with I49 in Zoom meeting, February–September 2021.
6. Interview with I38 in Zoom meeting, February–September 2021.
7. Interview with I86 in Zoom meeting, February–September 2021.
8. Interview with I22 in Zoom meeting, February–September 2021.
9. Interview with I21 in Zoom meeting, February–September 2021.
10. Interview with I35 in Zoom meeting, February–September 2021.

## References

Andrade, D. P., F. do A. Nogueira and G. Lotta, G. n.d. 'Missão dada é missão cumprida: management militar no governo Bolsonaro', *Gestão, Política & Sociedade*. Available at: https://politica.estadao.com.br/blogs/gestao-politica-e-sociedade/missao-dada-e-missao-cumprida-management-militar-no-governo-bolsonaro/. Accessed 6 May 2022.

Audi, A. 2023. 'Lula wants to boost public service numbers', *The Brazilian Report*.

Bersch, K. and G. Lotta. 2024. 'Political control and bureaucratic resistance: The case of environmental agencies in Brazil', *Latin American Politics and Society* 66(1): 27–50. https://doi.org/10.1017/lap.2023.22.

Brierley, S. 2020. 'Unprincipled principals: Co-opted bureaucrats and corruption in Ghana', *American Journal of Political Science* 64(2): 209–22. https://doi.org/10.1111/ajps.12495.

Carazza, B. 2023. 'Com reajuste e concursos, Lula tenta reverter "reforma administrativa silenciosa" de Guedes', *Valor Econômico*, 19 July 2023. Available at: https://valor.globo.com/opiniao/bruno-carazza/coluna/com-reajuste-e-concursos-lula-tenta-reverter-reforma-administrativa-silenciosa-de-guedes.ghtml. Accessed 28 March 2024.

Carpenter, D. 2001. 'The political foundations of bureaucratic autonomy: A response to Kernell'. *Studies in American Political Development* 15(1): 113–22. https://doi.org/10.1017/S0898588X01010069.

Cohen, N. and T. Arieli. 2011. 'Field research in conflict environments: Methodological challenges and snowball sampling', *Journal of Peace Research* 48(4): 423–35. https://doi.org/10.1177/0022343311405698.

Escobar, H. 2019. 'Brazilian institute head fired after clashing with nation's president over deforestation data'. Available at: https://www.science.org/content/article/brazilian-institute-head-fired-after-clashing-nation-s-president-over-deforestation. Accessed 29 April 2022.

Escobar, H. 2021. '"A hostile environment": Brazilian scientists face rising attacks from Bolsonaro's regime'. Available at: https://www.science.org/content/article/hostile-environment-brazilian-scientists-face-rising-attacks-bolsonaros-regime (Accessed: 29 April 2022).

Finer, S. E. 1962. *The Man on Horseback: The role of the military in politics*. New York: Praeger.

Guedes-Neto, J. V. and B. G. Peters. 2021. 'Working, shirking, and sabotage in times of democratic backsliding: An experimental study in Brazil'. In *Democratic Backsliding and Public*

*Administration: How populists in government transform state bureaucracies*, edited by M. W. Bauer et al. Cambridge: Cambridge University Press, 221–45.

Hirschman, A. O. 1970. *Exit, Voice, and Loyalty: Responses to decline in firms, organizations, and states*. Cambridge, MA: Harvard University Press.

Hunter, W. and D. Vega. 2022. 'Populism and the military: Symbiosis and tension in Bolsonaro's Brazil', *Democratization* 29(2): 337–59. https://doi.org/10.1080/13510347.2021.1956466.

Huntington, S. P. 1957. *The Soldier and the State: The theory and politics of civil-military relations*. Cambridge, MA: Belknap Press of Harvard University Press.

Jacobs, A. 2016. 'Dilma Rousseff, facing impeachment in Brazil, has alienated many allies', *The New York Times*, 1 May 2016. Available at: https://www.nytimes.com/2016/05/02/world/americas/brazil-president-dilma-rousseff-impeachment-allies-alienated.html. Accessed 29 April 2022.

Leite, F. 2020. *Com só 12 inscritos, plano de Aras para a Lava Jato fracassa*, *O Antagonista*. Available at: https://oantagonista.uol.com.br/brasil/com-so-12-inscritos-plano-de-aras-para-a-lava-ja to-fracassa/. Accessed 29 April 2022.

Lotta, G. and M. I. S. Costa. 2021. 'Use of political and social categorizations in policy implementation: Theoretical and analytical contributions', *Revista de Sociologia e Política* 28. Available at: https://scholar.google.com/citations?view_op=view_citation&hl=en&user=z kIjWYQAAAAJ&cstart=20&pagesize=80&sortby=pubdate&citation_for_view=zkIjWYQAA AAJ:oNZyr7d5Mn4C. Accessed 29 April 2022.

Lotta, G. and M. Silveira. 2021. 'Attacks on the bureaucracy within contexts of a democratic backsliding: Bolsonaro's government oppression and bureaucratic reactions', *PEX*. Available at: https://pex-network.com/2021/11/25/attacks-on-the-bureaucracy-within-contexts-of-a-democratic-backsliding-bolsonaros-government-oppression-and-bureaucratic-reactions/. Accessed 29 April 2022.

Lotta, G. S. et al. 2023. 'A resposta da burocracia ao contexto de retrocesso democrático: uma análise da atuação de servidores federais durante o Governo Bolsonaro', *Revista Brasileira de Ciência Política*, p. e266094. https://doi.org/10.1590/0103-3352.2023.40.266094.

Lotta, G., I. Alves de Lima, M. Costa Silveira, M. Fernandez, J. Paschoal Pedote and O. Landi Corrales Guaranha. 2024. 'The procedural politicking tug of war: Law-Versus-Management disputes in contexts of democratic backsliding', *Perspectives on Public Management and Governance* 7(1–2): 13–26. https://doi.org/10.1093/ppmgov/gvad008.

Marcello, M. C. 2019. 'Brazil decree weakens law aimed at holding government to account', *Reuters*, 24 January 2019. Available at: https://www.reuters.com/article/brazil-politics-tra nsparency-idUSL1N1ZO0Y3. Accessed 29 April 2022.

Michener, G. 2023. 'Transparency versus populism', *Administration & Society* 55(4): 671–95. https://doi.org/10.1177/00953997221147227.

Milhorance, C. 2022. 'Policy dismantling and democratic regression in Brazil under Bolsonaro: Coalition politics, ideas and underlying discourses', *Review of Policy Research* 39(6): 752–70. https://doi.org/10.1111/ropr.12502.

Mota, E. 2019. *Procuradores fazem manifestação em todo Brasil contra escolha de Aras*, *Congresso em Foco*. Available at: https://congressoemfoco.uol.com.br/amp/temas/judiciario/procura dores-fazem-manifestacao-em-todo-brasil-contra-escolha-de-aras/. Accessed 29 April 2022.

Oliveira, M. 2020. *Veja a íntegra do abaixo-assinado que questiona nomeação de Aras*, *Congresso em Foco*. Available at: https://congressoemfoco.uol.com.br/temas/judiciario/procuradores-manifestam-insatisfacao-com-aras-e-promovem-abaixo-assinado/. Accessed 29 April 2022.

Pearson, S. 2021. 'Brazilian Environment Minister Ricardo Salles steps down amid illegal logging probe', *The Wall Street Journal*. Available at: https://www.wsj.com/articles/brazilian-environment-minister-ricardo-salles-steps-down-amid-illegal-logging-probe-11624484322. Accessed 29 April 2022.

Peci, A. 2021. 'Populism and bureaucratic frictions: Lessons from Bolsonarism', *Journal of Policy Studies* 36(4): 27–35. https://doi.org/10.52372/kjps36403.

Phillips, T. 2021. 'Brazil's foreign minister, who bashed China and praised Trump, resigns', *The Guardian*, 29 March 2021. Available at: https://www.theguardian.com/world/2021/mar/29/brazil-foreign-minister-ernesto-araujo-resigns. Accessed 29 April 2022.

Rich, J. A., E. M. da Fonseca and L. Bower. 2024. *What Makes Bureaucracies Politically Resilient? Evidence from Brazil's Covid-19 vaccination campaign*. Comparative Politics 57(1): 25–48. https://doi.org/10.5129/001041524X17129370289167.

Salomão, A. 2023. *Governo prepara mais 10 mil vagas de concurso, diz ministra da Gestão, Folha de S.Paulo*. Available at: https://www1.folha.uol.com.br/mercado/2023/07/governo-prepara-mais-10-mil-vagas-de-concurso-diz-ministra-da-gestao.shtml. Accessed 28 March 2024.

Schuster, C. et al. 2022. 'Exit, Voice and Sabotage: Public service motivation and guerrilla bureaucracy in times of unprincipled political principals', *Journal of Public Administration Research and Theory* 32(2): 416–35. https://doi.org/10.1093/jopart/muab028.

Shalders, A. 2021. 'Com Bolsonaro, área ambiental do governo já perdeu 10% dos servidores', *BBC News Brasil*. Available at https://www.bbc.com/portuguese/brasil-55849937. Accessed 1 December 2021.

da Silva, F. A. B. and J. C. Cardoso Jr. 2020. 'Assédio institucional no setor público e o processo de desconstrução da democracia e do republicanismo no brasil'. In *Cadernos Reforma Administrativa: Assédio Institucional no Setor Público*, edited by F. A. B. da Silva and J. C. Cardoso Jr., 1–49. Available at https://www.servirbrasil.org.br/wp-content/uploads/2020/11/Cadernos-Reforma-Administrativa-N.-12.pdf.

Stargardter, G. 2021. 'Over 300 tax customs officials quit over Brazil's 2022 budget | Reuters'. Available at: https://www.reuters.com/world/americas/over-300-tax-customs-officials-quit-over-brazils-2022-budget-2021-12-22/. Accessed 29 April 2022.

Story, J., G. Lotta and G. M. Tavares. 2023. '(Mis) Led by an outsider: Abusive supervision, disengagement and silence in politicised bureaucracies', *Journal of Public Administration Research and Theory* 33(4): 549–62. https://doi.org/10.1093/jopart/muad004.

Stuenkel, O. 2020. 'The backlash against Brazil's politicised military', *Americas Quarterly*, 24 August 2020. Available at: https://americasquarterly.org/article/the-backlash-against-brazils-politicized-military/. Accessed 28 March 2024.

Stuenkel, O. 2024. 'Bolsonaro Coup Plans: U.S. pressure campaign kept Brazil's generals at bay', *Foreign Policy*, 20 February 2024. Available at: https://foreignpolicy.com/2024/02/20/brazil-bolsonaro-coup-us-biden-democracy-election-chips-lula/. Accessed 28 March 2024.

Tummers, L. and V. Bekkers. 2014. 'Policy implementation, street-level bureaucracy, and the importance of discretion', *Public Management Review* 16(4): 527–47. https://doi.org/10.1080/14719037.2013.841978.

*Valor Econômico*. 2019. 'We have to deconstruct a lot,' says Bolsonaro during dinner | Brazil | Economic value'. Available at: https://valor.globo.com/brasil/noticia/2019/03/18/nos-temos-e-que-desconstruir-muita-coisa-diz-bolsonaro-durante-jantar.ghtml. Accessed 29 April 2022.

Weber, M. 1978. *Economy and Society: An outline of interpretive sociology*. Vol. 1. Berkeley, CA: University of California Press.

# 5
# Autonomy as limitless freedom: authoritarian affordances in Brazil's Prevent Senior case

Katerina Hatzikidi

## Introduction

In the context of a high-profile controversy around the practices and health protocols used by Prevent Senior, a Brazilian health insurance and healthcare provider, during the Covid-19 pandemic, one term took centre stage in the unfolding debates: autonomy. This notion was repeatedly used, albeit differently appropriated, by the different parties involved in the fault line that captivated public attention over several weeks. Drawing on the findings of, and testimonies included in, the final report of a congressional panel investigating the federal government's handling of the pandemic, this chapter explores the different uses and understandings of 'physician's autonomy', a term mobilised by both physicians and the company's executive board. In discussing critically the dissenting interpretations of this notion, the term 'corporate autonomy' will be tentatively introduced to describe the specific translation of autonomy as unbridled freedom by Prevent Senior and to analyse the overarching context of neoliberal authoritarianism from which such practices emerged.

Two main questions will guide this analysis. Firstly, how did such a radical yet fundamental dissensus around autonomy between physicians on the one hand and the company's board of directors on the other come into being? Secondly, how did a conveniently shaped notion of autonomy, reduced to limitless freedom, acquire equal footing with a more conventional notion of autonomy as freedom within constraints? My hypothesis, which I will develop in what follows, is that the conditions of possibility for this discursive equivalence were enabled by a larger infrastructure of authoritarian affordances – accentuated, in this case, by the combined occurrence of a global health emergency and Jair Bolsonaro's administration.

The chapter begins by addressing briefly the main threads of the Prevent Senior affair within the broader pandemic context in Brazil, outlining the main controversy around autonomy. I will then explore the notion of 'physician's autonomy', as used in this case, mainly against the background of Cornelius Castoriadis's analysis. In the third and final part I will discuss the then socio-economic and political infrastructure, its authoritarian affordances and how it may have shaped the case under discussion. I will conclude with some reflections on the limitations inherent to autonomy and on the dangers attached to equating autonomy with unrestricted freedom.

## Prevent Senior, the pandemic context and the 'early treatment' to Covid-19

On 16 March 2020 the passing of a 62-year-old man who had been admitted to the Sancta Maggiore Paraíso hospital in São Paulo, one of Prevent Senior's units, was registered as the first Covid-19 related death in Brazil. This event drew the attention of local and state health authorities – not only because of its unprecedentedness (the official record was corrected, later that summer, to register the passing of a 57-year-old woman a few days earlier, also in São Paulo, as the first in the country), but also because the hospital had not previously reported any infections from the virus.

The health authorities began to investigate the case. Three days later the São Paulo State Health Secretary reported that all five confirmed Covid-19-related deaths in the state at the time had taken place in Prevent Senior's hospital units. By the end of March, as it emerged that the vast majority of registered deaths from the virus in São Paulo had taken place in Prevent Senior's network, the Minister of Health, Luiz Henrique Mandetta, was publicly expressing concern over hospitalisation conditions at the Sancta Maggiore, which he found problematic.

Prevent Senior is a private healthcare provider, founded in 1997 in São Paulo by the brothers Eduardo and Fernando Parrillo. The company quickly became one of the most important in the sector. It made headlines in mainstream Brazilian news outlets for apparently achieving the paradoxical feat of remarkable economic growth while preferentially attending to clients that no other health insurance provider would accommodate: those aged over 60. Although anyone over 39 can become a client, nearly 80 per cent of Prevent Senior's clientele was comprised of people aged 60 and above. Prevent Senior was thus praised for its unorthodox economic success despite its focus on an age group legally considered 'elderly' in Brazil, and so generally perceived as more costly to health insurance providers through being more likely to become ill. All this good publicity would drastically change from March 2020 onwards. A series of complaints and accusations for infractions were then filed against the company, prompting a wave of controversial and negative press.

The main accusations, brought to light by some of the company's former employees and patients alike, focused on two principal issues. Concerns were expressed, on the one hand, about the company's alleged coercion of its medical staff to prescribe a composition of drugs, such as hydroxychloroquine, ivermectin and azithromycin, included in the so-called Covid Kit, to all patients with flu-like symptoms, and on the other about the company's practice of dispensing with patients' consent to conduct unauthorised medical experiments – part of the company's Covid-19 health protocol known as 'early/initial treatment' (*tratamento precoce/inicial*).

A national congressional panel (Comissão Parlamentar de Inquérito or CPI), created by a Supreme Court decision in April 2021 with the aim of investigating the federal government's 'actions and inactions' in handling the pandemic, heard the testimony of Prevent Senior's executive director, Pedro Benedito Batista Júnior. In it he stated that about 4,000 patients had died of Covid-19 in the company's hospitals by September 2021. In fact this number may be significantly higher, as the private health insurance provider is under further investigation by different government bodies for under-notifying the number of infections and for changing the International Codification of Disease, so that the cause of death would appear unrelated to Covid-19. The congressional panel's final report called for the indictment of Prevent Senior's founders, its executive director, as well as of other people involved in the company, for committing, among others, crimes against humanity.

Prevent Senior's case, however scandalous, is far from unique. Different private healthcare and health insurance providers have been reported for promoting and using the 'early treatment', with or without patients' consent, as did several public hospitals across Brazil. Indeed, according to the CPI's report, the alt-scientific early treatment became 'a declared federal government health policy' from 20 May 2020 onwards, the date on which Eduardo Pazuello, an army general with no medical expertise, was appointed by President Jair Bolsonaro as Minister of Health (Senado Federal 2021, 102). Furthermore, one of the key findings of the congressional panel's investigations was the adoption by the federal government of a strategy that opted to favour the free circulation of Covid-19 with the aim of attaining 'herd immunity' through contagion. This strategy involved a fierce opposition to – even a boycott of – non-pharmaceutical interventions (such as social distancing, facial masks and lockdowns), a delay in the acquisition of vaccines and, most important to our discussion, propagation of the belief that a cure was available: there was consequently no significant danger from exposure to the virus. A swift 'return to normality' was the end goal.

In this sense, the general consensus around 'the imperative of health', seen as 'at once the duty of each and the objective of all' (Foucault 1984, 277), was inverted. The federal government created a sharp distinction between 'saving' the economy and human lives, apparently prioritising the former at the expense of the latter (Hatzikidi 2020). Official information campaigns launched (such as 'Brazil cannot stop', eventually banned by a Supreme Court decision) and policies introduced during the pandemic (the president used his discretionary powers to expand the list of 'essential services' that could remain open, authorising, among others, hair salons and lottery retailers) aimed to mitigate the sense of a health emergency and to encourage a return to business-as-usual.

In this scenario of pandemic malgovernance (Bastos Lima et al., 2025), in which 'neoliberal markets and morals' (Brown 2019) produce devastating effects by prioritising profit over human lives, and amidst growing pressure from patients, ongoing investigations and the press, Prevent Senior reached out to (informal) advisors working alongside and often parallel to the Ministry of Health for a helping hand. Such was claimed by Bruna Morato, a lawyer representing a group of physicians who had formerly worked for the private health insurance provider, in her testimony in front of the congressional panel. This group of physicians accused Prevent Senior of having made a pact with the Brazilian government on shared economic and ideological grounds. According to the plaintiffs, this pact, or informal agreement, involved an exchange around the early treatment: by adopting Prevent Senior's health protocol, the federal government would acquire a supposedly scientific basis for its defence of ineffective drugs and return to normality. Prevent Senior would meanwhile continue to run its ambiguous operations without interference from investigations.

Prevent Senior patients and family members, who testified for the CPI, denounced the company for restricting or obstructing their access to life-saving treatment, insisting instead on the use of the early treatment, which was based on anecdotal evidence (Furlan and Caramelli 2021, 2). The drugs' low cost and possibility for outpatient prescription compared to costly longer treatments for inpatients – such as Intensive Care Unit treatment – have been identified by critics as informing the company's decision to adopt the early treatment as its official protocol for treating Covid-19. This treatment would significantly reduce costs during a pandemic in which the vast majority of its clients came from 'at risk' groups. In Morato's words, the early treatment was a 'magic bullet' (*pílula de esperança*) that served the company's financial interests as well as those of the Ministry of the Economy (Senado Federal 2021, 839).

As the controversy of Prevent Senior's practice was unfolding, especially during the televised and livestreamed congressional hearings, the term 'autonomy' emerged as equally central and contentious. The company denied responsibility for the accusations, alleging that its 'official position is physician's autonomy' (Senado Federal 2021, 887), while physicians working for Prevent Senior accused the company of denying them their autonomy, understood in this context to mean their professional freedom to prescribe medication or to recommend treatment they considered adequate and appropriate for each patient. Both sides relied on the 'fundamental principles' of the Medical Code of Ethics, adopted by the Brazilian Federal Board of Medicine, which stipulate 'physician's autonomy' in the exercise of the medical profession. The concept is understood as ethically circumscribed freedom from all restrictions and impositions that may affect the efficiency and correct application of their work (Código de Ética Médica 2010, 30). However, the two sides had a strikingly diverse, if not directly opposite, understanding of how physician's autonomy operated at Prevent Senior. The company's managing director claimed physicians had 'full autonomy' while physicians claimed they were coerced and intimidated by their corporate superiors and had 'no autonomy' at all.

## Autonomy and its dissenting interpretations

In his testimony in front of the congressional panel, Walter Correa de Souza Neto, physician and former Prevent Senior employee, was emphatic about the company's coercion of its employees and about the lack of autonomy experienced by the latter. He gave detailed accounts of how medical staff were prohibited from using face masks at work in order not to 'scare the patients' and were instructed not to inform patients or their families about their treatment; some were even asked to work while infected themselves. 'The lack of autonomy [at Prevent Senior] is such that you do not have the autonomy to protect your own life,' he resoundingly stated (Senado Federal 2021, 909). He went on to describe Prevent Senior's internal policies as 'evangelisation politics' (Senado Federal 2021, 874), drawing attention to the continuous pressure experienced by medical staff from the company's board of directors to follow the established health protocol and prescribe the Covid Kit to *all* patients with flu-like symptoms.

Correa's testimony corroborates that of Morato, as well as accounts of former patients and physicians that came to light during the congressional hearings and in the press. Physicians reported feeling 'impotent' and deprived of autonomy, not knowing or understanding exactly why the protocol was imposed even against growing scientific evidence, their own will or case-by-case examination. Physicians also mentioned having their prescriptions tampered with and not having the liberty to prescribe drugs not included in the Covid Kit, or to order examinations when they wished (Senado Federal 2021, 882).

A culture of intimidation was appointed as the main reason behind physicians' compliance, despite many of them having serious doubts about the treatment's efficacy. Dissenting physicians were summarily dismissed (Senado Federal 2021, 907, 933) and medical staff were constantly reminded of the company's motto of 'loyalty and obedience' (Senado Federal 2021, 906). What is more, according to the plaintiffs, physicians were not able to report improper practices and irregularities in their workspace to the ethics committee of the Regional Board of Medicine, as the Brazilian Medical Code of Ethics dictates, because of a perceived 'proximity' between Prevent Senior and members of these boards.

Since the Covid Kits were sealed and physicians could not add or remove medication, some found leeway in confidentially recommending their patients not to take the prescribed drugs. Such practices of silent protest notwithstanding, former Prevent Senior patients spoke of being intimidated by physicians when manifesting resistance to taking the Covid Kit. Some reported being warned that if they did not take the drugs included in the Kit, their health plan would not cover them if their symptoms deteriorated and they needed hospitalisation (Senado Federal 2021, 900–2). It can be argued, then, that the culture of intimidation at Prevent Senior was not restricted to the relationship between employer and employees, but sometimes also informed that between physicians and patients.

Indeed, besides physicians and the board of directors, a third important agent in relation to autonomy is patients. In the CPI hearings, former Prevent Senior patients or their families testified they were given misleading or inadequate information, or no information at all, about the treatment they were undergoing. The same was corroborated by former Prevent Senior employees. Un- or misinformed, often coerced into or unable to consent to the treatment given to them, patients were denied their autonomy, a clear breach of international codes of medical ethics. The obligation to obtain consent from patients or their families is also stipulated in the Brazilian Medical Code of Ethics. Nevertheless, due to space limitations and because discussion of ethics would greatly exceed the scope of the present chapter, I focus here specifically upon the radically different appropriations of autonomy by physicians, on the one hand, and Prevent Senior's board of directors on the other.

Based on the testimonies discussed above, and on Prevent Senior's obstinate denial of liability, insisting instead that physicians had 'full autonomy' and consequently full responsibility for what they were prescribing, the CPI report concluded that the company used 'physician's autonomy' as a shield to protect itself from any accusations that might ensue from its corporate practices. In this sense an operational logic that interpreted physician's autonomy as full liability for the latter and unbridled freedom for the company was able to impose itself over medical ethics and limitations, which define physician's autonomy as freedom within constraints. I will schematically call this operational logic 'corporate autonomy'. In bending physician's autonomy to employ a health treatment against growing scientific evidence and the will of many physicians, Prevent Senior's corporate autonomy was backed both by the tacit but indispensable support of sectors in the federal government and by the April 2020 decision of the Brazilian Federal Board of Medicine. This decision, although cautioned against 'potential greater damages than benefits', indicated the prescription of chloroquine and hydroxychloroquine to patients with early or mild symptoms. In other words, corporate autonomy found fertile ground on an infrastructure of authoritarian affordances that will be further discussed below.

It is important to note that not only an expectation of successfully tackling a financial challenge but also a genuine hope in the success of their alt-scientific methods seem to have determined the company's internal policies vis-à-vis its Covid-19 health protocol, at least initially. Corporate autonomy effectively provided the conditions for experimentation unobstructed by accountability. If its health protocol proved successful, Prevent Senior would not only grow economically; it would also gain an international reputation. This ambition is well illustrated, for example, in an audio message that Rodrigo Barbosa Esper, appointed as coordinator of one of the unauthorised clinical studies, sent to Prevent Senior employees. In it he declared that the study would 'change the path of medicine' (Senado Federal 2021, 863).

The two main instances of autonomy in this context can thus be summarised as physician's autonomy on the one hand – equated to physician's responsibility for the prescribed treatment by Prevent Senior and perceived by physicians as lacking in the company – and corporate autonomy, in the sense of a company policy that combined unaccountability and denial of liability, on the other. Defence of physician's autonomy as a way of making medical doctors exclusively responsible for following the company's Covid-19 health protocol has been an essential element of how corporate autonomy operated. As will be shown below, conjunctural and structural factors provided the conditions of possibility for such radically dissenting views of physician's autonomy to co-exist at Prevent Senior. I will now discuss this discursive co-existence against Castoriadis's conception of autonomy.

## Autonomy as reflective activity and reason

The 'germ' of autonomy, argues Castoriadis (1991), 'emerges when explicit and unlimited interrogation explodes on the scene' (1991, 163). Whether social or individual, autonomy is 'a project' that begins with interrogation and creates, along the way, 'a new social-historical *eidos*: reflectiveness in the full sense, or self-reflectiveness' (Castoriadis 1991). Nothing is spared from interrogation, especially not what we regard as true, good and just, and our ways of knowing. Ultimately, therefore, autonomy for Castoriadis is a kind of reason that, far from being static, continuously creates itself in and through 'the reflective activity' (1991, 164). Put bluntly, without reflectiveness and questioning there can be no autonomy.

Such a process of reflection is also invoked by Foucault (1997) when he describes ethics as 'the conscious (*réfléchie*) practice of freedom' (1997, 284). Freedom, like autonomy, cannot be conceived of or discussed in isolation, but it is fundamentally relational: it concerns the ways in which an individual or group relates to other individuals or groups. Foucault proposes the concept of governmentality – understood in this context in a very broad sense as techniques of power relations – as one that 'bring[s] out the freedom of the subject and its relationship to others – which constitutes the very stuff (*matière*) of ethics' (Foucault 1997, 300). An ethical conduct, in this sense, takes the other into consideration, and often involves restraining one's own exercise of freedom.

Likewise Castoriadis shows that autonomy cannot be equated to any transgressive act; as *nomos*, even if given to one by oneself, it abides by specific rules and regulations. If autonomy is about 'being able to question everything' (Castoriadis 1981, 21) it is also, like governmentality, about self-limitation. That 'autonomy is, *ipso facto*, self-limitation' is in fact a tautology for Castoriadis (1991, 173). For self-limitation not to slide into self-oppression, however, an ethics of autonomous reason (which Castoriadis locates in the *paideia* of the citizens) is necessary. Individuals need to internalise 'both the necessity of laws and the possibility of putting the laws into question'; they need to be 'capable of interrogation, reflectiveness and deliberation', both 'loving freedom and accepting responsibility' (1991, 173–4). Consequently a careful balance between freedom from all constraints and absolute limitation is the product of conscious, reflective, autonomous reason and action.

In this sense, we can think of autonomy and freedom as gradational concepts, the practices of which depend on specific relational contexts. Indeed, for Foucault, 'relations of power', as 'a relationship in which one person tries to control the conduct of the other', can only exist insofar as there is 'at least a certain degree of freedom on both sides' (Foucault 1997, 292). The degree of freedom one enjoys is always relational and contextual: one may enjoy limited freedom in one context or set of power relations and more freedom in another. That is to say freedom is not an absolute value that can either be exercised fully or lost completely; some, little, or greater degrees of freedom can also be enjoyed, depending on the relations of power at work at a given moment. In the same vein, as discussed above, autonomy should not be confused with freedom from all limitation; it is rather the conscious exercise of free thinking and questioning – always enmeshed in, and constrained by, networks of power relations. Autonomy, in other words, is a reasoned exercise of relating to others, poised between (absolute) freedom and coercion. Historical conditions and conjunctural situations inform the margins of freedom and autonomy that specific practices may enjoy.

Autonomy, as a negotiated and gradational practice of reflectiveness and self-limitation, can be traced in Correa's CPI testimony. He acknowledged that at the beginning of the pandemic, when much was still unknown about Covid-19, ambivalence and uncertainty were prevailing among the medical staff with regards to the appropriate treatment (Senado Federal 2021, 872). Physicians might question the protocol's efficacy, yet expectations and hope that the clinical trials with hydroxychloroquine, ivermectin and other drugs and methods included in the early treatment might prove, to some degree, effective in treating Covid-19 shaped an atmosphere of confusion inside Prevent Senior, which contributed to tempering their resistance.

Nevertheless, even though there was some reflectiveness and interrogation on the part of physicians, and therefore some degree of autonomy, self-limitation prevailed under a climate of 'evangelisation', which asserted that the drugs worked in the absence of robust evidence against the early treatment at that phase of the pandemic. Therefore at the first moment, in the early stages of the pandemic, physician's autonomy (as autonomous reason in the sense discussed above) while present, receded, giving space to corporate autonomy.

After the first months of the outbreak, or during a second pandemic moment, international medical consensus was formed around the inefficacy of hydroxychloroquine, ivermectin and other drugs included in the Covid Kit and used as part of the early treatment for Covid-19. Despite this consensus, however, Prevent Senior continued to defend the early treatment and urge its medical staff to prescribe the above-mentioned drugs. In this scenario dissent was silenced by summary dismissals and a culture of intimidation. Eventually there was little or no room left for questioning. Under high-handed micro-management many physicians felt compelled to follow the company's directives, restricting any reservations to private or confidential conversations.

Feeling coerced to prescribe a treatment even when they considered it to be unsuitable, many physicians spoke of a complete lack of autonomy at Prevent Senior. Their descriptions corroborate Castoriadis's thesis: when there is no room for questioning (in this case, of the health protocol and instructions given), there is no space for autonomous action. Even though 'the reflective activity' might have emerged in private conversations (evincing *some* exercise of autonomy), it was not able to exceed the confines of intimacy and openly challenge the company's policies. To put it another way, physician's autonomy did not hinder corporate autonomy, which permeated through the medical practices at Prevent Senior.

We can therefore outline three moments which, although not entirely distinct, speak to the different dynamics of power relations and possibilities for autonomous action as these developed at Prevent Senior. At the beginning of the pandemic physician's autonomy, understood as the physicians' freedom to prescribe a treatment of their choice and to question the company's health protocol, while timid and reticent, was present and moderately challenged corporate autonomy. At a second moment during the pandemic, however, corporate autonomy appears to have swept physician's autonomy aside, leaving little or no room for questioning. It was only once physicians decided to denounce the company's practices and its health protocol that corporate autonomy encountered hindrance and physician's autonomy began to gain space.

At that third moment, guided by *proairesis* and *epistēmē* (choice and knowledge), not *anagkē* and *agnoia* (necessity and ignorance), physicians performed the 'virtuous act' (Foucault 2014, 105) of openly questioning corporate autonomy by exercising their own autonomous reason. As the CPI investigations were unfolding and the hearings captivated public attention, the constellation of power relations between the two types of autonomy discussed in the chapter was reconfigured; physician's autonomy was amplified and corporate autonomy was at last showing signs of reflectiveness and restraint. At the same time, however, Prevent Senior's board of directors insisted on their interpretation of physician's autonomy. In so doing they sought to establish a direct relation of accountability between physicians and patients, dissociating the company from the health protocol and denying liability for any irregular practices.

## Authoritarian affordances

As must have become clear by now, the discussion of the debate around physician's autonomy in the case of Prevent Senior does not aim at establishing whether those involved *actually* believed, or did not believe, in the efficacy of the early treatment against Covid-19. What interests me instead is the exploration of how such a conveniently articulated notion of autonomy, reduced to unregulated medical-ethical-legal licence to conduct experiments often without the patients' consent, prevailed over more conventional understandings of autonomy (as self-constraint, inherent in *nomos*)? How, in other words, did corporate autonomy, as discussed above, gain relevance and traction, and become Prevent Senior's *modus operandi*? Why was physician's autonomy sidelined, or even brazenly repressed, during a global health crisis? What were the conditions of possibility for such a configuration of power relations between physicians and the company's executive board, and what enabled some physicians eventually to come forward? Considering the coercive nature of such corporate autonomy, I frame the conditions of possibility for its emergence as authoritarian affordances.

A starting point in unravelling the infrastructure of authoritarian affordances that gave corporate autonomy such impetus is the 'confluence of interests' (Senado Federal 2021, 839) between sectors of the federal government and Prevent Senior. This 'confluence' reached a crescendo in the 'pact' agreed between the two. As Bruna Morato, the lawyer representing former Prevent Senior employees, maintained in her CPI testimony, physicians spoke of an 'ideological alignment' between Prevent Senior and interest groups inside or close to the government around the idea that:

> The economy could not stop and what they needed to do was the following: give hope so that the people could come out on the streets. And this hope had a name: 'hydroxychloroquine'. (Senado Federal 2021, 846)

According to former Prevent Senior employees, the company called a staff meeting to announce their 'collaboration' with the federal government on the use of the early treatment, which consisted in providing scientific basis for the government's 'return to normality' agenda.

One can speculate about what each side had to gain from that pact. Four desirable outcomes – contain fear amidst a health emergency, prevent an acute financial crisis, preserve its alliances with key stakeholders and maintain its popularity – are commonly understood to have been motivating factors for the federal government's defence of the early treatment (Ricard and Medeiros 2020; Casarões and Magalhães, 2021; Cavalcante et al., 2021). Prevent Senior, on the other hand, effectively shielded by the pact and enjoying an economically 'healthier' functioning of its hospital units by keeping as many patients as possible out, would also have had a lot to gain in the case of its health protocol being proved efficacious, namely international reputation and financial gain. One can assume, therefore, that on both sides there was a sincere desire that the early treatment should prove successful.

Yet the key factor in our discussion of authoritarian affordances is that in this case, independently of such wishful thinking, the early treatment *had* to work. The plaintiffs claimed that Prevent Senior agreed to produce data that would corroborate the theory that a Covid-19 treatment was available, and that there was therefore no reason to stay at home or even wear protective face masks. In other words, the early treatment's efficacy was predetermined; it would not be reached through clinical trials and empirical studies, and it was not liable to change. The stakes were so high that the possibility of admitting that the treatment was ineffective was ruled out; if the treatment did not work, then it would have to appear that it did.

As the CPI investigations demonstrated, Prevent Senior would consider a patient's death as 'discharge' (*alta*) and change the International Codification of Disease after a certain time in the hospital so that their death would appear unrelated to Covid-19. Using such methods, Prevent Senior under-notified Covid-19-related deaths and consequently appeared for some time to be successful in its pioneering health protocol. Members of the federal government, including the president himself, frequently commended the company's protocol, which they touted as panacea for Covid-19; they even rebuked the public healthcare system (SUS) for not seeking to adopt it. In the oscillation between Bolsonaro's public scepticism over vaccines and a pro-immunisation discourse, as examined by Barberia, Moreira and Costa Rosa in Chapter 6, the government's active and public engagement with Prevent Senior's health protocol is part of the former president's more sober and rational approach to the pandemic, as opposed to moments of denialism and refusal to take action.

The eagerness and determination of Prevent Senior and sectors of the federal government to defend the early treatment despite its results is well summarised in Rodrigo Nunes's (2021) description of 'freestyle entrepreneurship' – something that, he argues, has gained a new momentum under Bolsonaro's administration:

> [T]he shortest path to victory is the discovery, whether of a small marginal advantage or of the next big idea. And, naturally, where there are many people looking for a shortcut, there will always be quick-witted ones whose shortcut is convincing others that they found one. (Nunes 2021, online)

In this type of neoliberal subjectivity, where finance and influencer economy have an ever-increasing weight, the management of self-image – and the public perception of this – is a key mechanism of generating value. In this sense, rather than *proving* the early treatment's efficacy, it was essential to *convince* the Brazilian population that it worked.

To operate in such a framework, an interpretation of freedom as 'dirempted from the social' and hence 'not just unlimited, but legitimately exercised without concern for social context or consequences, without restraint, civility, or care for society as a whole or individuals within it' (Brown 2019, 42) becomes essential. Such conceptualisation of freedom, with its undemocratic imperatives and associated attack on the social, can be traced, as Wendy Brown (2018, 2019) shows, to the founding ideas of neoliberalism.

According to this rationality, which Brown identifies as specifically neoliberal, freedom is reduced 'to unregulated personal licence in the context of disavowing the social and dismantling society' (Brown 2019, 45). Instead:

> freedom is equated wholly with the pursuit of private ends, it is appropriately unregulated, and it is largely exercised to enhance the value, competitive positioning or market share of a person or firm. (Brown 2018, 62)

It is from this specific understanding of freedom that corporate autonomy emerges empowered and finds fertile ground to impose itself over other, more conventional notions of autonomy.

If limitless freedom is desired in principle, this does not equal an elimination of rules of conduct that reinforce specific values and ensure the continuation of neoliberal rationality. As Brown (2019) reminds us, for Hayek:

> Democracy's opposite is authoritarianism, concentrated but not necessarily unlimited political power. Liberalism's opposite is totalitarianism, complete control of every aspect of life. This makes authoritarianism compatible with a liberal society – freedom, traditional morals, a protected private sphere. (Brown 2019, 72–3)

In this sense (libertarian) markets and (conservative) morals are not incompatible, but articulated together and mobilised by an authoritarian neoliberal rationality that speaks in the name of freedom. While Prevent Senior pinned its hopes on 'physician's autonomy' to evade liability, its motto 'loyalty and obedience' did not allude to medical ethics but to a rigid corporate hierarchy that needed to be observed. The company was granted scope to test its health protocol with the government's backing and the acquiescence of some of its staff, but physicians were expected to follow orders without exercising any 'reflective activity'.

Just as the presence of rigid rules of conduct are part and parcel of the neoliberal rationality Brown analyses, the absence or strict limitation of governance and control mechanisms, especially when markets are concerned, is also an essential part of it. In this respect, different parties were enmeshed in the conjunctural configuration of authoritarian affordances; directly or indirectly, they enhanced the conditions in which corporate autonomy operated.

The 'Brazil cannot stop' campaign mentioned above, along with a government-launched smartphone application – with the ostensible aim of expediting diagnosis (TrateCOV), but which in fact only indicated the Covid Kit drugs independently of the symptoms input) – are but two notorious cases of active government mobilisation in favour of a swift 'return to normality' that strengthened the broader infrastructure of authoritarian affordances on which Prevent Senior's corporate autonomy relied. The Brazilian Federal Board of Medicine's decision in favour of the prescription of chloroquine and hydroxychloroquine to Covid-19 patients with light and mild symptoms also contributed to this infrastructure.

Indeed, President Bolsonaro referred to this decision in his UN address of September 2021, when he defended the early treatment in the name of physician's autonomy. Other medical associations, such as Physicians for Life (*Médicos pela Vida*), which was created to disseminate the early treatment, found favourable conditions both in the above decision and in the adoption of Prevent Senior's health protocol by the Ministry of Health (Furlan and Caramelli 2021, 2).

If we consider the operations outlined above as 'active' enablers of authoritarian affordances, there were also 'passive' ones: regulatory and auditing institutions, for example, such as the National Regulatory Agency for Private Health Insurance and Plans (ANS) and the Brazilian Health Regulatory Agency (Anvisa), who could have taken action to halt the consolidation of corporate autonomy. Walter Correa, physician and former Prevent Senior employee, underlined in his CPI testimony the critical role such institutions may have had in detecting and addressing irregularities and limitless freedom: 'Prevent Senior wouldn't exist if it wasn't for the omissions of such entities' (Senado Federal 2021, 894).

If the pandemic conjuncture was propitious for an emergency situation in which inspection could be suspended or restricted, it is also important to note that these were not entirely new problems. As Elias de Oliveira et al. (2020) show for the Public Prosecutor's Office and the Public Prosecutor's Office National Council, for example, little transparency and only weak accountability mechanisms are in place to evaluate the performance of prosecutors who appear to enjoy ample discretionary powers to select, assess or neglect individual cases.

By the same token, if authoritarian affordances, within the neoliberal framework described above, were exacerbated under the pandemic and Bolsonaro's administration, the conditions of possibility for their emergence had been in the making for quite some time. As others discuss in this volume, the weakening of different democratic institutions in recent years did not begin with Bolsonaro. Likewise, strategies of contestation and resistance to such changes (such as those against reduced bureaucratic autonomy discussed by Bersch, Lotta and Thomas in Chapter 4) go hand in hand with practices of repression and silencing.

A long authoritarian tradition (Schwarcz 2021) met with neoliberal policies, especially from the 1990s onwards, in Brazil (Hatzikidi and Dullo 2021, 7–10). It radically shaped political rationalities and reality principles that reach well beyond economic policy and capital enhancement. Undergoing continuous transformation under different historical periods and administrations, Brazilian neoliberalism appears to have morphed in recent years into an authoritarian (or even totalitarian, according to some analysts) hull, which

> defin[es] all social and political spheres not only as organisations, but as a specific kind of organisation that runs through society: the company; the school is a company, the hospital is a company, the cultural centre is a company. (Chauí 2020, 321; see also Saad-Filho 2020)

Having explored the conditions of possibility for the configuration of power relations and diverse interpretations of autonomy that emerged in the case of Prevent Senior, it is worth briefly considering the context in which some of its employees decided to come forward and denounce the practices at the company's hospital units. With their autonomy crippled even during a pandemic situation, physicians at Prevent Senior understood that financial aspects took precedence over health aspects within a broader politico-economic context that favoured such decisions. However, the creation of the congressional panel determined to investigate the federal government's handling of the pandemic, coupled with its remarkable success in capturing audience attention nationwide, were strong indications that a tide of dissent was gaining momentum. This context, which opened space for an independent examination of all sorts of wrongdoings related to the pandemic, was likely to have encouraged parties who may have been previously hesitant or intimidated to come forward and speak out against illicit acts and authoritarian attitudes.

## Concluding remarks

In exploring the case of Prevent Senior, a Brazilian private healthcare and health insurance provider, and the controversy around its health protocol for treating Covid-19, this chapter critically discussed the different instances of autonomy as they were mobilised and expressed by the two main parties involved – namely physicians and the company's board of directors. The radically dissenting interpretations of 'physician's autonomy' – generally understood as the physician's liberty to examine a patient and to prescribe an appropriate treatment to the best of their knowledge and in line with medical ethics – were discussed against the background of Castoriadis's theory of autonomy as reflectiveness and self-limitation. It was demonstrated that physician's autonomy, in the context of this debate, emerged as a sort of empty signifier which carried different meanings and associations for the two parties: while physicians claimed they were intimidated and coerced to follow Prevent Senior's health protocol without having room for autonomous action, the company mobilised it as synonymous to complete physician's responsibility, denying any corporate liability over medical malpractices.

Such corporate logic, which equated physician's autonomy with limitless freedom for the company, shaped the way in which relations of power were configured at Prevent Senior. I have tentatively called this operational logic 'corporate autonomy' in order to distinguish it from 'physician's autonomy', understood as freedom within limitations. Indeed, as a kind of law (*nomos*), autonomy implies constraint. As argued in this chapter, both freedom and self-limitation are inherent to autonomy, better understood as a reflective and relational process of conciliation between two diverging forces: unbridled freedom and coercion. Corporate autonomy, on the other hand, as a specific kind of logic afforded and enhanced by an authoritarian neoliberal rationality, negates 'the reflective activity', dictating instead loyalty and obedience.

The different logics or appropriations of autonomy in this case cohere with the paradoxical interpretation of democracy and freedom by the former president, as discussed in the introduction to this volume. In both cases, authoritarian practices steeped in a neoliberal rationality of (often unaccountable) action prioritise ends over means, discipline and hierarchy over autonomy and equality. In line with this book's broader themes, this chapter has delved into the intricacies and possibilities of manifesting dissent in a context of growing control and intimidation. In doing so, it has also engaged with the volume's desire to explore the different struggles over the meaning and practice of democracy.

Prevent Senior's case emblematically, if also tragically, exemplifies the dangers attached to an interpretation of autonomy as limitless freedom. Guided by a broader infrastructure of authoritarian affordances, which included the promise of unaccountability and impunity as discussed in the chapter, and led by its own aspirations to revolutionise medicine and achieve international fame and success, Prevent Senior relied on an understanding of autonomy as unrestricted freedom against a growing medical consensus in relation to its health protocol.

Both historical and conjunctural factors contributed to the emergence of such an infrastructure, which gained a new momentum under the Bolsonaro administration and the pandemic. In this context private ends and corporate profits often disregarded 'the imperative of health', leading to one of the deadliest responses to the Covid-19 emergency in the world. The ongoing investigations of this and other cases of suspected irregular practices and infractions are an important reminder that with autonomy comes not only freedom, but also responsibility and accountability.

## References

Bastos Lima, M., K. Hatzikidi and K. da Costa. 2025. 'Gore capitalism and necropolitics in Brazil's malgovernance of the COVID-19 pandemic', *Latin American Perspectives*. https://doi.org/10.1177/0094582X241311804.

Brown, W. 2018. 'Neoliberalism's Frankenstein: Authoritarian freedom in twenty-first century "democracies"', *Critical Times* 1(1): 60–79. https://doi.org/10.1215/26410478-1.1.60.

Brown, W. 2019. *In the Ruins of Neoliberalism: The rise of antidemocratic politics in the West*. New York: Columbia University Press.

Casarões, G. and D. Magalhães. 2021 'The hydroxychloroquine alliance: How far-right leaders and alt-science preachers came together to promote a miracle drug', *RAP: Brazilian Journal of Public Administration* 55(1): 197–214. https://doi.org/10.1590/0034-761220200556.

Castoriadis, C. 1981. 'From ecology to autonomy', *Thesis Eleven* 3(1): 8–22. https://doi.org/10.1177/072551368100300102.

Castoriadis, C. 1991. 'Power, politics, autonomy'. In *C. Castoriadis: Philosophy, politics, autonomy*, edited by D. A. Curtis, 143–74. Oxford: Oxford University Press.

Cavalcante, S., M. Miggiolaro Chaguri and M. Nicolau Netto. 2021. 'O conservadorismo-liberal no Brasil de Bolsonaro: A força da articulação no contexto de pandemia', *Brasiliana: Journal for Brazilian Studies* 10(1): 285–307.

Chauí, M. 2020. 'O totalitarismo neoliberal', *Anacronismo e Irrupción: Revista de teoría y filosofía política clásica y moderna* 10(18): 307–28.

Código de Ética Médica. 2010. 'Resolução CFM n.1931 de 17 de setembro de 2009'. Brasília: Conselho Federal de Medicina.

Elias de Oliveira, V., G. Lotta and N. Pires de Vasconcelos. 2020. 'Ministério Público, autonomia funcional e discricionariedade: Ampla atuação em políticas públicas, baixa *accountability*', *Revista de Estudos Empíricos em Direito* 7(1): 181–95. https://doi.org/10.19092/reed.v7i1.425.

Foucault, M. 1984. 'The politics of health in the eighteenth century'. In *The Foucault Reader*, edited by P. Rabinow, 273–89. New York: Pantheon Books.

Foucault, M. 1997. 'The ethics of the concern of the self as a practice of freedom'. In *Ethics: Subjectivity and truth. Essential works of Foucault, 1954–1984* (vol. 1), edited by P. Rabinow, 281–301. Translated by R. Hurley et al. London: Penguin Books.

Foucault, M. 2014. 'Lecture five; 6 February 1980'. In *On the Government of the Living: Lectures at the Collège De France 1979–1980*, edited by M. Senellart, F. Ewald and A. Fontana, 93–113. https://doi.org/10.22439/fs.v0i18.4654. Translated from the French by G. Burchell and edited by A. I. Davidson. New York: Palgrave Macmillan.

Furlan, L. and B. Caramelli. 2021. 'The regrettable story of the "Covid Kit" and the "Early treatment of Covid-19" in Brazil', *The Lancet Regional Health – Americas* 4, 100089. Accessed 28 June 2024. https://doi.org/10.1016/j.lana.2021.100089.

Hatzikidi, K. 2020. 'The worst is not over yet: The lives and deaths of the "self" and "others" in Brazil's response to the Covid-19 pandemic', *Bulletin of Latin American Research* 39(S1): 71–4. https://doi.org/10.1111/blar.13187.

Hatzikidi, K. and E. Dullo. 2021. 'Introduction: Brazil's conservative return'. In *A Horizon of (Im)possibilities: A chronicle of Brazil's conservative turn*, edited by K. Hatzikidi and E. Dullo, 1–33. London: University of London Press.

Nunes, R. 2021. 'Pequenos fascismos, grandes negócios: O bolsonarismo como empreendedorismo – e o que isso diz sobre a natureza da direita e do capitalismo hoje', *Revista Piauí*, ed. 181. Accessed 28 June 2024. Available online at https://piaui.folha.uol.com.br/materia/pequenos-fascismos-grandes-negocios/.

Ricard, J. and J. Medeiros. 2020. 'Using misinformation as a political weapon: Covid-19 and Bolsonaro in Brazil', *Misinformation Review*, Harvard Kenney School. Accessed 28 June 2024. Available online at https://misinforeview.hks.harvard.edu/article/using-misinformation-as-a-political-weapon-covid-19-and-bolsonaro-in-brazil/.

Saad-Filho, A. 2020. 'Varieties of neoliberalism in Brazil (2003–2019)', *Latin American Perspectives* 47(1): 9–27. https://doi.org/10.1177/0094582X19881968.

Schwarcz, L. Moritz. 2021. 'The past of the present'. In *A Horizon of (Im)possibilities: A chronicle of Brazil's conservative turn*, edited by K. Hatzikidi and E. Dullo, 37–55. London: University of London Press.

Senado Federal. 2021. Comissão Parlamentar de Inquérito (CPI) da Pandemia, Relatório Final. Accessed 28 June 2024. Available online at https://legis.senado.leg.br/comissoes/mnas?codcol=2441&tp=4.

# 6
# Regimes of truth: disinformation and conflicting on- and offline realities

Lorena G. Barberia, Natália de Paula Moreira and Isabel Seelaender Costa Rosa

## Introduction

Since the onset of Covid-19, incumbents quickly understood that their political careers and re-election prospects could be bolstered should they be perceived to lead their societies to winning the war against SARS-CoV-2 (Barberia, Plümper and Whitten 2021). The vast majority of government leaders across the globe moved quickly and remained steadfast in their support for the development, approval and procurement of Covid-19 vaccines. Indeed, leaders in high-income countries that account for only a fraction of the global population worked quickly to secure and hoard more than half of the projected early supply of doses, even before vaccines had been approved (Zhou 2022). In contrast to these leaders, President Jair Bolsonaro stands out for his reversal of previous efforts to promote and secure vaccines in 2020. We show how, starting in late 2020, Bolsonaro increased his rhetoric to dissuade the Brazilian population from protecting themselves with Covid-19 vaccines. He also refused to secure sufficient vaccines to ensure early coverage for the entire adult population.

Bolsonaro's stance contrasts starkly with many of his closest allies, including Benjamin Netanyahu in Israel (Tubi 2022) and Vladimir Putin in Russia (Baraniuk 2021). However, he shares some similarities with Donald Trump in the US (Lacatus and Meibauer 2021). While Putin invested in deploying Sputnik V across the developing world, and Trump pressured for vaccine approvals before the US presidential elections, Bolsonaro heightened his verbal attacks, vetoed or delayed the federal government's vaccine procurement agreements. In addition, he failed to allocate sufficient resources to ensure Brazilians had ready access to a diversified vaccine portfolio.

Like Trump, Bolsonaro was quick and persistent in condemning China as the source of the virus. Yet Bolsonaro went even further than Trump as he increased his attacks on vaccines in late 2020, including those of Chinese origin at a time clinical trials were already emerging, suggesting that vaccines would soon be authorised in Europe and the US, and when it became increasingly clear that vaccine supplies would be limited to a select number of nations in the developed West. As we illustrate in this chapter, Bolsonaro emphasised the experimental nature and adverse effects of Covid-19 vaccines produced by Pfizer, a large multinational pharmaceutical firm, and Sinovac, a private laboratory belonging to the Chinese pharmaceutical industry. We contend that Bolsonaro did so for strategic reasons.

In addition, we argue that several factors explain Bolsonaro's shift to delay further and reduce the likelihood that vaccines would be quickly adopted and used to help contain the pandemic's toll in Brazil. Firstly, an important factor contributing to Bolsonaro's U-turn concerns political rivalries – notably his dispute with João Doria, a centre-right politician who supported his presidential bid in 2018 but soon broke ties. As the governor of Brazil's largest and most powerful state, Doria was viewed as a potential rival in the 2022 elections. In 2020, early in the pandemic, Bolsonaro staked his bets on the Oxford/AstraZeneca vaccine, while Doria staked his claims on the CoronaVac/Sinovac vaccine. Both political leaders embarked on a competition to determine who would secure a political victory by distributing vaccines to Brazilians. Moreover, leaders in Brazil, as in other countries, politicised vaccines by country of origin.

Second, Bolsonaro became more critical of the safety of vaccines when scientific studies and news reports suggested that mRNA vaccines by Pfizer and Moderna might outperform rival vaccines, including the federal government's bet on the Oxford/AstraZeneca vaccine. Additionally, as the Brazilian government realised that securing additional vaccines from Pfizer and Sinovac would be much more costly (relative to the AstraZeneca agreement) and that deliveries would be delayed, Bolsonaro shifted from a discourse promoting vaccines to one that questioned their safety and efficacy at the beginning of the fourth quarter of 2020.

This chapter thus explains Bolsonaro's systematic efforts to delay and diminish the likelihood that vaccines would be quickly adopted and used to help contain the pandemic's toll in Brazil. Based on presidential speeches and social media interventions, we map Bolsonaro's contradictory vaccine discourse. For most of 2020 he remained supportive of vaccines. However, as news increased that these resources could soon be approved and distributed in other countries, Bolsonaro's strategy changed. He then began to question the highly favourable evidence that had emerged from clinical trials, choosing instead to emphasise that Covid-19 vaccination should not be mandatory. By late 2020 Bolsonaro repeatedly questioned the safety of Covid-19 vaccines and stressed their experimental nature. This rhetorical shift coincided with poor prognostics for Bolsonaro's vaccine technology 'bet' and his reluctance to shift the federal government's procurement to a larger portfolio of Covid-19 vaccines.

For this reason, in the second part of the chapter, we explore how Bolsonaro's change of stance is aligned with critical policy decisions regarding vaccine procurement and distribution. Early on, Bolsonaro failed to signal Brazil's leadership as a Covid-19 vaccine champion by acquiring a significant share of the country's required vaccines via COVAX. His government failed to sign contracts to guarantee sufficient AstraZeneca vaccines to inoculate all eligible Brazilians. He further refused to procure vaccines, including the CoronaVac and Pfizer vaccines, to diversify Brazil's vaccine portfolio. In fact Bolsonaro immediately vetoed a procurement agreement signed by the third Minister of Health, General Eduardo Pazuello, with the Butantan Institute and failed to back Ministry of Health (MOH) negotiations with Pfizer in 2020. The federal government's inertia hindered Brazil's ability to secure and quickly vaccinate adults against Covid-19. Without social and political mobilisation, Covid-19 vaccines would have encountered even further delays.

Finally, this chapter considers how Bolsonaro's rhetoric and actions affected the willingness of the population to accept vaccination, drawing on public opinion data for 2020.

## Bolsonaro's vaccine procurement and vaccination strategy: an analysis of public speeches, interviews and social media posts

To examine Bolsonaro's rhetorical strategic choices, we analysed his official and unofficial presidential speeches, tweets from @jairbolsonaro and press interviews from 10 January to 31 December 2020. This period is essential because it captures how Bolsonaro responded to increased uncertainty regarding vaccine development, efficacy and availability. On Twitter (now X) and in official speeches Bolsonaro was more reserved in his attacks. Between March and December 2020 President Bolsonaro gave 43 official speeches, mentioning Covid-19 immunisation only in eight. We also identified and analysed 26 Covid-19 vaccine-related tweets in this period.

Based on these texts, we show that the Brazilian right-wing populists' Covid-19 vaccine rhetoric can be separated into two distinct periods. In the first semester, Bolsonaro extolled clinical trials and vaccination. However, gradually in the second semester, and most critically in October, November and December of 2020, Bolsonaro shifted his discourse to raise concerns regarding vaccine safety and side effects, and to oppose mandatory vaccination.

## First semester of 2020

We coded Bolsonaro's tweets and speeches based on whether posts were in favour of, neutral towards or clearly against immunisation. In the first semester (Fig. 6.1), Bolsonaro did not mention vaccines in his public addresses, but his tweets were overwhelmingly favourable towards Covid-19 vaccines. Indeed, in the entire year Bolsonaro issued 13 vaccine-favourable tweets. Only six of his tweets manifested an unfavourable position towards Covid-19 vaccination. The remaining seven tweets were limited to providing information and are consequently coded 'neutral' regarding his position towards vaccination. In the first semester Bolsonaro tweeted the most about Covid-19 vaccines in June 2020; all of these messages supported vaccines. During the pandemic's first months, Bolsonaro emphasised both vaccine development and Brazilian procurement of these technologies.

Bolsonaro emphasised vaccination as part of a national crisis management strategy. In the first semester, his administration's pandemic response largely depended on partnerships with Oxford University and the US government. His tweets and speeches alluded to these partnerships as being fundamental to Brazil's pandemic response. Rather than citing the multinational pharmaceutical industry (such as the AstraZeneca-BioNTech), Bolsonaro cited partnerships with universities and countries (for example, the University of Oxford and the US) (Deutsche Welle Brasil 2020) in his speeches and tweets. His tweet on 1 June 2020 helps to underscore his view that Brazilian cooperation with the US (Poder 360, 2020) would be critical to the country's response:

> Brazil-US cooperation in the fight against COVID-19 continues to advance. Today, two million doses of hydroxychloroquine donated by the USA arrived in Brazil. We will collaborate with the US on the clinical research of hydroxychloroquine and the development of a vaccine.[1]

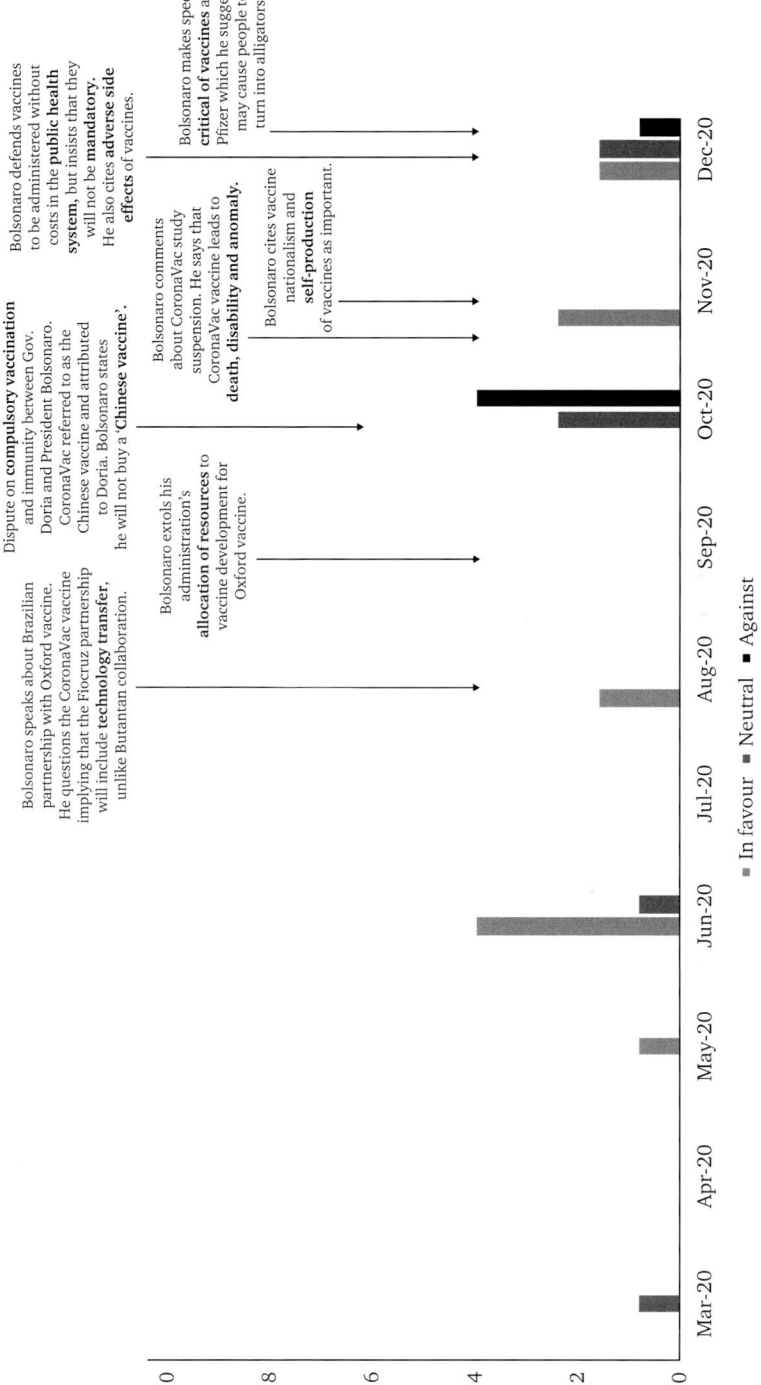

**Figure 6.1** Bolsonaro's tweets, speeches and key events relating to Covid-19 vaccines in 2020. Source: Twitter, Folha de Sao Paulo and official presidential speeches.

In the same week Bolsonaro also published several tweets extolling the Oxford/AstraZeneca vaccine. The first tweet celebrates the results of promising clinical trials; the second emphasises Brazil's leadership on vaccines as part of the Covid-19 pandemic response. This specific tweet, dated 6 June 2020, affirmed:

> @govbr takes another step towards the development of a vaccine against Covid-19. Anvisa decree authorises clinical trials of a potential vaccine by the University of Oxford.[2]

Bolsonaro also emphasised that Brazil's vaccine strategy would prioritise the nation's strategic interests and ensure that partnerships included technology transfer. On 7 August 2020 Bolsonaro sent celebratory tweets to mark the signing of an agreement between Oxford and Fiocruz to collaborate on vaccine development. In sharing this news, Bolsonaro emphasised:

> This partnership also aims at the entire transfer of technology to Brazil, so that the vaccine can be produced here at no further cost ... Once its effectiveness is proven, we will have 100 million doses from January 2021, which will be distributed free of charge.[3]

However, even if Bolsonaro generally supported Covid-19 vaccine clinical trials and committed to his government procuring these technologies, this does not mean he demonstrated an understanding of the virus and its dangers in his speeches and social media messages. Indeed, it is in this semester that Bolsonaro boasted that Covid-19 disease is a 'little flu' and that, as an athlete, he would not suffer severe health consequences if infected. Moreover, Bolsonaro insisted on affirming that other 'flus' had killed more people than Covid-19 (Folha de São Paulo 2021). Notwithstanding his minimisation of deaths and the severity of the pandemic, Bolsonaro signalled his acceptance that, like other 'flus', including the 2009 SARS pandemic, a vaccine was a critical development that Brazil needed to acquire and employ.

## Second semester of 2020

In the second semester of 2020 Bolsonaro's rhetoric changed significantly, especially starting in October. His new rhetoric relayed three key messages: vaccination should not be mandatory, vaccines may cause adverse effects and Chinese vaccines should be evaluated with increased scrutiny. This section explains how Bolsonaro relayed these messages to the public.

Initially Bolsonaro continued with the discourse he employed in the first semester of 2020. In September 2020, for example, Bolsonaro addressed the 75th Session of the United Nations General Assembly. There he affirmed:

> Covid-19 has become the centre of attention over the course of this year and, first of all, I wish to express my sorrow for each and every life lost. From the very beginning, in my country, I warned that we had two problems to solve, the virus and joblessness, and that both issues had to be addressed simultaneously and with the same sense of responsibility ... More than 100 billion dollars were allocated to cover health-related actions and help small and micro-enterprises; measures were also taken to offset the loss in revenue collection in state and local governments. More than 200 thousand indigenous families were assisted with foodstuffs and Covid prevention efforts. In close contact with healthcare professionals, we encouraged early treatment of the disease. 400 million dollars were dedicated to the research, development and production of the Oxford vaccine in Brazil. In Brazil, hospitals did not lack the means to cater to Covid patients.[4]

Gradually, however, a shift in rhetoric occurred. Bolsonaro started to insist that an individual's freedom of choice on whether to undergo vaccination should be respected; vaccine mandates should not be adopted by Brazilian authorities. Starting in October 2020, Bolsonaro began to tweet about mandatory vaccination. By October 2020 Russia had approved Sputnik V and was vaccinating the 'red zones' of Russian hospitals, which encompass healthcare workers and other high-risk groups. The Gamaleya Institute confirmed that 10,000 people had received the vaccine under this authorisation. In this same period Bolsonaro posted his second most popular vaccine tweet on 24 October 2020, proclaiming that only his dog *Faísca* should be submitted to mandatory vaccination: 'Good evening to all. Mandatory vaccines only for Faísca.'[5] Notably, Twitter users' engagement in response to these initial tweets rejecting Covid-19 vaccines and vaccination was substantially higher than to the ones in which he talks about the country's vaccine strategy, technology transfer or partnerships to develop a vaccine.

Bolsonaro also began to launch attacks on Chinese vaccines. The attack on these vaccines is linked closely to Bolsonaro's criticism of

São Paulo's former Governor, João Doria, the public research institute, Institute Butantan, and its partnership with Sinovac, a private Chinese laboratory, to develop vaccines. Of the tweets posted by President Bolsonaro in 2020, the one that generated the most significant repercussions was a post on 21 October. It ran as follows:

> João Doria's Chinese vaccine. For my government, any vaccine, before being made available to the population, must be scientifically proved by the Ministry of Health and certified by ANVISA. The Brazilian people will not be anyone's guinea pig.[6]

In other words Bolsonaro shifted tactics to attack specific vaccines and politicians who defended more aggressive vaccination programmes. However, this reversal only began in late 2020. The public following Bolsonaro on Twitter became increasingly responsive, engaging more with his rhetoric as the president's position emphasised opposition to vaccines and vaccination. Table 6.1 presents a summary of Bolsonaro's posts and their public repercussions. The highest impact was on posts against Covid-19 immunisation, which received 50,678 likes on average. Favourable tweets received 17,939 likes and those with a neutral position towards Covid-19 vaccines received 23,422 likes. Furthermore, tweets against Covid-19 vaccines also received most of the re-tweets (6,972), quotes (8,901) and replies (14,210).

One of the events most emblematic of the shift in Bolsonaro's official discourse regarding vaccination was his comments immediately following the suspension of the CoronaVac clinical trial, following the death of one of the participants in November 2020. Even though Anvisa issued a clearance allowing the clinical trial to resume, Bolsonaro and his allies launched a sustained attack against CoronaVac. On 10 November 2020 the president expressed his view on Facebook:

**Table 6.1** Positions of Bolsonaro's Covid-19 vaccine tweets and the public's engagement in 2020

| Position | Posts (Total) | Likes (Average) | Retweets (Average) | Quotes (Average) | Replies (Average) |
| --- | --- | --- | --- | --- | --- |
| Favorable | 13 | 17,939 | 2,835 | 512 | 1,964 |
| Neutral | 7 | 23,422 | 4,350 | 600 | 2,616 |
| Unfavorable | 6 | 50,678 | 6,972 | 8,901 | 14,210 |
| Average | 26 | 26,971 | 4,198 | 2,472 | 4,966 |

Source: Barberia, L. G. et al., 2023, 'Mapping political elites Covid-19 vaccine tweets in Brazilian Portuguese in 2020, 2021 and 2022'.

> Death, disability and anomalies. This is the vaccine that [Governor João] Doria wanted to force all São Paulo residents to take ... The president [Bolsonaro] said that the vaccine could never be mandatory. One more that Jair Bolsonaro wins.[7] (Della Coletta 2020)

Finally, in the second semester, Bolsonaro began to spread false vaccine information in his speeches. In several speeches and tweets he warns that Covid-19 vaccines could produce unwanted side effects, and that Pfizer will not accept responsibility for these collateral effects. In a speech in the city of Porto Seguro, Bahia, on 1 December 2020, made in the same week in which the FDA granted emergency use authorisation to Pfizer in the US, Bolsonaro stated:

> No one can force anyone to get vaccinated. I will not take it. I already had the virus. I already have antibodies. Why take the vaccine again? ... If you take it and become an alligator, it's your problem. If a man becomes a superman, if a woman grows a beard or a man speaks in a higher tone, they [Pfizer] have nothing to do with it.[8]

In sum, as this section has shown, a marked shift in Bolsonaro's rhetoric took place, starting in October 2020. He warned of side effects and hints that vaccines may lead to death. In these attacks, however, it should be noted that Bolsonaro is always careful to criticise two specific vaccines – Pfizer and CoronaVac. Even though there were investigations into adverse events, Bolsonaro expressed no concerns about possible side effects with Oxford/AstraZeneca. In the next section we discuss some of the reasons that may have contributed to Bolsonaro's adoption of a strategy critical to immunisation against Covid-19 by late 2020.

## Bolsonaro's vaccine procurement and vaccination policies in Brazil: chronicle of a death foretold

Table 6.2 summarises the dates, doses and amounts of the contracts for Covid-19 vaccines that the Brazilian federal government acquired in 2020 and 2021. In 2020 the Brazilian federal government hedged its bets on the Oxford/AstraZeneca vaccine. By September 2020 the Brazilian government had purchased enough doses to vaccinate 72 million Brazilians with two doses. Considering that 80 per cent of the over 210 million Brazilians are 16 and older, the Bolsonaro administration left 96 million Brazilians without vaccine coverage in 2020.

**Table 6.2** Brazilian Government Covid-19 vaccine purchase agreements in 2020 and 2021

| Procurement Date | Company | Vaccine | Quantity | Price/Dose (US\$) | Price/Dose (R\$) | Total Value (US\$) |
|---|---|---|---|---|---|---|
| Aug-20 | Fiocruz/AstraZeneca | ChAdOx1nCoV-19 | 10,04,00,000 | 3.16 | 16.97 | 31,72,64,000 |
| Sep-20 | CovaxFacility | AstraZeneca/Pfizer | 4,25,11,800 | 10.55 | 56.97 | 44,84,99,490 |
| Jan-21 | Fiocruz/AstraZeneca Instituto Serum | Covishield | 20,00,000 | 5.44 | 29.93 | 1,08,80,000 |
| Jan-21 | Fundação Butantan | Coronavac CHI-BRA | 4,60,00,000 | 10.82 | 58.2 | 49,77,20,000 |
| Feb-21 | Fundação Butantan | Coronavac BRA | 5,40,00,000 | 10.82 | 58.2 | 58,42,80,000 |
| Mar-21 | Pfizer/Biontech | Pfizer | 10,00,01,070 | 10 | 56.3 | 1,00,00,10,700 |
| Mar-21 | Janssen | Janssen | 3,80,00,000 | 10 | 56.3 | 38,00,00,000 |
| May-21 | Pfizer/Biontech | Pfizer | 10,00,00,000 | 12.25 | 56.3 | 1,22,50,00,000 |
| Total | | | 44,49,12,870 | | | 4,46,36,54,190 |

Source: da Fonseca, E.M. et al. (2021) 'Vacinas adquiridas e aprovadas para uso no Brasil contra COVID-19, Nota técnica 21', *Instituto de Estudos para Políticas de Saúde*.

Similar to crises that had occurred from insufficient supplies in hospital beds (Ranzani et al. 2021), testing (Barberia et al. 2023) and essential equipment during the pandemic, several state and municipal governments were actively seeking to explore opportunities to guarantee vaccines for their respective populations without relying on the Ministry of Health or the federal government's leadership (Castro et al. 2021). The most prominent and successful efforts occurred in the state of São Paulo. In early June 2020 the former São Paulo Governor João Doria, once a Bolsonaro supporter and now an aspiring candidate for the 2022 presidential election, successfully secured an agreement with Sinovac, a private Chinese pharmaceutical company. Under this deal the Butantan Institute, a state-owned research centre, invested 85 million reais ($16 million) to conduct a clinical trial of the Sinovac Covid-19 vaccine in Brazil (Reuters 2020). In exchange, the state of São Paulo's government, which runs Butantan, secured a commitment from Sinovac to secure priority access to the procurement of doses.

At the time, three months since the declaration of the pandemic, Brazil had already surpassed the number of deaths that China had experienced in its first month of the pandemic. Due to limited testing capacity, the Ministry of Health was restricting the detection of the virus only to hospitalised persons suspected of already having contracted severe infections (Ribeiro et al. 2023). Furthermore, even without testing, Brazil was already experiencing high infection rates, hospitalisation, and large numbers of deaths (Castro et al. 2021). By June 2020, while Bolsonaro debated with journalists about the severity of the virus, asserting it was only a 'little flu', the Ministry of Health was being administered by Eduardo Pazuello, an army general with no experience in health. In office as an interim appointee, Pazuello had become the third minister at the helm since the start of the pandemic (Barberia and Gómez 2020).

A full seven weeks after the Butantan-Sinovac agreement, Bolsonaro announced that the federal government had signed a memorandum of understanding with AstraZeneca. Under the agreement, the MOH committed to investing US $360 million in technology transfer and updating Fiocruz facilities in order to guarantee that the vaccine would be produced at Fiocruz. Under the agreement, the federal government committed to purchasing 100 million doses of the still-unproven vaccine at the cost of US $317 million (da Fonseca et al. 2021).

To put these milestones and contracted figures in perspective, by mid-August 2020 the US had secured 800 million doses of at least six vaccines in development. The UK had purchased 340 million doses of three vaccines and the European Union (EU) and Japan had each ordered hundreds of millions of doses. Brazilian efforts were timid and delayed compared to those of developed economies in the West.

On 17 January 2021, only 180 days after the beginning of the clinical trial that took place in Brazil, Anvisa granted the first Emergency Use Authorisation for two SARS-COV-2 vaccines in Brazil – the Oxford/AstraZeneca vaccine, to be deployed by Fiocruz, and the CoronaVac vaccine, to be deployed by the Butantan Institute. However, while both vaccines were authorised on the same date, Oxford/AstraZeneca vaccines were delayed. For the next three months CoronaVac remained the primary vaccine available to Brazilians in the first months of vaccination in 2021. As no other vaccine contracts had been signed there were limited options, so vaccine coverage was limited. The early arrival of vaccines could have been an important factor in impeding the devastation caused by the Delta variant in the second pandemic wave, which hit Brazil in late 2020 and early 2021. This second wave proved even more lethal than the first, tragically occurring while most of the developed world was vaccinating its adult population en masse. In Brazil there were long queues, with anxious Brazilians waiting for hours to secure a jab.

## Covid-19 vaccine hesitancy in Brazil and Bolsonaro's rhetorical strategy against vaccines

As we have shown above, President Bolsonaro's rhetorical strategy of raising significant concerns about the safety and efficacy of vaccines to combat Covid-19 was closely linked to his government's delay in procuring vaccines. In this section we present evidence to illustrate that these trends correlate with increased vaccine hesitancy towards Covid-19 vaccines in Brazil.

In the second semester of 2020, starting in October, Bolsonaro launched attacks on the safety and efficacy of the Covid-19 vaccines. Figure 6.2 depicts the percentage of Brazilian citizens who responded i) 'yes', ii) 'no' or iii) 'I don't know' to the question of whether they would get vaccinated if a COVID-19 vaccine was available (DataPoder 2020).[9]

In July 2020, 85 per cent of Brazilians declared that they would get vaccinated, while 8 per cent stated that they would not get vaccinated and 7 per cent were undecided (DataPoder 2020). A similar pattern was observed in August 2020. There was a slight decrease in the group that would take a vaccine (from 85 to 82 per cent) as well as

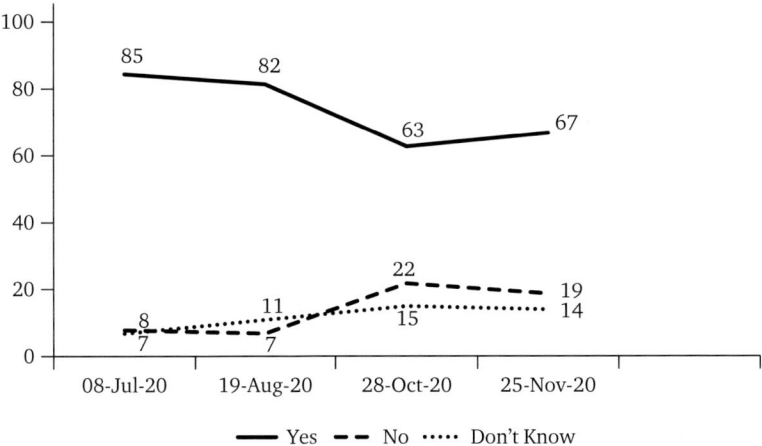

**Figure 6.2** Percentage of respondents willing to get vaccinated against Covid-19 in 2020, Brazil. Source: Data Poder. 2020.

an increase in the undecided group (rising from 7 to 11 per cent). Significantly, there is almost no change in the group that refused to accept a vaccination against Covid-19 (dropping from 8 to 7 per cent). However, a fundamental shift in the public's willingness to be vaccinated emerges when the same survey was repeated in October 2020. This survey reveals a substantial increase in the share of voters who express that they would not be vaccinated against SARS-CoV-2 and a decrease in the group willing to be vaccinated. Although several factors might explain such a change, the increase in the percentage of those reluctant to receive immunisation against COVID-19 coincides with the period in which President Bolsonaro started to criticise and raise doubts about the safety and efficacy of Covid-19 vaccines.

As discussed in the sections above, the first of Bolsonaro's tweets against Covid-19 vaccines were posted between 19 and 24 October 2020. As the public opinion data show, a dramatic change occurred in the support for getting vaccinated a few days after Bolsonaro's attacks. Before Bolsonaro's attacks the percentage of those willing to be vaccinated was above 80 per cent. Afterwards, however, the proportion was lower than 70 per cent in both the October and November 2020 polls.

As Figures 6.3a and 6.3b show, the most significant decline in the willingness to be vaccinated occurred among those who approved of Bolsonaro's job performance (Barberia and Rosa 2021).[10] In August 2020 (Fig. 6.3a), more than 70 per cent of the respondents said they would get vaccinated. This group was more prominent among those who did not support Bolsonaro's performance as president (84 per cent versus

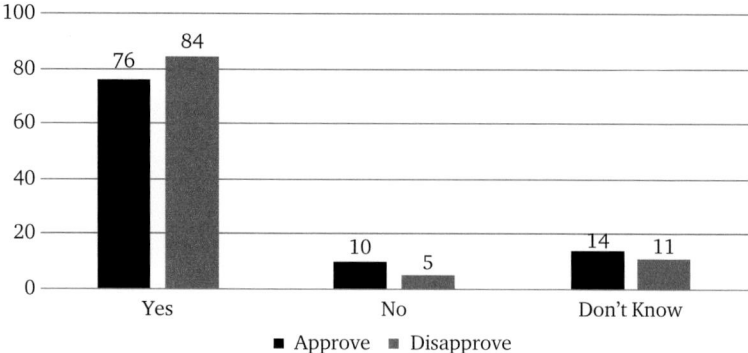

**Figure 6.3a** Willingness to be vaccinated against Covid-19 by those approving of Bolsonaro's government, August 2020. Source: Data Poder. 2020.

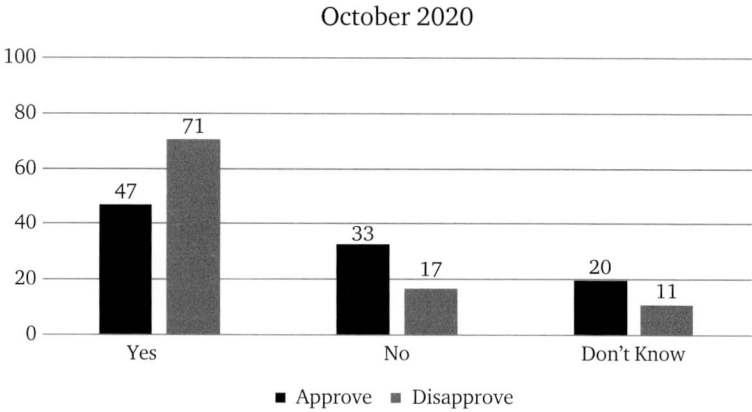

**Figure 6.3b** Willingness to be vaccinated against Covid-19 by those approving of Bolsonaro's government, October 2020. Source: Data Poder. 2020.

76 per cent). In October 2020 (Fig. 6.3b), however, only 47 per cent of those respondents who approved of Bolsonaro's performance as president declared themselves willing to receive a vaccine to protect them against SARS-CoV-2.

In contrast, 71 per cent of respondents who disapproved of Bolsonaro's job performance were willing to receive a vaccine. Among those who supported Bolsonaro's job performance, decline in the willingness to be vaccinated resulted in an increase of those who did not intend to be vaccinated (from 10 per cent to 33 per cent) or who did not know (from 14 per cent to 20 per cent). Significantly, among those who did not support the president's job performance there was again an increase in the group that did not intend to be vaccinated (from 5 per cent to 17 per cent). No change was observed in the undecided group. Overall, this evidence suggests that Bolsonaro's rhetorical strategy against vaccines increased vaccination hesitancy, and that such hesitancy was more pronounced among those who supported the president's job performance.

## Conclusion

During the COVID-19 pandemic, elected leaders presided over human history's most extensive vaccination campaign. This unprecedented situation required coordinated efforts as the pandemic spread across the globe. Leaders in different countries stepped up to promote and implement unparalleled national vaccination campaigns, starting in late 2020 and early 2021. In the case of Brazil, this chapter analysed President Jair Bolsonaro's discourse on vaccines and procurement policies in the year that Covid-19 vaccines were still under development, before progressing to receive emergency authorisation.

Our study helps to demonstrate how Bolsonaro failed to engage in the global race for vaccine procurement, either in words or actions, during the onset of the emergency. We show how his public rhetoric reflected conflicting views regarding SARS-CoV-2 immunisation, revealing a marked shift in the president's position by late 2020. After initially emphasising that Brazil would race to vaccinate its population, Bolsonaro reversed his position. He then stressed his scepticism concerning Covid-19 vaccines, their side effects and the benefits gained from natural infection.

While on holiday on the beach in the state of São Paulo, at a time when over 600,000 Brazilians had lost their lives to Covid-19, Bolsonaro spoke to journalists and a crowd of supporters. He declared:

> Why did many governors and mayors vaccinate young people between the ages of 12 and 17? Based on what? Anvisa's recommendation? The Ministry of Health? From whom? We are messing with lives. For kids under 20 the chance of having nothing, once contaminated, is 99.99 per cent. Is it worth the cost benefit of the vaccine?[11] (Richmond 2021)

In retrospect, Bolsonaro's actions to forestall and discourage Covid-19 vaccines are perplexing for a number of reasons. On the domestic front, the president's attacks against Covid-19 vaccines conflicted with historically widespread adherence and support for vaccines and vaccination in Brazil. Indeed, Brazil was home to four major Covid-19 clinical trials, selected in part by developers for the ease of quickly recruiting participants. Even if vaccine hesitancy was popular among his core supporters, Bolsonaro alienated a large share of the population in late 2020 with his discourse and actions. It is also contradictory bearing in mind his concerns about the pandemic's impact on the economy, as greater vaccination coverage and a faster rollout would ensure lower rates of hospitalisation and death.

On the international front, the president's actions raised tensions with China, Brazil's largest trading partner and a key player in global vaccine development and manufacturing (Agência do Senado 2021), and with Pfizer, one of the world's largest multinational pharma companies – precisely the type of firms that Bolsonaro and his economic team had promised to entice to invest in Brazil as part of the economic turnaround his administration would engineer.

Compared to most world and domestic political leaders who embraced vaccines and vaccination, Bolsonaro stands out as an exception, both in words and in programmatic policies, by the end of 2020. However, despite Bolsonaro's attacks toward Covid-19 vaccines, which began in late 2020 and continued throughout 2021, it is worth noting that Covid-19 vaccine procurement and population uptake was relatively high in Brazil in 2021. This fact was even acknowledged by Bolsonaro during his 2021 address to the 76th Session of the United Nations General Assembly. He boasted:

> To date, the Federal Government has distributed more than 260 million doses of vaccines and more than 140 million Brazilians have already received at least the first dose, representing almost 90 per cent of the adult population. Eighty per cent of the indigenous population has also been fully vaccinated. Until November, everyone who chose to be vaccinated in Brazil will be served.[12]

This quote confirms Bolsonaro's strategic rhetorical manoeuvres. When advantageous political gains were attainable through advocacy for Covid-19 vaccine development and dissemination, the political leader underscored his administration's endorsement of vaccine development, procurement and vaccination. Concurrently, Bolsonaro opted tactically to assail Covid-19 vaccines and specific brands when such a strategy was politically opportune. We posit that the right-wing leader's shift in mid–2020 from a predominantly favourable stance on Covid-19 to a markedly critical one was propelled by his rivalry with political adversaries, as well as the dividends he accrued for championing such perspectives among his supporters.

Furthermore, we have shown that this shift in rhetoric also coincided with the Bolsonaro administration's Covid-19 policy decisions and planning efforts. In mid–2020 the administration procured insufficient vaccine doses from a single supplier. The Ministry of Health only began to negotiate with the state of São Paulo and the pharmaceutical industry to secure additional doses in late December 2020/ early January 2021. This delay in securing a sufficient supply of Covid-19 vaccines to ensure coverage for the majority of the population, and a speedy rollout to deliver it, translated into a reduced supply of vaccines and considerable delays in Brazil's vaccination effort in 2021. Tragically death rates were far higher in 2021 than in 2020 due to the arrival of SARS-CoV-2 Alpha and Delta variants. Furthermore, the population's demand for vaccine coverage exceeded available supplies.

## Notes

1 Authors' translation of the following tweet in Portuguese: 'Cooperação Brasil-EUA no combate ao COVID-19 continua avançando. Chegaram hoje ao Brasil 2 milhões de doses de hidroxicloroquina doadas pelos EUA. Colaboraremos com os EUA na pesquisa clínica da hidroxicloroquina e no desenvolvimento de uma vacina'. This tweet generated 31,404 likes, 697 quotes, 3,274 replies and 5,411 retweets.
2 Authors' translation of the following tweet in Portuguese: 'DIVULGAÇÕES DIÁRIAS NAS REDES SOCIAIS DESDE O INÍCIO: A1.O @govbr dá mais um passo em direção ao desenvolvimento de uma vacina contra a covid-19. Portaria da Anvisa autoriza a realização de testes clínicos de uma potencial vacina pela Universidade de Oxford'. This tweet generated 21,734 likes, 194 quotes, 2,102 replies and 3,902 retweets.
3 Authors' translation of the following tweet in Portuguese: '2- Essa parceria visa também toda a transferência de tecnologia para o Brasil, de modo que a vacina poderá ser produzida aqui sem custos outros.3 – Comprovada sua eficácia contaremos com 100 milhões de doses a partir de janeiro de 2021, que serão distribuídas gratuitamente'. This tweet generated 15,146 likes, 82 quotes, 773 replies and 2,173 retweets.
4 https://www.gov.br/mre/en/content-centers/speeches-articles-and-interviews/president-of-the-federative-republic-of-brazil/speeches/remarks-by-president-jair-bolsonaro-at-the-general-debate-of-the-75th-session-of-the-united-nations-general-assembly-september-22-2020.
5 Authors' translation of the following tweet in Portuguese: 'Boa noite a todos. Vacina obrigatória só aqui no Faísca'. This tweet generated 77,624 likes, 6,340 quotes, 14,801 replies and 7,411 retweets.
6 Authors' translation of the following tweet in Portuguese: 'A vacina chinesa de João Doria. Para o meu governo, qualquer vacina, antes de ser disponibilizada à população, deverá ser comprovada cientificamente pelo Ministério da Saúde e certificada pela ANVISA. O povo brasileiro não será cobaia de ninguém'. This tweet received 83,164 likes, 36,862 quotes, 48,469 replies and 12,443 retweets.

7   Authors' translation of the following tweet in Portuguese: 'Morte, invalidez, anomalia. Esta é a vacina que o [governador João] Doria queria obrigar todos os paulistanos a tomá-la … O presidente [Bolsonaro] disse que a vacina jamais poderia ser obrigatória. Mais uma que Jair Bolsonaro ganha'.
8   Authors' translation of the following excerpt from Bolsonaro's speech in Portuguese: 'Ninguém pode obrigar ninguém a tomar vacina. Eu não vou tomar. Eu já tive o vírus. Já tenho anticorpos. Para que tomar vacina de novo? … Se tomar e virar um jacaré é problema seu. Se virar um super-homem, se nascer barba em mulher ou homem falar fino, ela [Pfizer] não tem nada com isso'.
9   Authors' translations of the following survey question in Portuguese: 'Se houver uma vacina contra o coronavírus, você: (i) com certeza tomaria, (ii) com certeza não tomaria ou (iii) não sabe'.
10  We consider respondents to support Bolsonaro's government if they evaluate it as 'excellent' or 'very good'. In contrast, we coded as a respondent who disapproves if s/he evaluates the administration as 'bad' or 'very bad'.
11  Authors' translation of the following tweet in Portuguese: 'Por que muitos governadores e prefeitos vacinaram jovens entre 12 e 17 anos? Baseados em quê? Recomendação da Anvisa? Da Saúde? De quem? Estamos mexendo com vidas. A molecada abaixo de 20 anos, a chance de não ter nada, uma vez contaminada, é de 99,99%. Compensa o custo-benefício da vacina?'
12  *G1*. 2021. Authors' translation of the following tweet in Portuguese: 'Até o momento, o Governo Federal distribuiu mais de 260 milhões de doses de vacinas e mais de 140 milhões de brasileiros já receberam, pelo menos, a primeira dose, o que representa quase 90% da população adulta. 80% da população indígena também já foi totalmente vacinada. Até novembro, todos que escolheram ser vacinados no Brasil, serão atendidos.'

## References

Agência do Senado. 2021. 'Fala de Bolsonaro sobre China causa polêmica em reunião da CRE com Chanceler', *Senadonotícias*. Accessed 30 July 2022. Available at https://www12.senado.leg.br/noticias/materias/2021/05/06/fala-de-bolsonaro-sobre-china-causa-polemica-em-reuniao-da-cre-com-chanceler. b – i.

Baraniuk, C. 2021. 'Covid-19: What do we know about Sputnik V and other Russian vaccines?', *BMJ* 372 (743): 1–2. https://doi.org/10.1136/bmj.n743.

Barberia, L., A. Boing, J. Gusmão, F. Miyajima, A. Abud, B. Kemp, M. Zamudio and T. C. and Moraes de Sousa. 2023. 'An assessment of the public health surveillance strategy based on molecular testing during three major pandemic waves of COVID-19 in Brazil', *PLOS Global Public Health* 3 (August). https://doi.org/10.1371/journal.pgph.0002164.

Barberia, L. and E. J. Gómez. 2020. 'Political and institutional perils of Brazil's COVID-19 crisis', *The Lancet* 396 (10248): 367–68. https://doi.org/10.1016/S0140-6736(20)31681-0.

Barberia, L., T. Plümper and G. D. Whitten. 2021. 'The political science of Covid-19: An introduction', *Social Science Quarterly* 102:5. https://doi.org/10.1111/ssqu.13069.

Barberia, L. and I. Seelaender Costa Rosa. 2021. 'De que maneira a ideologia afeta a disposição a se vacinar contra o Sars-Cov-2?', *Revista USP* 131: 47–64. https://www.revistas.usp.br/revusp/article/view/193315.

Barberia, L.G. et al. 2023. 'Mapping political elites COVID-19 vaccine tweets in Brazilian Portuguese in 2020, 2021 and 2022'.

Castro, M. C., K. Sun, L. Barberia, A. F. Ribeiro, S. Gurzenda, K. Braga Ribeiro, E. Abbott, J. Blossom, B. Rache and B. H. Singer. 2021. 'Spatiotemporal pattern of COVID-19 spread in Brazil', *Science* 372(6544): 821–26. https://doi.org/10.1126/science.abh1558.

Della Coletta, R. 2020. 'Ao responder sobre Coronavac, Bolsonaro afirma que ganhou de Doria', *Folha de São Paulo*. Accessed 30 July 2022. Available at https://www1.folha.uol.com.br/equilibrioesaude/2020/11/mais-uma-que-jair-bolsonaro-ganha-diz-presidente-sobre-suspensao-de-testes-da-coronavac.shtml.

DataPoder. 2020. 'Pesquisa de opinião pública, Brasil', DataPoder 360. Accessed 30 July 2022. Available at https://www.poder360.com.br/pesquisas-de-opiniao/.

*Deutsche Welle Brasil*. 2020. 'Brasil anuncia acordo com Oxford para vacina contra Covid-19', *Deutsche Welle Brasil*. Accessed 30 July 2022. Available at https://www.dw.com/pt-br/brasil-anuncia-acordo-com-oxford-para-vacina-contra-covid-19/a-53966779.

Folha de São Paulo. 2021. 'Relembre o que Bolsonaro já disse sobre a pandemia, de gripezinha e país de maricas a frescura e Mimimi', *Folha de São Paulo*. Accessed 30 July 2022. Available at https://www1.folha.uol.com.br/poder/2021/03/relembre-o-que-bolsonaro-ja-disse-sobre-a-pandemia-de-gripezinha-e-pais-de-maricas-a-frescura-e-mimimi.shtml.

Fonseca, E. Massard da, A. Davidian, C. Coutinho, N. Dias et al. 2021. 'Vacinas adquiridas e aprovadas para uso no Brasil contra COVID-19'. Instituto de Estudos para Políticas de Saúde', *Nota Técnica*, n.21, 1–7. São Paulo: IEPS. Accessed 30 July 2022. Available at https://ieps.org.br/wp-content/uploads/2021/11/IEPS_NT21.pdf.

G1. 2021. 'Veja e leia a íntegra do discurso de Bolsonaro na Assembleia Geral Das Nações Unidas', *G1*. Accessed 30 July 2022. Available at https://g1.globo.com/politica/noticia/2021/09/21/veja-a-integra-do-discurso-de-bolsonaro-na-assembleia-geral-da-onu.ghtml.

Lacatus, C. and G. Meibauer. 2021. 'Crisis, rhetoric and right-wing populist incumbency: An analysis of Donald Trump's tweets and press briefings', *Government and Opposition* 58: 249–67.

Poder 360. 2020. 'Bolsonaro diz que Trump vai enviar 2 milhões de comprimidos de Cloroquina', Poder 360. Accessed 30 July 2022. Available at https://www.poder360.com.br/governo/bolsonaro-diz-que-trump-vai-enviar-2-milhoes-de-comprimidos-de-cloroquina/.

Ranzani, O. T., L. S. L. Bastos, J. G. M. Gelli, J. F. Marchesi, F. Baião, S. Hamacher and F. A. Bozza. 2021. 'Characterisation of the first 250,000 hospital admissions for COVID-19 in Brazil: A retrospective analysis of nationwide data', *The Lancet. Respiratory Medicine* 9(4): 407–18. https://doi.org/10.1016/S2213-2600(20)30560-9.

Reuters. 2020. 'Brazil, hotbed for COVID-19 vaccine testing, may struggle to produce its own', 4 August 2020. Accessed 30 July 2022. Available at https://www.reuters.com/article/idUSKCN25028K/.

Ribeiro, A. F., M. C. Castro, G. Lotta and R. J. Carvalho. 2023. 'Early response to COVID-19 in Brazil: The impact of a targeted approach to suspected cases and on epidemiologic surveillance efforts', *IJID Regions*. Accessed 30 July 2022. https://www.sciencedirect.com/science/article/pii/S2772707623000528.

Richmond, K. 2021. 'Bolsonaro volta a questionar vacina contra Covid em adolescentes', *Folha de São Paulo*. Accessed 30 July 2022. https://www1.folha.uol.com.br/equilibrioesaude/2021/10/bolsonaro-volta-a-questionar-vacina-contra-covid-em-adolescentes.shtml.

Tubi, O. 2022. 'Infrastructural Capital in the Israeli vaccination campaign against COVID-19', *Social Science & Medicine* 303 (June 2022): 115022. https://doi.org/10.1016/j.socscimed.2022.115022.

Zhou, Y. R. 2022. 'Vaccine nationalism: Contested relationships between COVID-19 and globalization'. In *Post-Covid Transformations*, edited by Kevin Gray and Barry K. Gills, 82–97. London: Routledge.

# Part III
# God above all

# 7
# Mobilising charismatic evangelical Christianity: spiritual warfare and political activism amid the 2022 Brazilian elections

Manoela Carpenedo

In a climate of increased electoral violence due to one of the most polarised election campaigns in Brazilian history, Luiz Inácio Lula da Silva (Lula) narrowly defeated Jair Bolsonaro on 2 October 2022. Following Lula's very narrow victory, Bolsonaro's supporters organised several rallies to block roads and important highways across the country. These protesters rejected the results of the elections, claiming that the elections were rigged and open to electoral fraud. They also called for an urgent military intervention to save the country from Lula and from 'the left'. However, it was not only electoral discontent that moved people to protest against the election results. Forming an important part of Bolsonaro's voting base, conservative charismatic evangelicals strongly supported the rallies, framing these demonstrations as resistance to forces of evil that were trying to control the country. For them, the 2022 elections should be comprehended as spiritual warfare in which God is confronted by evil.

In this chapter I seek to unpack the role of religious imaginaries and theological narratives to understand Brazil's political scenario. While a socio-political reading is key to comprehending the rise of the authoritarian wave in Brazil, there is also a need to address the important role played by religion in the formation of contemporary regimes of truth/post-truth in Brazilian society. By tracing how religion can provide a corpus of discourses and practices to mobilise conservative masses, I investigate how religious imagination is infused into authoritarian political modalities.

While scholars have pointed out the importance of investigating the growing role of conservative charismatic evangelicalism in Brazilian politics through historical and sociological research, the interdisciplinary analysis of theological teachings, online evangelical activism and electoral mobilisation is not well explored in the literature. Based on a socio-cultural examination of theological ideas and virtual evangelical networks, this chapter considers how such discourses of spiritual warfare influenced evangelical political activism in the 2022 Brazilian elections, producing the condition of possibility for the promotion of authoritarian modalities.

## Charismatic evangelical Christianity and Brazil's authoritarian turn: 'the minorities must bend before the majorities'

In order to understand the authoritarian turn in Brazilian politics, the influence of religion upon new political actors must be considered (Burity 2018; Carranza 2020). Although the conservative wave that materialised in the election of Jair Messias Bolsonaro in 2018 was prompted by important economic and social problems – such as economic recession, skyrocketing urban violence, corruption scandals and political crises leading to the 2016 impeachment of Dilma Rousseff (Alonso 2019; Mariano and Gerardi 2019) – 'cultural disaffection' also played a key role in Bolsonaro's election. Performing an unconventional form of leadership characterised by nationalist rhetoric combined with an aggressive political style to defend the traditions and values of the *'cidadão de bem'*,[1] Jair Bolsonaro gained power in a climate of rising populism worldwide. In addition, attention must be paid to how politicians mobilised traditional Christian values. Before his election Bolsonaro declared his affinity with Christianity and Christian values in one of his speeches:

> God above all! There is no such thing as a secular state. The state is Christian, and the minority that is against it, let them move. The minorities must bend before the majorities. (IstoÉ 2018)

Deploying an anti-elite discourse in the name of 'the people', Bolsonaro articulated a strong religious imagination as part of his political persona. Although a self-declared Catholic, seen in Catholic churches and among Catholic clergy, Bolsonaro often visits evangelical services with his wife. He was baptised in the River Jordan in Israel in 2016, being what Freston described as 'the first pan-Christian president' (Freston 2020, 373).

By stressing the protagonism of conservative Christian world-views, Bolsonaro was able not only to secure the highest margin of evangelical votes in both the 2018 and the 2022 elections, but also to mobilise and nurture a particular form of Christian nationalism *à brasileira*. Most of Bolsonaro's charismatic evangelical base also remained supportive of his administration, and they were prominent in the rallies that inflamed the country after Lula's election.

The political importance of religion goes hand in hand with the rise in the number of evangelicals in Brazil. Many scholars have pointed out the successful capacity of charismatic evangelical Christianity to multiply itself worldwide. It is no wonder that such forms of Christianity, particularly influenced by Pentecostal tenets, have become the fastest-growing Christian movement worldwide. Since the 1970s, evangelical Christianity has become extremely popular in Africa and Latin America (Martin 2003), where approximately 425 million Pentecostals live (Johnson and Zurlo 2020). The Brazilian Institute of Geography and Statistics reported a steady growth in the evangelical population, which constituted 22.2 per cent of the total population in 2010.

Among these evangelicals, one-third can be defined as historical Protestants (Anglicans, Lutherans and Methodists, among others) and two-thirds as charismatic evangelicals (Pentecostal or Neo-Pentecostal). While charismatic evangelicals are a very heterogeneous group, they are mainly composed of disenfranchised sectors of the Brazilian population, being primarily, though not exclusively, composed of non-whites, women and individuals on low incomes (Freston 2020).

Historians of Latin American Christianity have shown us that the current authoritarian turn in Brazil is anything but surprising (Cowan 2021; Garrard 2020). This same historiography demonstrated that conservative right-wing moralists are not restricted to charismatic evangelical circles. From its mid-century bishops reacting against modernity and its values to the conservative rejection of the liturgical transformations proposed by the Vatican Council of 1962–5, some sectors of the Catholic Church in Brazil actively resisted changes promoted by liberal and secular values that threatened traditional and hierarchical principles (Cowan 2021). Paralleling these complaints but operating through their specific reasonings, evangelicals emerged from the 1970s as guardians of 'morality and good behaviour'. They formed the basis of shared Christian grievances that gained voice through a religious right promoting moralism, anti-ecumenism, anti-communism, an embrace of free-market capitalism, religious orthodoxy and a longing for supernaturalism (Cowan 2021).

While the participation of charismatic evangelicals in Brazilian politics and their alignment with conservative right-wing morality is not new, since the 1990s the evangelical political force has become increasingly visible and constitutive of the Brazilian political scene. Brazilian charismatic evangelicalism is unique in its electoral capacity, particularly in electing religiously affiliated candidates through the rise of the 'pastor-candidate' phenomenon (Guadalupe 2022) and utilising grassroots church support for canvassing votes.

Although the involvement of evangelicals in Brazilian politics cannot be generalised, as many evangelical politicians are interested in promoting the greater good of society, a significant number of evangelical politicians do seek to defend their religious interests and to act as an interest group (Guadalupe 2020). Founded in 2003, the so-called *'Frente Parlamentar Evangélica'* (Evangelical Front' or 'Evangelical Caucus') exemplifies the mobilisation of evangelical activism in Brazilian politics. After 2022 the evangelical caucus, including some Catholics, counts on 102 Congress members and 13 senators, amounting to 20 per cent of the Brazilian Congress.

Charismatic evangelicalism is also relevant in determining voting patterns. For instance, the evangelical support received by Bolsonaro in the 2018 election was very high, meaning that being an evangelical rather than a Catholic increased the odds of a person voting for Jair Bolsonaro (Amaral 2020, 13). Religious identities influence voting patterns, with evangelicals tending to vote for evangelical candidates ('in-group') and to reject candidates from other religious groups ('out-group') (Boas and Smith 2015). Therefore candidates who mobilise evangelical identities and adopt the prefix 'Pastor' during the campaign tend to obtain more votes from evangelical voters (Bohn 2007). In her study Smith (2019) also shows that politics and elections are openly debated in church services, as the church leadership advises followers to vote in certain ways.

However, while important, this influence is not always direct, as believers embracing more secular views can resist church political orientations. Surveys on evangelical voters also point to a high level of intolerance towards sexual minorities and towards women's freedoms (notably the freedom to have an abortion), low tolerance of civil rights for young offenders and a limited willingness to accord civil rights to groups with whom they disagree (Lehmann 2021, 105). While these low levels of tolerance align with the Brazilian public in general, evangelicals are growing increasingly apart from other citizens regarding issues concerning women's equality and rights, among them abortion and

LGBTQIA+ rights, developing 'the most active repertoires of political engagement' (Smith 2019, 129).

In Brazil, evangelicals played a crucial role in consolidating an 'Evangelical Christian Right' characterised by conservative values, an organisation surprisingly in tune with the growth of an international religious right-wing wave (Burity 2018). Inspired by their North American counterparts, who have battled feminist and humanist agendas in the US since the 1960s, the 'Evangelical Christian Right' in Brazil has gained political space, particularly after establishing the Constitution of 1988 (Carranza 2020). This evangelical political activism mobilises an 'anti-gender ideology' moral agenda by fighting against the sexual and reproductive rights of women and the LGBTQIA+ population. They also encourage military agendas and the need for strict public security policies to prevent urban violence. The movement thus openly reacts against cultural pluralism and gun control (Almeida 2017). The world-view propagated by this Christian right has also contributed to the rejection of the Workers' Party (the growth of 'anti-petismo'). This political activism mobilises a strong anti-pluralist and anti-communist rhetoric while promoting pro-family values (Machado 2018).

Bolsonaro's speech of 2017 highlighting the role of Christianity – and its values – in the subjugation of minorities to the 'Christian moral majorities' encapsulates religion's role in providing a possible grammar for Brazil's authoritarian turn. In this articulation we see tensions between the secular and the religious within the Brazilian political sphere. Although the separation between religion and politics is not always fruitful in social scientific analysis – as the analytical category of religion portrayed as a private and individual belief is inspired by Western European models (Asad 2003), which cannot be easily applied in Brazil – the emergence of a Brazilian Evangelical Christian Right is now a key player in governance.

To examine further the impact of charismatic evangelicalism in Brazil's authoritarian turn, I now explore how specific theological narratives are presented in the Brazilian public discourse.

## Theological imaginaries and political activism in Brazil

Theological understandings inspiring individual social actors are typically neglected in socio-political analysis because theologies and 'beliefs' are generally understood to be connected to an individual's private sphere. However, this position has changed with the growing mobilising power of religion in contemporary societies and the realisation that religions are becoming important forces in the public sphere (Wilson 2023). Through examining some theological narratives, this section unpacks how some theological teachings influence the public sphere in Brazil from the ground up, and with online and offline realities.

The first dimension to consider is the change in the position taken by charismatic evangelicals regarding electoral participation. Until the 1980s charismatic evangelicals usually adopted an apolitical position, as electoral politics was considered too worldly and contaminated for them to be directly involved. However, this position was gradually replaced by a more active posture, encouraging people to vote for candidates sharing the same world-view through the motto 'Brothers vote for Brothers' (Sylvestre 1986). Some scholars point out that a decisive factor in the growing participation of evangelicals in electoral politics was the theological shift embraced by certain Brazilian Pentecostal circles, moving from a pre-millennial Christian eschatology[2] to a post-millennial eschatology (Guadalupe 2020). While the embrace of the post-millennial vision has not replaced pre-millennial dispensational sensibilities as a whole, post-millennial influence inaugurated a new relationship between the church and the world, promoting different behavioural and social attitudes for church members.

Until the 1980s Brazilian charismatic evangelical churches mostly embraced a pre-millennial eschatology supported by a literal take on biblical prophecy, specifically Revelation 19–20. The pre-millennial interpretation of Revelation 19–20 teaches that the physical return of Jesus is in some way imminent (the so-called 'second coming of Christ') and that believers would be 'raptured' (literally, taken to heaven to meet God)[3] directly before the 'great tribulations'; they would thus be spared from a period of pain, horror and catastrophe. In this world-view life 'here and now' on earth should be understood by believers as insignificant, consisting simply of a 'waiting period' that leads to the rapture and subsequent eternal afterlife in heaven.

Because of the intense emphasis given to the rapture, the second coming of Christ and the looming destruction of the world, this eschatological view encouraged believers to disengage from worldly affairs, particularly politics (Guadalupe 2020; Garrard 2020). Believers did not need to involve themselves in politics at all, as the end of time was approaching and Jesus was soon to return. This apocalyptic view therefore promoted the rejection of the world (seen as sinful and impure) and withdrawal from the public sphere or from any popular articulation, crystallising an apolitical posture among believers (Carranza 2020).

However, with the emergence of Neo-Pentecostal churches during the 1990s, these attitudes dramatically changed. While still embracing many teachings from pre-millennial dispensational eschatology, many evangelical groups started to adopt some aspects of post-millennial eschatology, which teaches that Christianity should have an increasing influence in the world. In contrast to the pre-millennial interpretation, post-millennial eschatology teaches that the second coming of Christ is not imminent. For believers who embrace post-millennial teachings, Christ will only return after the transformation of the world into a better place. Christians must therefore gradually work out how to advance the gospel and its values worldwide to promote this transformation. In post-millennial eschatology, Christian believers must actively work to extend the Kingdom of God in the world through evangelisation and the active reform of societal institutions. In this view, the world does not need to be rejected or avoided; it should rather be enjoyed and transformed into an extension of heaven. Consequently, because of their transformative role, Christians have a duty to assume political roles (Guadalupe 2020; 2022).

While most Brazilian charismatic evangelical churches still strongly embrace pre-millennial dispensational eschatology, on a practical level the idea that Christian believers should not be apolitical, but rather become active players in the restoration of the reign of God on earth is now widely accepted in charismatic circles. Although most Brazilian evangelical circles still believe in core elements of pre-millennial eschatology, such as the imminence of the second coming of Christ (Rocha 2020), post-millennial sensibilities advocating for a political role for believers in the public sphere are currently infused in the religious imaginaries that support evangelical political activism in Brazil. From religious and social minorities not concerned with the nation's political life, evangelicals have thus gradually assumed the position of winning 'Brazil for Jesus'.

This new attitude paved the way for the intense evangelical political activity manifested from the mid-1980s onwards. The gradual growth of the evangelical caucus is an excellent example of the impact of this theological shift. Directly after Brazil's return to civilian rule, 33 evangelical representatives were elected as members of parliament in 1986. Their numbers have been steadily growing, with 90 members between 2015 and 2018 and 203 members between 2019 and 2022 (out of the 594 seats in the parliament).

In 1992 evangelical pastor Valnice Milhomens was one of the first religious leaders to emphasise in a church sermon the role of evangelicals in changing Brazilian politics. She declared that 'believers should be voting in brothers and sisters', maintaining that 'the solutions for the problems of the Brazilian nation would be in the church itself' (Romeiro 1999). While not mentioning Bolsonaro explicitly, in the 2022 elections the same pastor declared in her social networks that *crentes* (believers) should vote for politicians with a programme aligned to the Kingdom of God.

Another good example of contemporary evangelical electoral mobilisation is the case of Nikolas Ferreira, an extremely successful 26-year-old congressman. He received the highest number of votes in the 2022 election, gaining an astonishing 1.47 million votes. Nikolas Ferreira represents a new generation of highly engaged evangelical politicians who can articulate their offline and online presence very well. On the one hand, he utilises grassroots church networks to mobilise his electorate through well-polished religious-electoral rallies. By employing a range of religious jargon, these rallies are attended by a public from several churches; they ingeniously combine political teaching, personal anecdotes and religious faith. On the other hand Nikolas Ferreira has almost two million followers on Twitter (now X) and 1.38 million subscribers on YouTube, with videos achieving over three million views. On his YouTube website[4] the motto 'to rebel against tyranny is to obey God'[5] in his profile background illustrates his strong political commitment. He is also the author of the book *Christians and Politics: How to win the culture war*,[6] which explores the reasons why evangelicals should replace their former apolitical attitudes with an active role in contemporary Brazilian politics (Ferreira 2022a). In a podcast interview given in October 2022, Ferreira argues that:

> for a long time, the church did not want to be involved in politics because church leaders considered politics dominated by Satan, but what did the devil do? It dominated politics. (Ferreira 2022b)

According to Ferreira, the church did wrong in not getting involved with politics in the past; it has harvested bad fruit because of this apolitical attitude. In his view, believers should confront all institutions that jeopardise Christian values, such as those propagating abortion rights, gender ideology, desacralisation of the family, etc. According to the young congressman, the church has to be deeply involved in the public sphere, as there is a need 'to understand that the church is Christ's channel to change this generation' (Ferreira 2022b). In his sermon entitled 'Christians and politics', streamed online, he indicates that:

Christians have to take a political position as Jesus did. Jesus was no coward, and many Christians opt not to take a political standing … because they are afraid, are afraid to lose friendships or afraid to be a Christian … The life of a Christian is one of persecution, pain and suffering like Jesus suffered … Christians have to be bold and audacious even if the world is against us. (Ferreira 2022c)

With a remarkable talent for mobilising evangelical youth, Ferreira's words clearly exemplify the need for Christians to abandon former passive, apolitical standings and move towards a more active and effective role. In so doing they can address the perceived disjunction between the world and God's will. In this context, political participation is seen as a way to resist the misrepresentation faced by evangelicals in the media and the discrimination suffered by evangelical youth in many educational settings, as well as to fight against the demands of social movements (for example, feminist, socialist and LGBTQIA+) perceived to undermine Christian values. At the same time, as key social actors, evangelicals need to permeate politics and society with godly values to inspire the construction of a 'Christian nation' (see also Machado and Burity 2014).

The Christian Reconstructionism movement and the so-called 'dominion theology' are good examples of how post-millennial sensibilities are articulated in religious imaginaries and support for evangelical mobilisation activism in Brazil and Latin America as a whole (Garrard 2020; Carranza 2020; Guadalupe 2020). Deriving from fundamentalist Calvinist theology that can be traced back to the thinking of theologian Cornelius Van Til, then further elaborated and disseminated by Rousas Rushdoony in the 1970s, Christian Reconstructionism teaches that there is a need to re-create a society ruled by the premises of the Old Testament. Through the active role of Christians in political life and their 'dominion' over the earth, the unfolding of the end of time, which includes the second coming of Christ, could be hastened. Inspired by Genesis 1:28, conveying that humans have 'dominion' over the earth (its living beings, resources and institutions), this political, theological tradition teaches that Christian values should have 'dominion' over political life.

This Reconstructionist project would be undertaken through the election of an authentic Christian leadership able to replace secular liberal values with biblical ones (Garrard 2020; Marsden 2006). In this view, Christians have the mandate to conquer strategic positions and public spaces to influence the political life of society, being predestined to occupy influential positions in the world: as presidents, ministers, mayors and congressmen (Pérez 2006).

While the ideas of dominion theology are highly controversial, and viewed with deep suspicion within many evangelical denominations (Garrard 2020), they have gained traction within numerous Christian groups in the US and Latin America. Although many aspects of Christian Reconstructionism failed to find fertile ground in Brazil, the politicisation of the faith promoted by the notion of dominion was welcomed by charismatic evangelical circles. In Brazil, therefore, dominion theology assumed a charismatic evangelical face, mainly through its ability to relate to important elements of Neo-Pentecostal culture, such as the teachings on spiritual warfare.

## The spiritual warfare in a polarised nation

An essential dimension of dominion theology is the application of the dynamics of spiritual warfare to political life. The teachings about spiritual warfare can be localised within the Neo-Pentecostal theological developments. It is inspired by the idea that Christians are in a constant spiritual battle against Satan and his army of demons and evil spirits.[7] The theology of spiritual warfare was elaborated by North American Missiologist Peter Wagner, who describes how demons interact with individuals and territories. His book *Confronting the Powers: How the New Testament Church experienced the power of strategic-level spiritual warfare* (1996) was one of the outlets responsible for disseminating this Neo-Pentecostal world-view. According to theological narratives on spiritual warfare, the world is a battlefield between the forces of God and Satan. At an individual level, evil forces can possess believers by inhabiting a person's body and so provoking immense disorder (such as disease or financial problems); these need to be exorcised through deliverance rituals performed at the church.

While deliverance from evil forces is key for the 'wealth and health' of believers, the same logic is applied to the political life of nations. The so-called 'strategic level spiritual warfare' (Wagner 1996) suggests that Christians must identify 'evil territorial spirits' and engage in aggressive warfare prayer to set the spirits possessing a specific territory free. These territorial evil spirits are assigned to geographic locations, nations and governmental institutions (Lowe 1998). In this sense, a legion of evil spirits can control countries, regions and specific social groups. In light of these spiritual cartographies, evangelical believers see themselves as having an important role in getting rid of all satanic dispositions that are against God's law within the nation.

It is understood that the devil operates ingeniously within a country's culture, media and politics (Ramirez 2017). Having established the projection of demonic influence into the political sphere, believers embracing 'strategic level spiritual warfare' feel obliged to participate actively in a Crusade of purification in order to liberate the nation and politics from Satan's influence. This, they believe, can take different forms, including corruption, economic deprivation, the advancement of feminist and LGBTQIA+ agendas and the growing influence of secularism or other religions. There is consequently a need for Christians to achieve 'dominion' over political life and to re-take the territories lost to Satan. In this way biblical values can replace wicked secular values.

During the 2022 elections I was able to map how this 'strategic level spiritual warfare' took shape in the narratives and bodily dispositions of evangelical believers. By identifying Jair Bolsonaro as the candidate aligned with biblical values and Lula as the representative of evil forces, evangelical pastors, influencers and politicians understood the 2022 Brazil elections as a spiritual battlefield. These narratives can be easily found in many evangelical online outlets. For instance, 'Povo da Fé', the popular YouTube channel[8] with an estimated 700,000 followers and numerous videos with over one million views, features a series of livestreams exploring how the 'Bolsonaro X Lula' electoral dispute could be interpreted as a spiritual battle.

The channel streams a series of prophetic readings. It openly advocates voting for a candidate with Christian values who can promote patriotism and will not sabotage traditional family values, for example by supporting the legalisation of abortion. In one of their videos a prominent pastor of the 'Povo da Fé' channel portrays the left as aligned with evil forces, claiming that Karl Marx was a Satanist who wanted to destroy Christianity and Christian values; consequently any politician who aligns with the left, such as Lula, will be against the Christian faith. The pastor concludes that no Christian should consider voting for a candidate on the left. By invoking examples of socialist countries, the 'Povo da Fé' YouTube channel claims that the dissemination of the Bible and evangelisation are likely to be suppressed under left-wing governments.

The theological grammars provided by the spiritual warfare help believers to give new meanings to national politics and to create new regimes of truth based on charismatic evangelical imaginaries. As explored by O'Donnell (2020) in his study on charismatic demonology in US politics, the political imaginaries around spiritual warfare enable the construction of physical, social and institutional realities embedded in specific discursive practices. These practices not only produce and reproduce relations of domination; they also 'construct' or 'constitute' these same realities (Hjelm 2014). In this vein O'Donnell (2020) warns that spiritual warfare, as a discourse, defines the limits of social relations and viable subjectivities by commending or condemning specific models of social organisation, ideologies, individual world-views and practices.

Evangelical devotee and former first-lady Michelle Bolsonaro illustrated the discursive dynamics of spiritual warfare during the 2022 Brazilian electoral campaign. In a religious service at an Assembly of God in Rio de Janeiro, shortly before the second round of the elections, she declared:

> This is not about a politician. It is about an ideology of good versus evil. It is about what Satan wants to do with our nation. And we have prayed a lot for this moment. However, many Christians need to realise this. You do not need to look at my husband; look at me. I am a servant of the Lord. I bend my knees and am aware of the spiritual world. (Bolsonaro 2022)

Michelle Bolsonaro's appeal clearly exemplifies how spiritual warfare discourses construct the political realities of believers. Nevertheless, such dynamics reach beyond narratives, as the discursive dynamics of spiritual warfare also take shape in the embodied religious practices of believers. Good examples of these are the virialised requests for fasting and prayers orchestrated by many evangelical leaders and politicians days before the second round of the elections. For instance, congressman Nikolas Ferreira (p. 00) asked for his followers to adhere to 21 days of fasting and prayers for Bolsonaro:

> I believe that this war is not a material but a spiritual one. We cannot understand adversaries as mere political adversaries. On the contrary, for people who want to kill unborn babies, it is way more dangerous than a political adversary. There is something spiritual about this dispute. We see people trying to legalise drugs and threatening the freedom of religion, like Lula's friend Ortega in Nicaragua, who is prohibiting the celebration of mass. I invite you to this challenge of fasting and praying for the future of our country (…). This is biblical and will prevent us from being governed by those who want to destroy our nation. (Ferreira 2022d)

Some of Ferreira's followers responded enthusiastically to his YouTube appeal by saying:

> I am a member of the church, and we will fast 12 hours daily in the name of the family, the nation and our freedom. I am evangelical. I am with you, my brother Nikolas! I believe, and I am sure, that this fight is not human but spiritual.

By adopting a series of embodied religious disciplines such as fasting and prayer, believers could transform their bodies into vehicles of political electoral action. In this context, fasting and prayer can be understood as a technology of the self (Foucault 1997). In performing a certain number of operations in their 'own bodies and souls, thoughts, conduct and way of being' (Foucault 1997, 242), believers would construct their subjectivities, becoming moral subjects in line with evangelical values. Therefore, by complying with fasting and prayer regimes in 'the name of the nation', believers mobilise religious disciplines as a political act. For evangelicals the body thus becomes a privileged place to imprint the dynamics of spiritual warfare and to convey electoral choices.

While bodies and religious disciplines were re-signified in light of spiritual warfare teachings during the 2022 electoral campaign, spaces and places were also affected by religious practices and political narratives. After the electoral defeat of Jair Bolsonaro, many of his supporters started to organise rallies and block roads in protest. Claiming that the elections were rigged, they called for urgent military intervention to prevent the left from overtaking the country. Such demonstrations were concentrated especially in front of military establishments, which became the locations of choice for political demands and religious displays.

For instance, Forte Imbuhy, a military headquarters located in Niteroi, Rio de Janeiro, was transformed by pious Bolsonaro supporters into what was called the 'Wailing Wall'.[9] In front of this military headquarters, with their outstretched hands, numerous supporters could be found praying, speaking in tongues[10] or even crying on their knees. These religious displays aimed to awaken the military to answer their demand for a military coup d'état. The emergence of such a 'Wailing Wall' demonstrates how political mobilisation and religion could convey new forms of religious spatiality. The believers invest sacred meanings in ordinary places by kneeling and praying in front of military headquarters (Finlayson 2017). Because of these manifestations, the Forte Imbuhy demonstration became a receptacle of hope and resistance in the spiritual battle that evangelical supporters of Bolsonaro imagined being fighting. It shows how places and spaces can be re-signified through the performance of religiosity and collective political mobilisation (Woods 2019).

In this juxtaposition between visible and invisible realms, and between demonic threats and godly presence, believers espousing discourses of spiritual warfare reconstruct their realities, investing their political sympathies and actions with spiritual significance. In the following section I explore further how discourses of spiritual warfare are articulated with broader, post-truth political claims and aims.

## The demonisation of the left and the rise of Christophobia

Anti-leftist and anti-communist discourses are not new within the Brazilian conservative evangelical milieu (Martelli 2010; Cowan 2021). Analysing how anti-communist sentiments and eschatological imaginaries were intertwined in the Assemblies of God in Brazil, Martelli (2010) argues that anti-communist discourses could be traced back to the first part of the twentieth century. Drawing on key church printing presses and newspapers, Martelli reveals how Pentecostal eschatological narratives understood the spread of communist ideologies as a sign and enabler of the end of time, together with atheism, violence, idolatry, trade unionism and the decline of the family (Martelli 2010). In such as interpretation, communist ideas and leaders would be compared to evil forces, the anti-Christ or Satan himself. Strongly influenced by North American missionary activity, communist ideologies were represented by symbols connected with beasts, dangerous animals, pathological agents and civil chaos (Martelli 2010). Based on these interpretations, discourses on spiritual warfare would be used to repress socialist ideologies, as its atheist ideals challenged Christ and Christian values.

Even after the fall of the Berlin Wall in 1989, these anti-communist discourses, revamped as anti-leftist sentiments, found fertile ground among conservative evangelicals in Brazil. Today important charismatic evangelical leaders still consider Marxism and leftist ideologies as one of the greatest dangers to the church and Christian values. For instance, in many of the 'lives streams' broadcasted by the YouTube channel 'Povo da Fé', we find pastors discussing how leftist ideologies are being used to promote atheism and the active persecution of Christians. For them, many left-wing politicians were influenced by the anti-Christ and its demons, who would try to prohibit the Christian faith while imposing gender ideology that threatens family values.

In evangelical imaginaries, left-wing politicians would also endorse the end of nationalism and patriotism; in addition, they would promote gun control policies, preventing individuals from protecting their private properties. Aware of these interpretations among conservative evangelicals, Jair Bolsonaro, during his electoral campaign, called Lula a 'capeta' (a devil). He goes on to say

> We have something evil ahead, a demon who wants to impose communism in Brazil. Someone who was recognised internationally by his systematic corruption. (*Correio Brasiliense* 2022)

Discourses on spiritual warfare create a dichotomy between right-wing sentiments, as aligned with godly values such as family, capitalism and patriotism, against leftist inclinations, as connected with Satan, the end of the traditional family and social and economic chaos. In the 2018 elections evangelical leaders systematically attacked the leftist Workers' Party, PT, and their presidential candidate in 2018, Fernando Haddad (Mariano and Gerardi 2020). Such leaders also blamed the left for the economic crisis and corruption scandals, and disseminated fake news[11] about the 'gay kit' (Mariano and Gerardi 2020).

The 'gay kit' refers to the project entitled 'School without homophobia', conceptualised in 2004 during the Workers' Party (PT) administration. The project consisted of training schoolteachers to deal with sexual diversity issues including homophobia. Needleless to say, the 'School Without Homophobia' project triggered numerous controversies, particularly among conservative religious actors. Bolsonaro and many other conservative politicians gained many supporters after denouncing the supposed 'erotisation of children' and the 'sexual deviations' that the 'School Without Homophobia' project would incite. Identified as emerging from communist ideas and part of a broader left-wing agenda, reproductive and LGBTQIA+ rights would represent how evil forces could threaten Brazilian society.

However, it is not only through the advancement of reproductive and LGBTQIA+ rights agendas that conservative evangelicals localise satanic forces in Brazilian politics. For this group, the left is attacking the freedom of expression of the Christian faith through the emergence of Christophobic narratives and anti-Christian strategies. Recent years have seen a growth of discourses claiming an alleged rise of 'Christophobia' in Brazil. This term is used to designate 'hatred of Christians' and/or a broader 'aversion to the Christian religion'. While it is a valid category in many contexts, such as North Korea, Afghanistan, Somalia, Libya, Pakistan and Egypt, all countries where Christians are persecuted because of their faith, this expression generates a certain discomfort in Brazil, where Christianity forms the religion of 88 per cent of the population.

In 2015 the term was used by congressman and pastor Marco Feliciano, who defined the Gay Pride parade as a Christophobic manifestation because of its threat to Christian family values. He later affirmed that the media and Brazilian politics openly persecute Christians. Marco Feliciano was not alone. In 2016 the City Council of São Paulo approved a bill celebrating the 'Day to Combat Christophobia' in the city's official calendar. The mayor later vetoed the bill. Connected to these events, in 2019 congresswomen Chris Tonietto proposed a bill to increase judicial sentences for crimes of religious intolerance. The bill, which sought to defend Christianity and to fight against Christophobia in Brazil, stated that:

> Christianity is the very face of the Brazilian people, and has been mocked daily by most of the media and in various academic circles ... To protect it [Christianity] is to defend the moral support of our democracy.

During the 2022 electoral campaign, numerous items of fake news linking the Workers' Party and Lula to the persecution of Christians and threats of church closures were heavily disseminated in religious digital media. For instance, Congressman Marcos Feliciano spread fake news during a sermon in São Paulo. He claimed that if PT were to win the elections, evangelical groups would be persecuted and forced to close their churches (*O Globo* 2022). While no candidate connected with the left articulated this threat, many believers assumed that the PT would try to close churches, as 'the left' does not like 'evangelical people'. Silas Malafaia, a well-known pastor of the Assembly of God, has also said that the PT and Lula personally persecuted him. According to Malafaia, this persecution was evil for him and the church (*Estadão* 2022). Moreover, widely disseminated fake news among evangelical networks informed believers that Lula claimed that 'in my government, the Bible will adopt a neutral pronoun and will no longer have the name of Jesus' (*G1* 2022).

The wave of fake news accusing the PT of Christophobia and persecution of Christians was so intense that Lula had to write an open letter stressing his commitment to evangelicals (*G1* 2022). Published right before the second round of the elections, the letter emphasised Lula's commitment to the values of religious freedom. The letter also promised that no action against freedom of worship would be taken under his administration. The statement emphasised that Lula is personally against abortion rights and reminded voters that it was under his administration that both the 'March for Jesus' and the 'National Day of Evangelicals' were created. Despite these efforts, the evangelical community did not receive his letter well. Believers interpreted the letter as a dishonest, desperate act from the left to win evangelical votes.

Operating within a regime of falsehood, these examples show how religious imaginaries and 'post-truth' politics overlapped in the 2022 Brazilian elections. The logic of spiritual warfare delineates a clear distinction between opposing forces, categorising and classifying what is considered truth and falsehood, identifying threats and enemies, as well as recognising allies and representatives. It operates within a framework that recognises both the visible and invisible, as well as forces perceived as godly and evil. Such a dichotomy plays a crucial role in the discourse, influencing perceptions and guiding actions within the context of this theological narrative. By demonising and accusing the left of Christophobia, discourses of spiritual warfare pave the way not only for new relations of domination, but also for reconstructing political realities by giving spiritual meanings to political actors.

## Conclusion

This chapter examines the ways in which theological imaginaries and online evangelical activism provide a corpus of discourses and practices that inspire authoritarian political modalities in Brazil. By stressing the role of religious grammars in Brazil's authoritarian turn, it investigates how charismatic evangelical imaginaries contribute to the formation of contemporary regimes of truth in Brazilian societies. In this web of post-truth politics, I stress the role played by discourses of spiritual warfare in assigning spiritual meanings to political actors in the Brazilian public arena.

While authoritarianism is a complex phenomenon with multiple contributing factors, my analysis suggests that religion can significantly influence the establishment of certain 'regimes of truth' that foster authoritarian tendencies. Bolsonaro's advocacy for 'cidadão de bem' values – characterised by his opposition to reproductive and sexual rights and to cultural pluralism, as well as his intolerance toward religious and ethnic-racial minorities, in addition to his anti-communist stance and support for military agendas – exemplifies the creation of an 'us versus them' narrative that fuels authoritarian modalities and practices. When encountering some teachings of charismatic evangelical

Christian theology, these narratives not only promoted conspiratorial thinking, but also invited believers to rally against progressive ideologies in order to uphold 'Christian moral majorities', thus reinforcing authoritarian tendencies.

This chapter invites readers to understand the 2022 Brazilian electoral campaign as a spiritual battlefield. In doing so, it reveals how discourses of spiritual warfare, in combination with evangelical online activism, served to endorse the demonisation of the left. In this view, the left is portrayed through images of apocalyptic beasts and evil forces. Furthermore, the left is seen as responsible for imposing a diabolic culture driven by the forces of evil, promoting the end of traditional family values and the persecution of Christianity through encouragement of Christophobic practices.

This study also maps how discourses of spiritual warfare and political activism affected the spaces, places and bodily dispositions of believers during the 2022 Brazilian electoral campaign. By fasting and praying in 'the name of the Brazilian nation', believers transformed their own bodies into vehicles of religious and political electoral action. The analysis also shows how these discourses shaped the sacralisation of certain urban spaces, for example military buildings. By capturing the influence of these spiritual cartographies in political modalities, this chapter demonstrates the pervasive role of religious imaginaries in contemporary Brazilian politics.

While producing a viable grammar for authoritarian modalities, charismatic evangelicalism cannot be conceived as a monolithic driving force of authoritarianism within Bolsonarism. Although this study stresses how theological narratives can be mobilised to promote authoritarian modalities, charismatic evangelicalism is in fact a very multifaceted movement in Brazil. For example, various evangelical groups have both endorsed Lula and strongly condemned Bolsonaro and his approach to governance, which they term 'necropolitics' (Rede Brasil Atual 2021). In a statement by certain evangelical leaders, Bolsonaro is denounced as the 'Anti-Christ' due to his actions and speeches of hate, which contravene the teachings of Christ (*Brasil de Fato* 2022). Rather than equating charismatic evangelicalism with authoritarianism outright, I therefore encourage scholars to investigate the particular ways in which theological narratives, such as spiritual warfare, are mobilised to create the condition of possibility for authoritarian modalities.

# Notes

1. The idea and term for the 'good citizen' emerge in Brazilian society vis-à-vis the 'delinquent'. In the contemporary context, the concept is attached to the defence of neo-conservative ideas.
2. Derived from the Greek term ἔσχατος (*eschatos*), meaning 'final', 'last' or 'end', eschatology refers to theological elaborations that reflect ideas about the end of the world and the end of time.
3. 'For the Lord himself will come down from heaven, with a loud command, with the voice of the archangel and with the trumpet call of God, and the dead in Christ will rise first. After that, we who are still alive and are left will be caught up together with them in the clouds to meet the Lord in the air. And so we will be with the Lord forever' (1 Thessalonians 4:16–17).
4. https://www.youtube.com/@NikolasFerreiraO.
5. 'Revoltarmo-nos com a tirania é obedecer a Deus'.
6. 'O Cristão e a Política: Como vencer a guerra cultural'.
7. 'For we do not wrestle against flesh and blood, but against principalities, against powers, against the rulers of the darkness of this age, against spiritual *hosts* of wickedness in the heavenly *places*' (Ephesians 6:12).
8. https://www.youtube.com/@prgeovanidias.
9. The 'Wailing Wall', or Western Wall, is the holiest place for Jews because its proximity to the Temple Mount. At the Western Wall Jews pray and display their religiosity.
10. Speaking in tongues, or *Glossolalia*, is one of the 'gifts of the spirit' in Pentecostalism. The person is touched by the Holy Spirit in a trance and starts to speak in an unknown language.
11. Fabricated stories resembling news, circulated on the internet or other media platforms, often designed to sway political opinions.

# References

Almeida, Ronaldo de. 2017. 'A onda quebrada. Evangélicos e conservadorismo', *Cadernos Pagu* 50. https://doi.org/10.1590/18094449201700500001.

Alonso, A. 2019. 'A comunidade moral bolsonarista'. In *Democracia em risco*, edited by S. Abranches et al., 52–70. São Paulo: Companhia das Letras.

Amaral, O. 2020. 'The victory of Jair Bolsonaro according to the Brazilian electoral study of 2018', *Brazilian Political Science Review* 14(1): 1–13. https://doi.org/10.1590/1981-382120 2000010004.

Asad, T. 2003. *Formations of the Secular*. Redwood City, CA: Stanford University Press.

Boas, T. and A. E. Smith. 2019. 'Looks like me, thinks like me: Descriptive representation and opinion congruence in Brazil', *Latin American Research Review* 54(2): 310–28. https://doi.org/10.25222/larr.235.

Bohn, S. R. 2007. 'Contexto político-eleitoral, minorias religiosas e voto em pleitos presidenciais (2002–2006)', *Opinião Pública* 13(2): 366–87. https://doi.org/10.1590/S0104-627620070 00200006.

Bolsonaro, J. 2017. 'Jair Bolsonaro diz que a minoria tem que se adequar a maioria'. YouTube. Accessed 16 December 2022. Available at https://www.youtube.com/watch?v=BCkEwP8 TeZY.

Bolsonaro, M. 2022. 'Não olhe para meu marido, olhe para mim'. YouTube. Accessed 16 December 2022. Available at: https://www.youtube.com/shorts/cVKjr2Cs6WE.

*Brasil de Fato*. 2022. 'Setenta líderes evangélicos declaram apoio a Lula: "Bolsonaro é um anticristo"'. Accessed 16 December 2022. Available at https://www.brasildefato.com.br/2022/10/28/setenta-lideres-evangelicos-declaram-apoio-a-lula-bolsonaro-e-um-anti-cristo

Burity, J. 2018. 'A onda conservadora na política brasileira traz o fundamentalismo ao poder'. In *Conservadorismos, fascismos e fundamentalismos: Análises conjunturais*, edited by R. Almeida and R. Toniol, 15–66. Campinas: Editora da Unicamp.

Carranza, B. 2020. 'Evangélicos: O novo ator politico'. In *Novo ativismo político no Brasil: Os evangélicos do século XXI*, edited by J. L. Pérez Guadalupe and B. Carranza, 171–92 Rio de Janeiro: Konrad Adenauer Stiftung.

Casanova, J. 2011. *Public Religions in the Modern World*. Chicago, IL: University of Chicago Press.

*Correio Brasiliense*. 2022. 'Em comício, Bolsonaro chama Lula de "capeta" e diz que vencerá no 1º turno'. Accessed 16 December 2022. Available at https://www.correiobraziliense.com.br/politica/2022/09/5036477-em-comicio-bolsonaro-chama-lula-de-capeta-e-diz-que-vencera-no-1-turno.html.

Cowan, B. 2021. *Moral Majorities across the Americas: Brazil, the United States and the creation of the religious right*. Chapel Hill, NC: University of North Carolina Press.

*Estadão*. 2022. 'É #FAKE que Lula disse que em seu governo Bíblia vai adotar pronome neutro e não terá mais o nome de Jesus'. Accessed 16 December 2022. Available at https://g1.globo.com/fato-ou-fake/noticia/2022/06/13/e-fake-que-lula-disse-que-em-seu-governo-biblia-vai-adotar-pronome-neutro-e-nao-tera-mais-o-nome-de-jesus.ghtml.

Ferreira, N. 2022a. *O Cristão e a política: Como vencer a guerra cultural*. Editora Central Gospel.

Ferreira, N. 2022b. 'Nikolas Ferreira – Cristianismo X Política'. Accessed 16 December 2022. Available at https://www.youtube.com/watch?v=dw574pP2AG8.

Ferreira, N. 2022c. 'O cristão e a política'. Accessed 16 December 2022. Available at https://www.youtube.com/watch?v=u8ScSzYSvEc&t=1010s.

Ferreira, N. 2022d. '21 dias de Jejum e oração pelo BRASIL'. Accessed 16 December 2022. Available at https://www.youtube.com/watch?v=FxEQQcXjQYo.

Finlayson, C. 2017. 'Church-in-a-box: Making space sacred in a non-traditional setting', *Journal of Cultural Geography* 34(3): 303–23. https://doi.org/10.1080/08873631.2016.1264262.

Foucault, M. 1997. *Ethics, Subjectivity and Truth. The essential works of Foucault: 1954–1984*, Vol. I., edited by P. Rabinow. New York: New Press.

Freston, P. 2020. 'Bolsonaro, o populismo, os evangélicos e América Latina'. In *Novo ativismo político no Brasil: Os evangélicos do século XXI*, edited by J. L. Pérez Guadalupe and B. Carranza, 371–91. Rio de Janeiro: Konrad Adenauer Stiftung.

Garrard, V. 2020. 'Hidden in plain sight: Dominion theology, spiritual warfare and violence in Latin America', *Religions* 11(12): 648. https://doi.org/10.3390/rel11120648.

*G1*. 2022. 'Leia a íntegra da carta divulgada pela campanha de Lula a evangélicos'. Accessed 16 December 2022. Available at https://g1.globo.com/politica/eleicoes/2022/noticia/2022/10/19/leia-a-integra-da-carta-divulgada-pela-campanha-de-lula-a-evangelicos.ghtml.

Guadalupe, J. 2022. *Pastores y políticos: El protagonismo evangélico en la política Latinoamericana*. Lima: Konrad Adenauer Stiftung.

Guadalupe, J. 2020. 'Brasil e os novos atores religiosos da política latino-americana'. In *Novo ativismo político no Brasil: Os evangélicos do século XXI*, edited by J. L. Pérez Guadalupe and B. Carranza, 17–109. Rio de Janeiro: Konrad Adenauer Stiftung.

Hjelm, T. 2014. 'Religion, discourse and power: A contribution towards a critical sociology of religion', *Critical Sociology* 40(6): 855–72. https://doi.org/10.1177/0896920513477664.

*IstoÉ*. 2018. 'Frases de Bolsonaro, o candidato que despreza as minorias'. Accessed 16 December 2022. Available at https://istoe.com.br/frases-de-bolsonaro-o-candidato-que-despreza-as-minorias/.

Johnson, T. and G. Zurlo. 2020. *World Christian Encyclopaedia Online*. Leiden: Brill.

Lehmann, D. 2021. 'Ritual, text and politics: The evangelical mindset and political polarization'. In *A Horizon of (Im)Possibilities: A chronicle of Brazil's conservative turn*, edited by K. Hatzikidi and E. Dullo, 103–20. London: University of London Press.

Leite, V. 2019. 'Em defesa das crianças e da família': Refletindo sobre discursos acionados por atores religiosos "conservadores" em controvérsias públicas envolvendo gênero e sexualidade', *Sexualidad, Salud y Sociedad: Revista Latinoamericana* 32: 119–42. https://doi.org/10.1590/1984-6487.sess.2019.32.07.a.

Lowe, C. 1998. *Territorial Spirits and World Evangelisation. A biblical, historical and missiological critique of strategic-level spiritual warfare*. Bristol: OMF International.

Machado, M. 2018. 'O discurso cristão sobre a 'ideologia de gênero', *Estudos feministas* 26(2): 1–18. https://doi.org/10.1590/1806-9584-2018v26n247463.

Machado, M. and J. Burity. 2014. 'A ascensão política dos pentecostais no Brasil. Na avaliação de líderes religiosos', *Dados – Revista de Ciências Sociais* 57(3): 601–31. https://doi.org/10.1590/00115258201419.

Mariano, R. and D. Gerardi. 2020. 'Apoio evangélico a Bolsonaro: Antipetismo e sacralização da direita'. In *Novo ativismo político no Brasil: Os evangélicos do século XXI*, edited by J. L. Pérez Guadalupe and B. Carranza, 329–50. Rio de Janeiro: Konrad Adenauer Stiftung.

Marsden, G. 2006. *Fundamentalism and American Culture*. New York: Oxford University Press.
Martelli, L. 2010. *Escatologia e anticomunismo nas Assembléias de Deus do Brasil na primeira metade do século XX*. Federal University of Santa Caterina (UFSC), MA thesis. Florianopolis: Federal University of Santa Caterina.
Martin, D. 2003. *Pentecostalism: The world their parish*. Oxford: Blackwell.
O'Donnell, S. J. 2020. 'The deliverance of the administrative state: Deep state conspiracism, charismatic demonology and the post-truth politics of American Christian nationalism', *Religion* 50(4): 696–719. https://doi.org/10.1080/0048721X.2020.1810817.
*O Globo*. 2022. 'Fake News sobre fechamento de igrejas em caso de vitória da esquerda tem respaldo de deputado'. Accessed 16 December 2022. Available at https://oglobo.globo.com/politica/eleicoes-2022/noticia/2022/08/fake-news-sobre-fechamento-de-igrejas-em-caso-de-vitoria-da-esquerda-tem-respaldo-de-deputado.ghtml.
Pérez, R. 2006. *Las iglesias, el campo religioso y la plaza pública*. Lima: Instituto de Estudios de la Comunicación.
Ramirez, J. 2017. *Armed and Dangerous*. Bloomington: Chosen.
Rede Brasil Atual. 2021. 'Cresce movimento evangélico contra Bolsonaro: "Ele não tem ideia do que causou na base da fé cristã"'. Accessed 30 June 2024. Available at: https://www.redebrasilatual.com.br/cidadania/cresce-movimento-evangelico-contra-bolsonaro-ele-nao-tem-ideia-do-que-causou-na-base-da-fe-crista/.
Rocha, D. 2020. 'Faça-se na terra um pedaço do céu: Perspectivas messiânicas na participação dos pentecostais na politica brasileira', *Perspectiva teológica* 52(3): 607–32. https://doi.org/10.20911/21768757v52n3p607/2020.
Romeiro, P. 1999. *Evangélicos em crise: Decadência doutrinária na igreja brasileira*. São Paulo: Mundo Cristão.
Smith, A. E. 2019. *Religion and Brazilian Democracy: Mobilizing the people of God*. Cambridge Studies in Social Theory, Religion and Politics. Cambridge: Cambridge University Press.
Sylvestre, J. 1986. *Irmão vota em irmão: Os evangélicos, a constituinte e a Bíblia*. Brasilia: Pergaminho.
Wagner, P. 1996. *Confronting the Powers: How the New Testament Church experienced the power of strategic-level spiritual warfare*. Raleigh, NC: Regal Books.
Wilson, E. 2023. *Religion and World Politics: Connecting theory with practice*. London: Routledge.
Woods, O. 2019. 'Religious urbanism in Singapore: Competition, commercialism and compromise in the search for space', *Social Compass* 66(1): 24–34. https://doi.org/10.1177/0037768618805871.

# 8
# Opacity and anxiety: how disruptive ritual may offer a clue to certain evangelical affinities with political authoritarianism

David Lehmann

Preaching in the neo-Pentecostal Universal Church of the Kingdom of God (subsequently IURD – Igreja Universal do Reino de Deus), from which the evidence in this chapter is drawn, is dominated by the moral decadence of modern life. It repeatedly dwells on the misery suffered by lives plagued by suicidal thoughts, depression, financial problems, addiction and family breakdown, as well as on the diabolic forces that cause those miseries. The response to these threats is twofold: faith in God, which is concealed in each person's own inner life, and church services. The latter enable that faith to be materialised by attending services that follow a themed weekly rota, reflecting its vocation as a '*pronto socorro espiritual*' (spiritual emergency room) for people in need.[1] Thus Monday is for financial problems, Tuesday for healing, Wednesday for Bible study (also known as the School of Intelligent Faith – Escola da Fe Inteligente), Thursday for emotional problems ('Love Therapy'), Friday for 'deliverance' (from the forces of evil). Saturday for the 'impossibles' – making the impossible become possible – and Sunday for the Holy Spirit. In London the services have slightly different titles, though the content is the same: Congress of Success (Monday); Health Day (Tuesday); School of Faith (Wednesday), Family Day (Thursday); Spiritual Cleansing (Friday); Impossible Causes (Saturday); Empowerment (Sunday).

Individuals attending services participate in a range of ritual activities. These involve a commitment to return to the church bringing trinkets, tokens, a loaf of bread and a bottle of water or slips of paper with messages for the Holy Spirit. In many places the church's branches are advertised publicly as help centres, though inside the visitor will find a full programme of usually four religious services a day. Consoling visions of eternal happiness, of sunny uplands, of the return of the Messiah and the end of time, or even eternal salvation, are advertised on screens and wall decorations.

The question for this chapter is whether specifically religious features of the beliefs and practices about the supernatural, disseminated by the church, encourage followers to interpret societal phenomena in terms of hidden forces or conspiracies. These in turn may stimulate distrust of the formalities of democratic procedure, for example the law and bureaucracy, and also of the accuracy of electoral outcomes – a distrust that favours authoritarian dispositions in the political field. I first studied the church in 1991 (Lehmann 1996), but the primary data quoted here come from attending services of the Igreja Universal in Brazil in London since 2020, as well as from conversations – and occasionally interviews – with bishops and pastors in Brazil (São Paulo), Chile (Santiago and Valparaíso), Argentina (Buenos Aires, Matadero and Lanus), Israel (Tel Aviv), Mexico (Oaxaca) and the USA (Brooklyn, New York) between 2020 and 2023. The services of this church follow a standard format and ritual procedures are very similar across the world. The content of pastoral discourse is also broadly similar from one country to the next. This consistency is assured not only by the frequent mobility of pastors, but also by weekly sessions over the internet, in which pastors gather at local centres to listen to an address from the leader, Edir Macedo. As a result, the illustrations and quotations provided here can be taken to be as representative of the church in Brazil as anywhere else.

The church is present in 142 countries, in locations ranging from Moscow to Papua New Guinea, California to Israel. It has a regularly updated internet presence, the contents of which vary from reports of healing to advice about marriage and relationships; it publishes testimonial and didactic material on YouTube, Facebook and Instagram, and makes films and television series known as *novelas bíblicas*. In Brazil its founder and leader, Edir Macedo, owns the second largest free-to-air television network (Record TV) in terms of audience size, and a bank (Banco Digi+). Its bishops number about 300 worldwide and it has thousands of – mostly Brazilian – pastors, supplemented by tens of thousands of volunteer assistants, known as *obreiros*. The church's followers join women's groups, youth groups, groups for older people, therapeutic groups such as 'Depression can be cured' (*Depressão tem Cura*) and prison and hospital visiting groups, whose activities are carefully programmed and recorded – as I have observed at London's flagship establishment in Finsbury Park. A news item on its Brazilian website in 2019 stated that the church had 7 million followers in Brazil and 2.8 million in other countries.[2]

Since 2014 the church has been headquartered at its Templo de Salomão in the Brás district of São Paulo. This monumental building, inspired by the Temple described in 1Kings 6, but on an incomparably larger scale, has seating for 10,000. The pioneer of what has become known as neo-Pentecostalism, the church's highly centralised and global structure marks a departure from classic Pentecostalism. The scale and breadth of its activities, which can be charted on many dimensions, merit astonishment and, in some quarters, apprehension. However, in this chapter I will only focus on what pastors tell their followers about how they can shape their lives, and the ways in which they can deal with the forces of darkness that seek to undermine the Holy Spirit. Through the pastoral discourse I engage with the core theme of this book, raising the question whether such discourse contributes to shaping an authoritarian political disposition among its followers.

## Anxiety and the Holy Spirit

Members of the Universal Church are expected to follow a demanding path through what they call the 'reconstruction of the self', leading to their possession by and of the Holy Spirit, culminating in the 'death of their old selves' whereupon they will be born again. The prize is inestimable:

> If the Holy Spirit is inside you, then you will overcome the world. The sin that controlled you no longer controls you. Then nothing is impossible ... Imagine the creator of the whole universe inside you. Once you receive the Holy Spirit you have the power of the creator of Heaven.[3]

Besides the moral self-examination, the journey also includes the ritual counterpart of baptism by full immersion. In the church's branch in Nazareth, Israel, in April 2022, I heard from the highly experienced Brazilian pastor that sometimes people are baptised quickly, soon after they start to attend a church. They get them off to a swimming pool or a river, anywhere with water: it is a rite of passage and it marks a stage and a commitment in the person's journey towards possession of the Holy Spirit. Long drawn-out preparation is not a prerequisite.

Usually the sequence is more gradual, however, and in any case baptism in water does not guarantee the true presence of the Spirit in that person. It is but a moment on a journey that, even after rebirth, is not entirely irreversible. We must constantly watch out for the devil, who is especially eager to target people who have received the Spirit. The ambiguity of the message, poised between a ritual with possibly magical effects and the individual's struggle with self-doubt, is a hallmark of the church's preaching: you should follow prescribed ritual and practical steps, even though you can never be sure that you will gain possession of the Holy Spirit. There is no 'guarantee'.

Even our best efforts may be irrelevant, for the Spirit may descend independently of a person's actions.[4] 'The people whom God chooses are not the ones with Diplomas: they may even have a criminal past and had never thought the Holy Spirit would choose them'. Beware those who think they can achieve spiritual outcomes by good works or sacrifice: we may perform acts of repentance, such as the 12-day Fast of Daniel, during which we should forsake superficial pleasures and live frugally, but we should not succumb to the illusion that the blessing of the Holy Spirit is brought by a kind of exchange: that by fasting we will somehow come to 'deserve' it. On the contrary, we are placing ourselves at God's mercy. We can only offer a highly unequal exchange: 'I can give only my broken life, yet in return I want to receive the Holy Spirit that will change my life for ever.'[5] Prayer and vigilance are permanent exigencies.

The same pattern is observed when pastors invite people to anoint their bodies with oil in places that are causing them pain. This example took place in the Buenos Aires suburb of Lanus in February 2023:

> At the door an *obreira*[6] offers me a swab with oil to anoint parts of the body which are giving me pain. She says I can go to the bathroom if I like and do it there. But she is also careful to remind me that it is not the oil which cures – rather God, or my faith, cures.

In his autobiography Macedo writes that at first he had doubts about the need for such gestures. Referring to a miracle in which Jesus cured a 'man who was deaf and could hardly talk', he wondered why it was necessary for him to 'put his fingers into the man's ears' and why he then 'spat and touched the man's tongue' (Mark 7:33). Macedo concluded that there are people whose faith is awakened only when they are anointed with oil on the place where they feel pain, or when they are touched by other gestures that can help them in their homes or their businesses. This insight brought untold number of people to the church – although, in a remark left unexplained, he claims it also cost him dear in his personal life (Macedo 2013, 122).

Naively, I asked the Nazareth pastor how one can tell that a person has received the Spirit. Since it is a marker on their progression towards full membership, that is conversion and rebirth, can one 'take their word for it'? I also posed a similar question – typical of my secularist/empiricist cast of mind – to an *obreira* in London: 'What is the difference between being "baptized in the Spirit" and "receiving the Spirit"? Although more theologically minded interlocutors might have responded in the terms in which the question was framed, to this person it just did not make sense to ask her to define the undefinable, nor to describe a state of mind or of the soul as if it was an item to be picked off a shelf. Maybe she thought I was splitting hairs.

The Nazareth pastor found a clearer response: he said it is through its effects on a person that the presence of the Spirit can be observed. That person exudes an aura. However, he also advised discretion: it is 'not something one talks about'. A Brazilian pastor at the Fulton Street church in Brooklyn used almost the same words, telling us that when we go about our lives, we bear witness not by saying we attend the church, or even by what we say, but by lighting up our inner selves from within.

Then, as if to redescribe the presence of the Spirit in terms more understandable to my mindset, the Nazareth pastor gave his own story as an example: he got rid of his houses in Brazil and in Israel, put aside frivolities and bad habits and dedicated himself to God and the church, though for many years he also had had a job.[7] The church offers parallel spiritual and material 'tracks' in the pursuit of spiritual ideals: despite rituals such as the anointment of the body or baptism by full immersion, there is no conventional ritual nor any sign that definitively marks a person with the presence of the Spirit. Nonetheless an individual can also be convinced that they do possess the Holy Spirit. A pastor in Santos (Brazil) told me in January 2023 how his conversion experience left him with an 'indescribable' feeling, almost a state of shock, for a whole day. Some people simply say they experience an inner sense of conviction that they are possessed of the Spirit, while others describe it in quite matter-of-fact ways.

Edir Macedo himself holds out an idealised version – but it is so idealised that he also questions people, including pastors, who give the false impression that they are possessed of the Spirit. In a volume entitled *The Ministry of the Holy Spirit,* he opposes 'the natural man' and 'the spiritual man': 'one lives to please the world, the other lives to please God'. Those who have been 'regenerated … have the Holy Spirit, the source of wisdom living inside them'. Partnership between a natural and a spiritual man can never work in any sphere of life. 'The decisions made by the spiritual mind can readily agree with the will of the Spirit of God' so long as they are not influenced by emotions or secularism (Macedo 2020, 62–3). Numerous passages that place the spiritual man and spiritual woman on an ineffable pedestal also cast doubt on the sincerity, or simply on the faith, of those who lead an apparently spiritual life:

> I have known people who've spent years in the Gospel, baptised in the Holy Spirit, and who even serve God, but are close to death and waiting for a miracle because they don't use their faith. On the other hand, I see others coming to the church for the first time, or after a prayer over a radio or TV programme, being healed from the same problem afflicting those who are just hoping for a miracle, even though they work for God. (Ministry of the Holy Spirit, 66)

At the same time, in a contrast frequently drawn by pastors in front of their congregations, he denounces 'emotion': faith has to be 'intelligent'.

> This shows it is not enough to be faithful, sincere, to serve in the work of God as a pastor, an assistant or even as a Bishop, since the requirements for us to be blessed go beyond these titles and apply to everyone. (Macedo 2020, 66–7)

The spiritual and material tracks are in tension, though probably not a tension that torments the faithful. Macedo is taking up an ancient motto, often reiterated in the Gospels and repeated by IURD pastors, that no amount of learning or even sacrifice is a substitute for innocent, unconditional faith. Yet he is also casting doubt on the faith of his own pastors, whose service in the work of God is 'not enough'.

Prayer meetings are peppered with cries from congregants imploring the Holy Spirit to descend upon them: no one seems to be thinking 'oh well, I have the Holy Spirit so now I am free, I don't have to pray for him'. The preaching does not refer to possession of the Holy Spirit as a permanent state – save perhaps in another world, where the soul will survive.

We are told that baptism in or receiving the Spirit marks a rupture in our lives, and it would seem to open up all manner of new beginnings, but we also know that our personal struggles do not let up; we may well backslide or fall by the wayside. Above all, we can never really know.

Followers are under constant pressure: to watch out for their own failings, to watch out for the traps laid by the forces of evil, to pay the tithes that are their obligation and to give more on top of that, to fundraise, to visit the sick, to visit people in prison, to go to suicide spots and discourage people who want to kill themselves, to distribute *City News*, the church's UK publication, or its equivalents in other countries.[8] For the core of faithful, belonging is not a once-a-week affair. Pastors and assistants bring people into the core by encouraging them to become an assistant or to take on any one of a myriad of responsibilities – for example, sorting out vegetables for the weekly soup kitchen.

The rhetoric gives with one hand and takes away with the other: pastors call for donations, but cast doubt on people's motivations. Prosperity is an illusion, yet every Monday a service is dedicated to solving financial problems. This may sound paradoxical, but the financial success in question is more like financial stability, requiring sacrifice and competence as emphasised by pastors during the Monday Congress for Success, which features much practical advice about how to run a business. To quote a phrase frequently repeated by pastors on the most varied subjects: 'faith in God is not enough – you too must do your bit'.[9] They do not believe that they will become billionaires.

Sometimes videos are screened portraying people who, after many struggles – with addiction, with crime, with family conflict or with an intangible emptiness at the heart of their lives – give away all their possessions and start anew, emerging as a happy and comfortable family. One video I have seen shown at the Finsbury Park church depicts a couple from humble origins who achieve a comfortable lifestyle and then, discovering the emptiness at the heart of their lives, sell everything and resolve to devote their time and energy to the church. While the manifest message is one of renunciation, the latent message of material reward does not require comment, for the video shows them now living in comfortable circumstances: not wealthy, but comfortable.

Followers of the Universal Church are told, in a high octane, unforgiving style, that the Holy Spirit is there, waiting for them. But they can never be quite sure; even if they have received the Holy Spirit, the devil will be targeting them. A preacher in the Portuguese service at the Rainbow Theatre told his listeners 'If you think that by giving your life to God nothing bad will happen, you are wrong'. This sounds like a battery of double binds. People are invited to pray for financial security, but they are told of others who gave away all their possessions (presumably to the church) and only then found peace and financial security. At the same time there is the parallel, practical way of belonging, such as joining the Youth Victory group or the Caleb groups for seniors,[10] evangelising and, above all, contributing their tithes – according to some reports, more than the minimum 10 per cent of their income. (The tithe is an obligation, but transfers beyond that count as a 'sacrifice'.)

I should note that the balance between the spiritual and the material or practical may not operate similarly everywhere in the church's empire. Among followers of the Universal Church in Cape Town, in a country where the church, as of 2023, claimed 400 branches, the one study we have describes a pervasive sense of vulnerability and mutual suspicion. This is reinforced by fears of pollution and witchcraft, triggered or transmitted especially by family members. In Ilana van Wyck's troubling ethnography, conducted during the first decade of the century, the material activity of giving did not offer a relief from the challenges and setbacks that people faced in the supernatural sphere in the way I have outlined for Latin America and for London. On the contrary: 'monetary sacrifices became tangled up with the essence of their givers' because money was tarnished with *muthi* – a Zulu word denoting dirt from a person's body that can leave openings where demons penetrate (van Wyck 2014, 124, 216).

## Anxiety and disruption

Pentecostal preaching in general is known for its high volume and even punitive quality, but the Universal Church style is distinctive in its own way. Preaching sounds standardised: pastors' voices rise and fall in pitch and volume, hammering away at their listeners as if added insistence in their tone can bring forth the love and miraculous works of the Almighty, even screeching to summon devils, seeking to release a person from their grasp. Although the pastors take care to be approachable before and after, their rhetoric during meetings is disruptive, more demanding of respect than love – offset by occasional bursts of humour. Their fluency is impressive and they routinely command a congregation for up to two hours. Services follow a flexible liturgical sequence. Fixed standard elements – the collection of donations and tithes, the Lord's Prayer and priestly blessing to conclude – are few. Oratory is so standard that one might regard it as ritual in itself.

Symbolic procedures are constantly changing, such as the distribution of tiny models of a chalice or a small kerchief to take home and then bring back, or the rose that we bring and then take home and bring back again for burning to purge the harmful spirits that haunt our homes. Followers are introduced to new procedures, their attention drawn to ever-changing manifestations of the malign supernatural forces in their lives.

'Mainstream' religion routinises and regularises ritual so that it can be performed daily, weekly or annually as if sleepwalking. Questions of meaning and substance are left to professional theologians in specialised institutions, removed from the everyday life of the faithful. Linda van de Kamp, drawing on Karla Poewe, contrasts charismatic Christianity, in which signs 'manifest and make the power of the Holy Spirit palpable', with the symbolic apparatus of, for example, Orthodox Christianity, in which signs perform a function of representation: in Pentecostalism they actually 'make things happen' (van de Kamp 2016, 125).

But Universal Church pastors do explain their symbolism to the faithful. This concretisation, peeling away the aura of mystery from the symbolism, is also disruptive – in the sense that it breaks with the veil of mystery ritually shrouded in what pastors contemptuously call 'religion', with its apparatus of learned people who know nothing of the Holy Spirit and its appeal to mere emotions. It is a further dimension of the disruptiveness of which Joel Robbins speaks in one of his accounts of Pentecostalism (Robbins 2020). According to Edir Macedo and his pastors, emotional impulses are no guide to the Holy Spirit: they advocate a faith partnered with rationality and intelligence, even while their oratory dwells on listeners' feelings of despair and insignificance, to be combated by rituals of deliverance.

Evangelical preachers tell us that forms of sacrifice – whether fasting or tithing – are not an exchange with God: they do not constitute a 'deal'. No ritual or material gesture entitles us to anything. As we saw in discussing the Holy Spirit, pastors prod their listeners to question whether their actions truly reflect their inner feelings, whether they are being honest with themselves. Ritual cannot be a matter of 'going through the motions', yet there is no question but that we should go through those motions. They say one should not give only out of a sense of obligation, but we are constantly reminded that the first 10 per cent of anything we receive (salary, pension, Christmas presents) belongs to God and should take precedence over all one's own necessities or even those of one's family. To do otherwise is to 'steal from God'. Theirs is indeed a ritual of interruption.

Pastors denounce the habits of religion as empty formalism, or worse, 'The devil uses religion to lead us astray and to believe that we can be saved or receive the Holy Spirit by performing all sorts of ritual, like obeying the 613 commandments or lighting candles or reciting the rosary'. When I mentioned that I had spent a week in a monastery and how much I appreciated the rituals, the chanting of the monks and the atmosphere, the reply was sharp: 'There is all sorts of filth behind those appearances'.[11]

A more specific example of disruptive ritual is the worldwide 'Novena of Spiritual Cleansing'. This event, as announced in London in May 2022, stretches over nine Fridays as indicated by its name. Members are given a booklet and each Friday over nine weeks they bring a page from the booklet on which they have written their 'purpose' or resolution.[12] The booklet is prefaced with a brief text about the sin-ridden biblical cities of Sodom and Gomorrah, located near the Dead Sea – and the Dead Sea provides the salt for the 'Valley of Salt'. The Valley consists of a white sheet laid along the space in front of the altar: we walk in file under a temporary white arch and then proceed along the sheet flanked by assistants. Floor lights flank the sheet. Most people have written on the page, which they give to one of the assistants or drop on the sheet. There is a page and a theme for each of the nine weeks, starting with Physical Cleansing and followed by Mind, Emotional, Financial, Family, Professional, Love Life, Social Life and Spiritual Life.

Evangelicals reject or avoid the ritualised iteration that enables mainstream religion to circumvent literal interpretations of the discourse of faith. For an adherent to Anglican or Catholic Christianity, or for a Modern Orthodox Jew, it is not necessary to believe that the Torah was 'literally' handed to Moses on Mount Sinai;[13] nor is it necessary to believe that by praying for the sick a priest or a congregation will cure them. Yet they still follow the Torah and say prayers for the sick. In his first autobiographical book *Orixás, caboclos e guias: deuses o demónios?* Macedo wrote that as he embarked on building the church he was thinking 'If Jesus healed the sick, this is what I too should do' (Macedo 1988). Again, in a more recent text, he criticises Christians who 'rely on easy access to health insurance rather than on faith … I am not against medical care, but we can't simply trust in [doctors] more than in God's healing power'. This was not only a matter of sickness and health: as mentioned above, he believed that there is a need for such devices if a church is to attract followers in large numbers.

In the IURD these ambiguities are channelled into symbolic procedures such as the Valley of Salt that are constantly renewed and reinvented, triggering mechanisms of reciprocity that create a sense of obligation and are designed to bring people back regularly.

## Healing

Healing forms part of a web of relationships. When people come down from a podium after a summary healing gesture from a pastor, can we assume that by agreeing that their pain has subsided they 'truly believe' they have been cured? When the pastor asks whether they feel better now?' people can hardly say 'no', if only because they would themselves then look foolish and naive. If they volunteer from among the congregation to present themselves for the summary cure, they must be prepared to recognise its effectiveness. This is not a short-term instrumental relationship: those people have not walked in off the street to get a 'quick fix'. I have never seen anyone throw away their crutches and shout 'Hallelujah!' On one occasion an *obreiro* of the Universal Church in Recife told me that they had stopped distributing plastic bags of 'water from the River Jordan' precisely because people would take them home and never return. Where they saw a fix the church hoped to start a relationship with a community of the faithful, with supernatural entities (the Spirit), with the pastor and with the church.

Nor are healing ceremonies to be equated to a consultation with a medical professional; certainly the pastors advise followers to consult a doctor if they are ill.[14] People are sometimes invited to bring their medicaments to church and place them on the altar, or podium, during the service – then reminded not to forget them at the end of the service.[15] As in Macedo's sentence quoted above, they would have it both ways.

Few people will know, or even claim to know *for sure*, whether they owe their recovery to the mysterious healing procedure. If it fails, they, or their bereaved relatives, will accept this, saying 'at least we tried'. In that case they will conclude that something went wrong, but that on another occasion the pastor's cure might work (Sperber 1996, 51–2).

Unlike the authority of a pastor, that of medical practitioners is based on independent professional certification of their expertise. The authority of a pastor is based on trust in the religious organisation, and yet pastors from this church want something more. They wear white lab coats on Fridays, when the theme of the meetings is deliverance – especially deliverance from the forces of evil.

The lab coats are presumably intended to exude not just trustworthiness but also expertise. My requests for explanation of their significance received varying responses. In London I was told that it was intended to denote a 'certain distance', since in the service of deliverance they are performing something resembling a professional role. In Renca, a suburb of Santiago de Chile, I was told that wearing white on a Friday signified 'sanctity' (*santidad*).

An episode on TV Templo in São Paulo in February 2023 depicts a prolonged session combining therapy with exorcism in a crowded hall. The pastor, wearing a white lab coat, sits in an armchair and listens to a woman describing her very bad relationship with her mother, who has said she wishes she had never given birth to her. Eventually he proceeds to an hour-long exorcism, holding her down as she groans and grunts until eventually the spirit is released. The pastor says her suffering is spiritual. He says the neutralisation of the devil that possesses her will also change her mother.

On another occasion (February 2023) at the church in Lanus, a suburb of Buenos Aires, in front of a small congregation of 20, mostly middle-aged or elderly women, a pastor asks whether any of them have experienced improvements in their health. An elderly and very bent woman volunteers, so he asks her to walk a few paces, which she does, though my sense was that she did so with difficulty and somewhat reluctantly.

Maybe the television episode was staged, but if not it illustrates how submission to pastoral authority is consubstantial with healing. The vignette from Lanus was less melodramatic but illustrative, and in a small way distressing.

The pastor in Nazareth mentioned at the start of this paper provided a different sort of illustration. He told me that he and his wife have an autistic child who is now a teenager. He said the child had been on Ritalin, but has gradually evolved from an acute case to a high functioning one – he knew all about 'the spectrum'. He hinted at the role of the Spirit in improving the child's condition, but did not insist on it, and also said that the intelligent care received from the parents had a role. He did not mention medical professionals, although presumably they had also been consulted.

The aforementioned bishop told me of the recovery of his sister-in-law, who had been taken to hospital in São Paulo following a stroke. At the time he was outside Brazil. The surgeon had said that the clot could be removed, but that she would afterwards be paralysed for life. So he called his brother, over whom he seems to have had strong influence, and told him to stop the operation and start a *corrente de oração* (a prayer circle). Three days later the doctor opened up her brain and found no clot. He did not explicitly offer an explanation: he just looked at me as if to say 'you see?'.

He then told me of a man who works with him, who also had had conflicts with his father and who had overcome severe psychological and addiction problems. Determined to free himself of psychiatrists, therapists, drugs and methadone, he had persuaded his doctor to reduce methadone gradually over a period of a month. He said the process was extremely painful, but it relieved him of his addiction.

He now had a job as a security guard in a hospital, as well as working with the Bishop in church administration. He took care not to say his improvement was due to a miracle cure: he believed that he had overcome his addictions, and the demons that underlay them, by the application of reason.

The pastor's sister-in-law, for her part, may well not have had a tumour on her brain at all: that is, the doctors' initial diagnosis may have been mistaken. Even if the outline of events was correct, this was an *ex post* story. Had she died or remained sick, it would not have been recounted.

Twice, on different occasions several years apart, the same Bishop also recounted his own story, which involved family violence and suicidal thoughts as a teenager, until he heard a pastor speak about how he needed to cleanse his heart and to forgive: 'that was the turning point … there was more I still had to do and to learn, to live a faithful life to God…'. His emphasis was on the motivating effect of participation in the church and he did not mention any supernatural agency.

The healing space emits ambiguity on several dimensions. If the sufferer is making their own contribution, for example by unsupervised withdrawal from drugs, is that thanks to the church, to a pastor, to their encouragement or moral support? Or is it the result of a spiritual transformation involving a supernatural element?

The physical performance of exorcism serves as an illustration of pastoral authority not only over the forces of evil that possess the sufferer, but also over sufferers themselves. Church is a separate authority space. When members enter a church they adopt an attitude of submission, expressed when together they all rise to their feet on the pastor's entry (always exactly on time).

The pastors and bishops of the Universal Church proclaim the healing powers of faith, but much less, if at all, the powers of gestures or charms. In order to underline the power in their recovery of the individual's faith – as distinct from performances and devices – they frequently quote the 'miracle of the bleeding woman' that appears in the Gospels of Matthew, Mark and Luke.[16] In each case the woman is healed merely by touching Jesus's cloak and each time the text uses the same phrase: 'your faith has healed you'. It is in the intangible sphere of deliverance that pastors exercise healing powers of gestures and imprecations, for that is also the sphere in which the subjects' sufferings are psychological and emotional, in which improvements are hard to detect. They say that it is the sufferer's own faith that heals, or perhaps that Jesus has healed them, but in any case the pastor does not claim healing powers.

*Obreiros* circulate in the church at certain points during these rituals, placing their hands on our heads, then suddenly lifting them as if releasing a demon, crying 'Out! Out!' (*Sai!*). It is a summary gesture, accompanied with a brief prayer for the person to be freed of pain and bad things.

In short, although the church proclaims its powers of healing and deliverance in the headlines, the practice is quite ambiguous. In one interpretation one might say that, concerned to avoid accusations of *charlatanismo* (a legal term in Brazil subject to criminal proceedings), its people avoid exposing themselves to charges of unlicenced medical practice. Yet in another one can say that these are ritual performances that express hope, blessing or consolation. They are performed by a person authorised by the church and follow a prescribed sequence of words and gestures.

Nevertheless, it is wrong to take the path of relativisation by claiming an equivalence between these rituals and the prayers for the sick that are an essential ingredient of proceedings in Catholic, Protestant and Jewish services. In the Universal Church, as in Pentecostalism generally, people are encouraged to bridge the gap between ritual (that is, psychological) and practical efficacy, and to follow those words of Jesus: 'Your faith has healed you'. To be sure, there is a subtext: 'If you have faith in God, then God may heal you', but, once again, 'there is no guarantee'. By 'bridging the gap', words, procedure and pastoral discourse combine to introduce the supernatural into the banality of everyday life, which is why one could describe this treatment of ritual as 'banalisation'.

## 'Fake'

Sceptics wonder whether there is not an element of deception in performances of healing, deliverance and speaking in tongues. The pastors, for their part, are more attentive to the harm people may suffer by deceiving themselves, rather than by deceiving others. Someone who prays ostentatiously may not be sincere.[17] Congregants are advised not to partake of the Lord's Supper 'if you continue thinking in the same way: be sincere (*sejam sinceros*)!'.[18] The faithful must distinguish between '*arrependimento consciente*' and '*arrependimento de coração*' – that is, between reciting the words and procedures associated with repentance and true repentance of the heart.[19]

Although they sometimes seem to promote the so-called 'theology of prosperity', the pastors of the Universal Church are far from indifferent to the Christian critique of materialism. While they point to a comfortable life as a sign or even a reward for the born again (as in the videos mentioned above), they also draw attention to the illusion of wealth as illustrated by high suicide rates among the rich or by posing the question 'what use is a diamond if you find yourself without water in the desert?' And since followers are obliged to contribute 10 per cent of all that they own, there is an in-built limit on their road to prosperity. (A London informant who had left the church after a decade told me that this limitation on members' economic advancement had lain behind many departures.)[20]

The call to donate, but 'only with a pure heart', places followers in another double bind. You have to sacrifice, and if you do not see the results you are not *really* sacrificing. Jesus said: 'Give and it will be given unto you' (Luke 6:38), but it has to be 100 per cent. Even if you give 99 per cent you will still receive zero benefit.[21] The test of the sincerity of your prayers lies in whether they have been answered – something that places the member under further stress if they take the admonition seriously. However, again in accordance with the parallel tracks, the majority of followers attending do give and do so publicly, although (unlike in Cape Town) donations in London and Brazil are confidential.

The description of a ritual performance triggers a question about its authenticity, even as a donation invites a questioning of the donor's motivation and a declaration of love can conceal all manner of perfidy. Pastors hammer away at this theme, insistently and sometimes loudly evoking the dark side of relationships, in tones that go beyond a routine reminder of human frailty. They tell their listeners that despite an appearance of peace and love, their marriage may be threatened by evil spirits, especially by infidelity. A caring neighbour who seems so kind to their children may be concealing sinister intentions. Edir Macedo and his daughter and son-in-law advise their followers that emotions are a poor guide to rational decision-making. Appearances, including the beauty and charm of a prospective life partner, can deceive.

These warnings are reinforced in Brazil by the influence of possession cults in the country's culture. Although subject to intermittent persecution over many decades until the postwar period, varieties of *candomblé* and *umbanda*, and the ideas of possession and mediumship derived from West Africa which they have incorporated (among others such as indigenous Brazilian sources) are deeply embedded in Brazilian culture, encompassing all social classes. Pentecostal churches have long denounced these expressions of the supernatural for bringing harm into intimate spheres of people's lives, but the Universal Church has elevated derision into open warfare. The *terreiros* where priests and priestesses of camdomblé hold court and conduct their rituals, and *the umbanda* centres, have become targets of the church's animosity, occasionally boiling over into physical attacks. There results something resembling a feedback loop in which *terreiros* and centres are under siege, sometimes literally, while their followers and sometimes their officiants migrate to evangelical churches where their occult expertise can be both reviled and valued (Birman 1996; Birman 1997; Birman 1998; da Silva 2007; Lehmann 2023a; Vital da Cunha 2015; Vital da Cunha 2021).

## Disruption and authoritarianism

The well-known pattern of evangelical voting – veering in favour of the victorious candidate in 2018, slightly less so in 2022 – does not constitute evidence that the message of evangelical pastors and the dispositions of their followers as they relate to the supernatural are themselves causes or facilitators of an authoritarian streak in their political dispositions. I express this in a roundabout way because I want to avoid formulating the question as 'does evangelical religion encourage political authoritarianism?' It is possible after all that the causation runs in the opposite direction – namely that evangelical churches tend to attract people of an authoritarian disposition.

We are dealing here with serial correlations which can be misleading: there are indications that evangelicals tend to vote on the right (Araujo 2022), that they tend to oppose the rights of the accused in criminal proceedings, that they tend to oppose abortion, that they oppose 'gender ideology' and that they distrust vaccine campaigns, but we do not have ways of unpacking these trends to see how closely they are bound up with one another. One sample survey from 2013 indicates that support for severe criminal punishment of abortion, for example, is by no means confined to either evangelicals or Catholics (Prandi and dos Santos 2017).

I was concerned that asking pastors or others about their political choices might undermine their confidence in my good intentions. I have therefore avoided the subject, just as I avoided inquiring about the church's financial arrangements. Maybe I have been too cautious, but my intention was rather to concentrate on their religious, or supernatural, lives. In a video broadcast shortly after the election but now unavailable, Edir Macedo, without mentioning names, consoles his followers on account of their disappointment with the result.

In contrast to other prominent evangelical pastors, Macedo wields his widely recognised political influence with discretion; he has not figured prominently in ideological campaigns or 'culture wars'. His political party (Republicanos), like many in the congressional soft centre or '*centrão*', seems to be ideologically moderate, although Record TV was widely regarded as biased in favour of the last President. Republicanos's successful candidate for Governor of the State of São Paulo in 2022 is an engineer who served as Minister for Infrastructure in the previous government but also held senior positions in that Ministry under Dilma Rousseff. By 2024 he has emerged as a strong chance to be the right-wing Presidential candidate in 2026, Bolsonaro being forbidden from standing by the Supreme Electoral Court because of his past misdemeanours.

Nonetheless there is a connecting thread between the diabolic forces, or simply 'the devil', and the theme of 'fake' as described in this chapter and the conspiracy theories that have been running amok in the public sphere, especially on the subject of sex and gender, targeting the PT and Lula.[22] An affinity between those themes and ideas about hidden forces in political life could underwrite a connection between evangelical ideas about the presence of harmful supernatural forces in people's lives and the emergence of an ideological right wing with a significant evangelical component.

I have not myself witnessed political preaching in the Universal Church. However, the persistent, sometimes ear-splitting warnings about the omnipresence of diabolic or evil spirits in their lives may well affect congregants' responses to politics, notably at a time when social media are shaping their political environment. Social media feed on deep-seated fears and unleash panic through memes experienced as threats to people's most intimate lives. Such a scenario was observed in Brazil's 2018 election, when scare stories about the PT's intention to encourage children to express their own gender preference around age 10 were disseminated in bulk WhatsApp messaging. Openness to such campaigns may be stimulated by pastors telling people they must not trust appearances and must not take even their own professions of faith and love at face value. This language encourages receptivity to conspiracy theories, as well as an attitude of distrust vis-à-vis the opaque formalisms of the bureaucratic apparatus and the impersonal professional and judicial expertise that form an essential part of democratic politics. Such distrust tends to be reinforced when those professions are staffed by people from relatively privileged classes. A conspiratorial persuasion, like the scheming of the devil, encourages people to think that institutions are designed to confuse the masses paving the way to support for authoritarianism – a politics in which the links binding the masses to their leaders are direct and empathetic, unmediated by institutions.

## Acknowledgements

I wish to thank Manoela Carpenedo and Katerina Hatzikidi for their very helpful comments on earlier drafts, as well as the Leverhulme Trust for awarding me an Emeritus Fellowship to conduct fieldwork in 2023. This chapter is a sequel to my contributions to a previous volume edited by Katerina Hatzikidi and Eduardo Dullo and to the online journal *Brésil(s)* (Lehmann 2021a; Lehmann 2021b). It shares some material with my recent article in Portuguese and English in *Religião e Sociedade* (Lehmann 2023a; Lehmann 2023b).

## Notes

1. On 30 November 2022 the UCKG announced on its Portuguese-language Facebook page the opening of a new UK branch in Nottingham: 'Mais um pronto socorro espiritual foi aberto para todos … as portas estão abertas diariamente para socorrer o aflito, dar ânimo ao cansado e ser esse ponto de contato entre Deus e o ser humano' ('Another spiritual emergency room has been opened for everyone … the doors are open daily to help the afflicted, give a boost to the weary and act as a point of contact between God and human beings'). Accessed 13 March 2023. https://www.facebook.com/story.php?story_fbid=6408811425796671&id=248641745147034&m_entstream_source=permalink.
2. https://www.universal.org/noticias/post/diplomatas-estrangeiros-participarao-da-solenida de-de-troca-das-bandeiras-no-templo-de-salomao-2/.
3. Preacher at the Universal Church's London Headquarters, Rainbow Theatre, Finsbury Park, London, 3 April 2022.
4. The point is illustrated by the incredulity of people of a secular cast of mind who cannot understand the popularity of Donald Trump, a man who makes no pretence of living a Christian life, among evangelicals in the US. However, the evangelical is quite prepared to believe that an individual can serve as the instrument of divine will independently of their behaviour or their beliefs.
5. Preacher at the Universal Church's London Headquarters, Rainbow Theatre, Finsbury Park, London, 12 August 2021.
6. *Obreiras* and *obreiros* (Portuguese; Spanish *obreras* and *obreros*) are volunteers who form an essential part of the church's apparatus. Known as assistants in English and mostly women, they wear uniforms, lead church groups (women's, youth, older people etc.), patrol services, collect tithes and much more. On a Sunday service at London's Rainbow Theatre they might number around one hundred, supporting between three and five pastors and the bishop. Women cannot be pastors, but pastors have to be married and their wives are full-time collaborators in their role.
7. His was an unusual case: he had come to Israel as a professional footballer, first in Nazareth and then in Haifa, and eventually became a football scout. I think he was already a member of the church when he arrived, and may indeed have been encouraged by them. It is not easy to get missionaries into Israel, whereas professional footballers probably get exemptions from ethnic or religious restrictions.

8   *Folha Universal* in Brazil; *Stop Suffering* in South Africa etc.
9   'Você tem que fazer a sua parte'.
10  The name comes from Ecclesiasticus 46: 9–10: 'The Lord gave Caleb strength, which remained with him in his old age, so that he went up to the hill country, and his children obtained it for an inheritance, so that all the Israelites might see how good it is to follow the Lord.'
11  Tel Aviv, 17 February 2022. The Jewish tradition speaks of 613 Commandments contained in the Pentateuch, and the lighting of candles on Shabbat eve is a weekly ritual in even moderately observant households.
12  A novena is a Catholic cycle of prayers offered on nine consecutive days. The Universal Church uses the word to refer to nine weekly events.
13  Some strands of Ultra-Orthodox Judaism do adopt a literal reading.
14  The website of the Rainbow Theatre Help Centre states that 'The UCKG Help Centre does not claim to heal people, but believes that God can heal through the power of faith'. This warning originates in the shocking case of Victoria Climbié, a child tortured and murdered in 2003 by her great-aunt who was involved tangentially in the church. This case led both to an inquiry into the performance of the local social services and to an examination by the UK Charity Commissioners of whether the church had contributed to the child's abuse by claiming to practice healing. The Commissioners subsequently absolved the church of those accusations. Accessed 16 April 2021. https://www.uckg.org/press/exorcism-and-healing/.
15  Observation at the Fulton Street church, Brooklyn.
16  Matthew 9:20–2; Mark 5:25–34; Luke 8:43–8.
17  Interview, Brooklyn, 21 October 2021.
18  Church in Vargem Pequena, Bairro Recreio, Rio de Janeiro, 12 February 2023.
19  'Conscious repentance' and 'repentance of the heart'. Rainbow Theatre, Finsbury Park, London (Portuguese service), 8 August 2021.
20  For bitter criticism by aggrieved former members see https://www.theguardian.com/world/2022/nov/29/young-uk-people-speak-out-against-evangelical-church-universal-kingdom-god.
21  Rainbow Theatre, Finsbury Park, London, 4 December 2020.
22  To the extent that in 2022 the Electoral Court that manages elections issued Resolution 23,714, sanctioning the 'dissemination or sharing of knowingly false or grossly decontextualised facts that affect the integrity of the electoral process', with fines of between BRL 100,000.00 and BRL 150,000.00 per hour for non-compliance, plus harsher measures, against 'systematic production of disinformation, characterised by the persistent publication of false or decontextualised information about the electoral process' (Art. 4). This, of course, raised further questions concerning freedom of speech and the limits of the court's powers (Pereira et al. 2022).

# References

Araujo, V. 2022. 'Pentecostalismo e antipetismo nas eleições presidenciais brasileiras', *Latin American Research Review* 57(3): 517–35. https://doi.org/10.1017/lar.2022.29.

Birman, P. 1996. 'Cultos de possessão e pentecostalismo no Brasil; passagens', *Religião e Sociedade* 17(1–2): 90–108. https://religiaoesociedade.org.br/wp-content/uploads/2021/09/Religiao-e-Sociedade-N17.01-02-1996.pdf. Accessed 23 January 2025.

Birman, P. 1997. 'Males e maleficios no discurso neopentecostal'. In *O Mal, a cultura e as religiões populares*, edited by P. Birman, R. Novães and P. Crespo, 62–80. Rio de Janeiro: EdUERJ.

Birman, P. 1998. 'Feminine mediation and Pentecostal identities', *Cambridge Anthropology* 20(3): 66–83. http://www.jstor.org/stable/23818811. Accessed 23 January 2025.

da Silva, W. G. 2007. 'Neopentecostalismo e religiões afro brasileiras: Significados do ataque aos símbolos da herança religiosa africana no Brasil contemporâneo', *Mana* 13(1): 207–36. https://doi.org/10.1590/S0104-93132007000100008.

Lehmann, D. 1996. *Struggle For The Spirit: Religious transformation and popular culture in Brazil and Latin America*. Oxford: Polity Press.

Lehmann, D. 2021a. 'L'Église universelle du Royaume de Dieu et la reconfiguration de la religion', *Brésil(s)* 20. https://doi.org/10.4000/bresils.11207.

Lehmann, D. 2021b. 'Ritual, text and politics: The evangelical mindset and political polarization'. In *A Horizon of (Im)possibilities: A Chronicle of Brazil's Conservative Turn*, edited by K. Hatzikidi and E. Dullo, 103–20. London: Centre for Latin American and Caribbean Studies and University of London Press.

Lehmann, D. 2023a. 'Ansiedade e reciprocidade: A Igreja Universal do Reino de Deus além das fronteiras', *Religião e Sociedade* 43. https://doi.org/10.1590/0100-85872023v43n3cap12.

Lehmann, D. 2023b. 'Anxiety and reciprocity: The Universal Church of the Kingdom of God across frontiers', *Religião e Sociedade* 43. https://doi.org/10.1590/0100-85872023v43n3cap12EN.

Macedo, E. 1988. *Orixás, caboclos e guias: Deuses o demónios?* Rio de Janeiro: Universal Produções.

Macedo, E. 2013. *Minha biografia 2: Nada a perder. Meus desafios diante do impossível*. São Paulo: Planeta.

Macedo, E. 2020. *The Ministry of the Holy Spirit*. São Paulo: Edições Horebe.

Pereira, F. B., N. Bueno, F. Nunes and N. Pavão. 2022. 'Fake news, fact checking and partisanship: The resilience of rumours in the 2018 Brazilian elections', *Journal of Politics in Latin America* 84(4): 188–201. https://doi.org/10.1086/719419.

Prandi, R., and R. W. dos Santos. 2017. 'Quem tem medo da bancada evangélica? Posições sobre moralidade e política no eleitorado brasileiro, no Congresso Nacional e na Frente Parlamentar Evangélica', *Tempo Social* 29(2): 187–213. https://doi.org/10.11606/0103-2070.ts.2017.110052.

Robbins, J. 2020. *Theology and the Anthropology of Christian Life*. New York: Oxford University Press.

Sperber, D. 1996. *Explaining Culture: A naturalistic approach*. Oxford: Blackwell.

van de Kamp, L. 2016. *Violent Conversion: Brazilian Pentecostalism and urban women in Mozambique*. Woodbridge, Suffolk: James Currey.

van Wyck, I. 2014. *A Church of Strangers: The Universal Church of the Kingdom of God in South Africa*. New York, NY: Cambridge University Press.

Vital da Cunha, C. 2015. *Oração de traficante: Uma etnografia*. Rio de Janeiro: Garamond.

Vital da Cunha, C. 2021. 'Cultura pentecostal em periferias cariocas: Grafites e agenciamentos políticos nacionais', *Plural* 28(1): 80–108. https://doi.org/10.11606/issn.2176-8099.pcso.2021.188462.

# Part IV
# Political peripheries at the centre

# 9
# Corruption models and the appeal of left- and right-wing politics in rural Brazil

Aaron Ansell

In 2010 a rural Brazilian friend of mine was apprehended by the head policeman of a rural municipality in the northeastern state of Piauí, my field site since 2003. My friend, 'João', had colluded with a junior cousin in the theft of another villager's goat. Having caught João but not his accomplice, the delegate took him to the margins of the village reservoir and tied him up beside a *jurema* tree. He used a branch of the tree to beat João's legs until the latter gave up the name of his cousin, after which both men were charged. My field assistant, Cícero, told me the story during one of my return fieldwork trips to the region in 2012. However, when I vented my outrage at the policeman's behaviour, Cícero pushed back: 'Aaron, if the police don't do a little torture, then nobody's livestock is safe'.

A few years later, in 2018, Brazil elected as its president the former military captain Jair Bolsonaro – a man who advocated police torture for witnesses (Werneck 2021), celebrated the legacy of the military regime (1964–85) and suggested that the more thieves a police officer killed, the more decorated they should be (*O Globo* 2018). While Bolsonaro had served as a Rio de Janeiro congressman for some 20 years, he billed himself as a political outsider, as a devoutly Christian 'Tropical Trump' and as a staunch opponent of the corrupt 'old politics of give-and-take' (*toma lá dá cá*).

Bolsonaro had found his moment. Since 2014 hundreds of career politicians from a wide range of parties had been stripped of office, fined and imprisoned by the anti-corruption taskforce known as Car Wash. The taskforce's leader was especially keen to go after officials affiliated with the left-wing Workers' Party (*Partido dos Trabalhadores*, hereafter 'PT') that had ruled the country from 2003 to 2016, and then returned to power again in 2023. Indeed Judge Sérgio Moro who led the taskforce even colluded with the prosecution to convict the still-popular former PT president, Luis Inácio 'Lula' da Silva, for allegedly accepting a town house as a kickback from a government contractor (Greenwald, Demori and Reed 2019). Bolsonaro relished the 12 year-sentence Lula faced (and made Moro a Supreme Court Justice), just as he had relished the 2016 impeachment of Lula's successor, Dilma Rousseff, for 'tricky accounting'. Hailed as the leader of Brazil's 'new right' (aka. 'extreme right' or 'populist right'), Bolsonaro promised a regime of uncompromising and heavy-handed Christian moralism: 'Brazil above everything. God above everyone' was his 2018 campaign slogan. His second-round defeat of the PT candidate (Fernando Haddad) was a landslide in every state ... except those in the northeastern region, Piauí included.

In this chapter I draw on some 36 months of ethnographic fieldwork in rural Piauí State, beginning in 2003, to analyse the ambivalence that rural Piauienses felt toward then-president Jair Bolsonaro (2018–22), as well as their overwhelmingly positive regard for PT politicians. My argument is that the logic of municipal politics shapes Piauienses' perceptions of these national-scale politicians. More specifically, I claim that local patronage relations furnish Piauienses (and many other Brazilians) with folk models of political corruption that differ from the normative (read 'liberal') model of corruption undergirding Car Wash and other modern anti-corruption institutions. Considered through this local folk model, Lula appeared a morally upright patronal leader. The case of Bolsonaro is more complex, however. Depending on how Piauienses apply local ideas of corruption and moral governance, Bolsonaro appeared to epitomise either corruption or its opposite.

First, I offer an analytic framework for assessing and comparing the various folk models of corruption at issue in this chapter. Then I discuss the politics of small-scale patronage in rural Piauí State and the folk model of corruption associated with patronage. Next I show why, through this local political lens, Lula did not seem to be corrupt, despite many Piauienses believing that the kickback allegations against Lula were true. I then turn to President Bolsonaro, arguing that his status as Lula's nemesis and his cuts to PT-era social policies cast him in the role of corrupt villain within established rural narratives. But I also show how Bolsonaro's anti-human rights and anti-LGBT positions had the opposite effect for some Piauienses (mainly Pentecostals), making him appear as a redemptive antidote to the PT's corrupt attack on the family, the elementary unit of a world organised by patronage.

I wrote most of this reflection in May 2022, just before the official start of the campaign period preceding the state/federal elections in October. Those elections saw another Bolsonaro-PT showdown, this time involving Lula himself (who was exonerated and released from prison in 2019). Lula went on to beat Bolsonaro in the second round, carrying about 70 per cent of the northeastern vote (Tenente 2022). While the PT may enjoy a wide margin of support in this region, I hope that my analysis serves as a warning against any complacent trust in the northeast as an enduring redoubt of PT support.

## Corruption: folk models and transcultural frameworks

Corruption, when defined in liberal-cosmopolitan terms, refers to 'the appropriation of public resources for private gain' (Fukuyama 2014, 83). However, as many scholars of corruption have noted, the validity of this Eurocentric definition is 'dependent on the distinction between public and private' such that 'it made no sense to talk about corruption in [a] context [where] there was no concept of a public sphere whose resources could be misappropriated' (Fukuyama 2014, 83). In this section I offer a more robust framework for studying corruption transculturally. It's not that I wish to compare various geographically disparate cultures; it's that various cultures are now to be found 'on the ground' in rural Piauí among what is now a smartphone-using, social media-savvy populace attuned to news from around the world.

Despite the worldliness of Piauienses, theirs is a setting in which the public and the private spheres are not strongly delineated. Certainly this case has been made of the region's history. One seminal theorist traces Brazil's national culture to the foundational structure of rural life, lamenting that

> certain sentiments appropriate to the domestic community … dominated all other social relationships; the private sphere invaded the public, the family invaded the state. (Buarque de Holanda 2012 [1936], 53)

The concept of patronage expresses this 'invasion'. While patronage is often conceived by scholars as a form of governance based on personalist transactions between those of lesser and greater rank (as in 'political clientelism'), I use the term to refer to the transposition of the principles of family hierarchy (patriarchy and gerontocracy) onto larger spheres of collective self-governance.

Because patronage principles afford senior kin (men especially) the prerogative of allocating resources as they see fit (without transparency or accountability), and because patronal figures prioritise kin over non-kin in their alliances and distributive decisions, patronage constitutes a form of corruption according to the liberal model defined above. Indeed, both the PT and Bolsonaro railed against the patronage (*patronagem*) and clientelism (*clientelismo*) notoriously endemic in rural northeastern culture, especially among the poor. Yet as compelling as those liberal allegations of patronage-style corruption might be to cosmopolitan readers, they often overlook the fact that patronage, as a moral logic of self-governance, prefigures its own folk model of corruption.

In order to assess the patronage model of corruption, to compare it to the liberal model and to show how these different models of corruption can synthesise or cancel one another out, one needs a broader analytical framing of corruption, of which these folk models appear as variations on a theme. While some argue that such a transcultural corruption framework would be doomed to ethnocentrism (Bratsis 2003; Muir and Gupta 2018, S6), I find that position unwarranted. I submit that all governance structures imply a morally laden distribution of value down a moral gradient of some kind, such that worthy people at higher levels of social organisation (such as the national government) legitimately channel value down towards worthy people at lower levels (for example, municipal governments, family heads). Within this transcultural framework, corruption names those illicit practices that effect a perverse re-routing of value in ways that erode (degrade) such gradients (Kockelman 2016; Ansell 2022).

This analytic framework renders commensurable the liberal model of corruption defined above, the patronage model of corruption endemic to rural Piauí, and Bolsonaro's new right model of corruption. That is, all of these folk models can be reckoned in terms of the specifics of their central moral gradients (what kinds of people or relations are positioned closer or further from value's source), the value-forms (money, jobs, fertility and so on) that flow across those gradients and the perverse modes of re-routing value (graft, usurpation and so on) that threaten a given gradient.

For example, in the liberal model of corruption, the moral gradient is organised around the relative and situational public-private binary, such that an agent represents the 'public' interest relative to another agent who stands as the 'private' interest. The downward flow of value (government grants, contracts, benefit cheques, among others) from 'the people' to particular people (or institutions) is the basis for modern social reproduction. That downward flow must be achieved in ways consonant with the principle of impartiality with respect to the parties' private interests (see Rothstein 2011).

In the case of Piauiense patronage, the moral gradient guiding local governance is differently construed. So too are its concomitant corruption models, which differ from the liberal model and others. As I show, Piauienses coordinate and synthesise these different folk models of governance and corruption. Indeed, to explain the local appeal of one or another national politician I look to precisely the articulations and mutual amplifications among disparate models of moral degradation.

## Patronage morality and its attendant folk model of corruption

The moral gradient central to Piauiense patronage runs from senior kin (whose age puts them closer to God) to junior kin, more distant from the divine. The former owe the latter value in the form of love, blessings and material support. The latter owe the former deference, loyalty and gratitude. Harsh punishment for defiant children is the norm, though even the wayward are defended in the kinship idiom 'They never stop being part of the family'. When transposed to the realm of electoral politics, ordinary people vote for (prototypically male) candidates who show them care (*carinho*) and provide them with the assistance (*assistência*) they need to propagate their families, fields and livestock over transgenerational time. They 'adhere' to these politicians' factions (often labelled 'families') on that basis and not for 'ideological' reasons (Heredia and Palmeira 2006). The very idea that a person would have an ideology (a discrete and contestable set of moral norms) differing from that of their neighbour was alien when I began my fieldwork in 2004. My initial question, 'Are you more right or left?', was utterly incomprehensible to them.

A politician's virtuous assistance need not accrue to private individuals or households. Goods benefiting villages (dams, watering holes, paved roads) or even the entire municipality (gymnasium, school construction, basic health centres, etc.) are valid demonstrations of patronal munificence, often called 'work'. What matters is not so much what a politician gives, but the fact that they avail themselves to those in need when they come knocking. Thus politicians who simply buy votes with cash on the eve of an election only to 'disappear after being elected' are viewed as self-seeking 'adventurers' (L'Estoile 2014; Villela 2004). By contrast, a good politician is one who shows constant 'presence' (*presença*) in the municipality. Here 'presence' is a kind of religious concept, associated not only with the ubiquity of Christ in the lives of the poor (Dullo 2015; Lebner 2011) but also, in the wake of liberation theology, as a revolutionary battling alongside the poor (Lowy 1996). Building infrastructure, visiting families, walking 'among the people', leaving their front doors open for petitioners – these are all signs of 'presence'.

Patronage thus names a political formation organised by a familial order of precedence in which all people are metaphorical children who belong to other people who are metaphorical parents. Enhancing the prestige of one's patron is simultaneously an act of self-aggrandisement because the patron's identity transfers downward to his or her followers. As Piliavsky has observed

> By giving, (the patronal person) absorb(s) their gifts' recipients, becoming ... bigger people, socially enhanced. (2021, 33)

Essentially, as a Piauiense woman boasted in 2004, 'We are people of Henrique', a reference to the mayor. Such references allow an ordinary person to mobilise 'the social projection of his *patrão* ... as a cloak for his own social position' (DaMatta 1991 [1979], 144). By being absorbed into a greater person's identity a nobody, a *cidadão qualquer* ('any old citizen') becomes a somebody (Holston 2008, 4). Concomitantly, this same logic of identity-absorption explains the endurance of a good patron's power long after their term in office has ended. Their successor is seen as an extension of their identity, a relation framed in a parent-child idiom, sometimes as the father working through the son.

When Piauienses allege that a politician is 'corrupt' (*corrupto*), that indictment points to some form of absent fatherhood. This may be figurative: the patron-politician has failed to leave their mark by 'working for the people'. The absence may also be literal. The rural northeast, and Piauí State in particular, has a notorious history of absentee landlordism (see Caio Prado Júnior 1957, 187) – one that transfers into the political realm when mayors live elsewhere, enjoying the comforts of cities (air-conditioning, running water, reliable electricity, restaurants, brothels) over the sparse amenities of their rustic municipalities. The bad father-politician redirects his resources outside the factional channel leading to the loyal needy, re-routing them to prostitutes and other luxuries for selfish reasons; he is described as 'eating his salary' while 'his own people go hungry'.

Alternatively, corruption can take the form of another person's breaking down (*derruba*) of a good father. Such 'envious' saboteurs are said to 'know only how to destroy' the good works of their betters. Either way, the corrupt agent disrupts the proper flow of value, re-routing it to less-worthy recipients and giving worthy juniors cause to stop showing the upward-looking respect on which the entire moral edifice depends.

Let this serve as an overview of patronage's inner logic and its associated folk model of corruption. I turn now to the way in which this logic influenced Piauienses' favourable interpretation of President Lula, Dilma Rousseff (Lula's successor) and Fernando Haddad (Rousseff's intended successor). After that I'll discuss how it shaped Piauienses' ambivalent appraisal of Jair Bolsonaro.

## Lula, a present father

On 8 February 2022 a story appeared in *The Intercept* concerning the ongoing popularity of the Workers' Party, and Lula especially, in an important municipality. Located in rural Piauí, a few hundred kilometres south of my field site, Guaribas Municipality had been one of the pilot towns for the PT's flagship anti-poverty initiatives in 2003. As in much of the rural northeast, this town became a redoubt of PT electoral support during Lula's first term (2003–6). Why? Because, as one resident told reporters, 'Lula was a present father' (Felizardo 2022).

When Lula took office in 2003 he immediately launched massive anti-poverty policies (most famously *Bolsa Família*) that reduced both poverty and social inequality in record time – all the while appeasing big domestic capital and foreign investors by maintaining low inflation and a high growth rate (French and Fortes 2012). Lula's 'Light for All' programme brought electricity to Piauí's rural interior (including the village where I had once taken notes by candlelight). This amenity that allowed for small-scale irrigation and refrigeration and proved wildly popular with people who 'had been living in the dark', an oft-repeated phrase that suggested a connection between electricity and technologically-mediated knowledge. Lula's '1 Million Cisterns Program' built submerged 16,000-litre cisterns adjacent to virtually every rural household to ensure potable water and to spare women and children the daily chore of fetching water from far-away reservoirs. When I asked one older Piauisense how Lula's government compared to those that had preceded it, she responded, 'Here there was no government before Lula. The government was for the cities, for the people of means. This place was abandoned'.

When Lula's second term ended, there was no question that rural northeasterners, such as my associates in Piauí, would vote for his intended successor, Dilma Rousseff (2011–14, 2014–16). As one man said, 'Dilma is Lula. It's Lula behind her commanding, right?' 'Dilma', as she is called, was not regarded as a puppet in a diminutive sense. Rather Piauienses saw her (and later Haddad) as avatars of Lula. Piauienses regarded Rousseff's helpful policies as her own doing, while also viewing these as a manifestation of Lula's ongoing presence.

Rousseff's second term ended badly. Global economic changes following the 2008 financial collapse led to a crash of commodity prices, leading to a falling rate of growth, foreign capital flight and increased inflation (Anderson 2019, 140–1). In 2013 President Rousseff faced popular revolts in the big cities that originally targeted fare hikes in public transport but then spun out into numerous grievances. What was an initially diverse set of protesters evolved into a largely right-wing movement demanding that she be ousted. After Rousseff's impeachment in 2016 on trumped-up charges of 'tricky accounting', her vice president (and one-time ally) Michel Temer, of the catch-all Brazilian Democratic Movement Party (PMDB), sided with the impeachers. He took over as Interim President and implemented a host of neoliberal measures. Temer proved so unpopular that when the 2018 election came around, the traditional conservative parties had no choice but to abandon him. This created the power vacuum that forced them to endorse the wild-eyed Bolsonaro as their 'high pitched obbligato' (Anderson 2019, 165).

As for who my Piauiense associates would vote for in 2018, most of the sentiments I heard chimed with the lyrics of one popular song (artist unknown) making its way across YouTube and Facebook:

| | |
|---|---|
| Eu voto num cambito | I'd vote for a ham |
| Num jegue, num passarinho | for a donkey, a little bird |
| Num burro, num porco espinho | for a mule, a hedgehog, |
| Numa cabra ou num cabrito… | a goat or a kid |
| Se o velho Lula mandar | If old Lula commands me to… |

The idioms through which Piauienses explained their readiness to embrace Haddad as another Lula avatar revolved around creative constructs of 'presence'. Across a range of social media platforms, several before-and-after memes emerged that depicted the rural landscape

**Figure 9.1** Facebook Meme.[1]

pre- and post-PT rule. One such meme, shared on Facebook by the left-wing group *Democráticamente* (Figure 9.1), featured four rows of two before-and-after photos of the northeast. Two of these photos (the bottom two) carried clear references to PT social policies, 'My House My Life' (a house construction programme), and the 1 Million Cisterns Program.

Such images worked to offset disappointment in Lula's corruption, implying that corruption refers not to the practice of taking a kickback, but to the abandonment of 'the people'. It's not that Piauienses approved of kickbacks, but rather that such modern peccadillos were less morally salient than questions of patronal presence or absence.

Another factor causing widespread reverence for Lula was the ex-president's own northeastern background. He was easy to cast as the hero of an archetypal northeastern narrative: the bright-eyed youth flagellated by drought-induced poverty flees the semi-rural arid region to seek their fortune amidst the dangers and temptations of the city. It can go badly. The young man may fail, or he may succeed but stay away forever, 'forgetting' their family. In the happy ending version the prodigal youth returns with wealth to redeem their parents and siblings from poverty. *Lula, Son of Brazil*, as he was called in one titular documentary (2009), fulfilled the allegorical narrative of a Christ-like son whose love for the poor sets the bar to which other, more flawed, fatherly politicians aspire (Lebner 2012). Indeed, Lula's many telegenic appearances across the blighted northeastern landscape were didactic, guiding other politicians to a path of moralisation that required direct presence among the real-world suffering of the poor (Dullo 2015).

In sum, Piauienses' overwhelmingly positive reception of Lula can be explained as a function of his activation of the moral matrix of local patronage relations. (This is not to say that Lula used his social policies to 'buy votes', as Bolsonaro alleged.) Within that patronage matrix Lula was the furthest thing from 'corrupt', even among those people who had no trouble believing that he had illegally accepted the kickback. However, the warm glow cast over Lula by the lights of patronage did not preclude his enemies from enjoying those flattering lights themselves.

## Bolsonaro, a heavy-handed (would-be) father

For most Piauienses I came to know, Lula's imprisonment was an outrage of religious proportion, a sabotage of paternal munificence committed by those (Temer, Moro and Bolsonaro) who 'know only how to destroy'. Yet despite their generally negative perceptions of Bolsonaro, Piauienses are disposed to sympathise with him in certain regards. Both Pauienses' support and their antipathy for Bolsonaro derive from the same model of patronal family governance (and its corrupt degradation) that underlay their positive reception of Lula.

Bolsonaro's cuts to PT-era social policies did not escape the attention of rural Piauienses. Nor did his pension reforms (which raise the retirement age), his privatisations of parastate businesses, his necropolitical dismissal of the Covid-19 'little flu' (Muniz, Ferradas, Gomez and Pegler 2021) or his general failure to curb the soaring cost of fuel. President Bolsonaro seemed to be destroying the 'work' that the PT did during its 13 years in office. Perhaps Bolsonaro's two greatest policy failings (in the eyes of my Piauiense associates) pertained to the PT-era Bolsa Família cash grant and fuel costs.

As for rising fuel costs, Piauienses know perfectly well that these are largely driven by complex, macro-economic factors. However, they also understand that, through mechanisms such as executive influence over Petrobrás, President Bolsonaro had the means to lower prices at the pump artificially. That he chose not to is construed as further evidence that he did not 'care about the people'. More pointedly, Bolsonaro had campaigned on this issue in 2018 when high fuel prices under Interim President Temer spurred a wave of truck-drivers strikes in May and June, just before the campaigns. When a subset of the strikers demanded 'Military Intervention Now', Candidate Bolsonaro quickly latched onto their cause, while suggesting that a militarisation of the government needed to happen through the vote (UOL 2018).

Bolsonaro was right to intuit that the military enjoyed a high degree of institutional credibility among the poor (who often view promotion in the ranks as a key vehicle for social mobility). After becoming president, however, he followed his neoliberal finance minister's lead and proposed only tax cuts to fuel (and basic foods) as the solution to high costs. Prices continued to rise during his administration, which became the target of another truckers' strike in 2021, this time aimed at Bolsonaro. But as much as fuel costs drive Piauienses' dislike of Bolsonaro, that dislike rarely takes the form of corruption allegations.

This was different in the case of Bolsa Família. That monthly cash stipend was perhaps the most famous and successful of the PT-era social policies. Piauienses and others often cite it as the reason why 'when Lula was president, we didn't lack food in the pan', as one older woman said – a phrase suggesting that Lula was, in some sense, inside people's homes as a kind of second husband-father-provider. The very name of his flagship cash grant bespoke the PT's awareness that family reproduction was the touchstone of popular morality, with its food preparation aspect being the traditional responsibility of the woman of the house. (The female household head was indeed the primary beneficiary of Bolsa Família.) As a congressman, Bolsonaro had made many derisive remarks about the programme, claiming that the poor were addicted to their benefit payments and were unwilling to find employment (UOL 2021), that the PT's motive in distributing the grant amounted to cynical 'vote-buying' (UOL 2019) and so forth.

Once in office, President Bolsonaro moderated his tone, fearing Bolsa Família's popularity among the poor would bring dire consequences to his approval ratings if he discontinued it. Nonetheless, under the advice of his finance minister, Bolsonaro cut many so-called welfare fraudsters from the ranks of Bolsa Família, later replacing the programme entirely with his own cash subsidy, Auxílio ('Renda') Brasil. This was an emergency measure, created during the COVID-19 pandemic, that Bolsonaro declared would remain permanent (Resende and Garcia 2022). (When Lula regained the presidency in 2023, he resurrected Bolsa Família.)

The case of Auxílio Brasil is instructive because just as President Lula had obviously relied on Bolsa Família to boost northeastern support for his re-election in 2006, Bolsonaro used Auxílio Brasil in 2022 as 'the main platform to seek support in the region [where] (h)alf (47 per cent) of the beneficiaries of the program' resided (Rossi 2022). Bolsonaro met with some modest success. Comparing just the first rounds of the 2018 and 2022 elections, northeastern support for Bolsonaro increased by 1.3 million votes, but it was still a landslide: about 22 million northeastern votes for Lula as compared to about 9 million votes for Bolsonaro (Rossi 2022). Explaining Bolsonaro's gain in votes is easy enough. Auxílio Brasil increased substantially (by as much as 20 per cent in some cases) the monthly stipends that families had previously received from the federal government through Bolsa Família. Indeed, several increases to Auxílio Brasil occurred during the election year 2022, putting the government 42 billion *Reais* over its spending ceiling (Papp 2022).

The harder question is why this cash increase failed to secure *more* votes for Bolsonaro in this region so notorious for its morally disassociated 'vote-buying'. I think the answer is that those northeastern voters who were unmoved by Bolsonaro's evangelical moralism (see below) were uncompelled by his increases to their cash stipends. In effect, these increases failed to convince them that Bolsonaro was truly invested in the wellbeing of the region's people. In addition to Auxílio Brazil's policy shortcomings (mainly its unpredictability), the 'electoralist' timing of the grant and the absence of other complementary social programmes to address problems in the region (illiteracy, child labour, water scarcity, under-resourced healthcare, etc.) gave northeasterners the impression that Bolsonaro was not attentive to the region's needs. He was not really 'present' for them as Lula (and the PT in general) had been.

Not only did Bolsonaro fail to embody the image of a present father, but his support for Lula's prosecution and Rousseff's impeachment also played directly into a northeastern messianic narrative that predicts the persecution of a good father, who truly 'works' and 'cares' for the people, by envious rivals who 'only eat their salaries' and destroy the good work of others. Bolsonaro slotted himself into a hagiographic story that read Lula's imprisonment as martyrdom and Bolsonaro as the envious villain who 'knows only how to destroy things'.

Nevertheless the two main pillars of Bolsonaro's moralism, 'the bible and the bullet', held some appeal and for reasons related to the ethics of patronage.

The same 2022 article from *The Intercept* that reported widespread approval of Lula ('a present father') in Guaribas Municipality also featured a countercurrent:

> new churches with affinity for Bolsonaro with pastors influencing people's voting intentions in this once most pro-PT of all cities.

When the reporter asked one pastor (from the Assembly of God Church) why he supported Bolsonaro, he answered 'because he defends the family'. I continually heard similar utterances in my conversations with Bolsonaro supporters in southeast Piauí.

Itamar, one of my pro-Bolsonaro, Pentecostal (Assembly of God) field assistants, elaborated the political significance of family values and the value of 'the father of the family'. He is worth quoting at length:

> Bolsonaro defends the family, defends the right of a father of a family to keep a gun to defend his family from assault, in the house, on the street. He is against the PT's Statute of Adolescence, which teaches homosexuality to our children, which would make a father who disciplines his child leave the house. He defends good citizens (*cidadão de bem*) from bandits, from this redirecting of public monies to bandits [a reference to the PT-era Penitentiary Stipend that went to prisoners' families], from drugs and criminality. Morally, Brazil has degraded significantly. Now in the elections [of 2018], we are seeing politicians with a new vision. Bolsonaro is seen as a friend of the family and an enemy to corruption … They take money that was supposed to be public, but they take it themselves. People are indignant with the Left for this.

Notice the parallelism in Itamar's discourse across the domains of (homo)sexuality, criminality (banditry) and graft – all of which appear as homologous symptoms of Brazil's moral degradation (see Ansell 2018). Nested in such talk of 'defence of the family' is a folk model of successful child socialisation to gender-typical desire, law-abiding productivity and abstemiousness from drugs, premarital sex and the allures of graft. The central agency of this socialisation is patriarchal discipline – a discipline that, in order to work, requires discretion and a licence to mete out pain in order to 'straighten-out' wayward children. Just as importantly, Bolsonaro grants to fathers the licence to use heavy-handed means to protect and discipline their dependents (wives and children) from the immoral incursions of outsiders, whether these are the state-sponsored teachers who espouse 'gender ideology' or the highway 'bandits' whose nests are feathered by PT human rights policies that, as one Piauiense Pentecostal explained, 'are more concerned with the lives of the bandits than with the lives of families and the police'.

Bolsonaro, like Lula, argues for a scaling up of primordial parental functions from the level of the household to the level of the polity. If Piauienses prized PT-era policies that supported the nourishing function of parents (especially mothers), Bolsonaro 'defends' the punitive, normalising function of the family, especially fathers. Even Bolsonaro's push to make the police immune from charges of torture and extrajudicial killing – 'the policeman who doesn't kill isn't a policeman' (Veja 2018) – scales up and exaggerates his push to afford fathers the discretion of 'energetic discipline' (read corporal punishment). His discourse and policy profile appeal to the patronage model of political culture foregrounded by the agency of disciplinary fathers.

Poll results from the 2018 and 2022 elections suggest that Bolsonaro's support in the northeast (as with the poor in general) was more or less restricted to Pentecostals and to law enforcement personal (military included). However, I suspect that his appeal is far wider than those polls indicate. Put differently, were it not for northeasterners' admiration of Lula and Bolsonaro's symbolic position as Lula's usurper, I speculate that many Piauienses would support him, believing, along with Cícero, that they 'have a little of Bolsonaro inside' themselves.

It's not that Piauienses (and other northeasterners) are simply given to atavistic authoritarianism. Rather, an authoritarian aspect of their patronal model of self-governance was catalysed by the insecurity brought about by Brazil's economic and political crises (see Anderson 2019, 173). Both paternal care and discipline have indeed been undermined by economic hardship, making ordinary people vulnerable to right-wing anti-corruption discourses that locate the cause of paternal jeopardy not in the complexities of the market but in the 'marginal' figures of the bandit and the homosexual.

It is true enough that some forms of violent criminality increased during the PT era (Soares and Guindani 2017), just as it is true that the LGBT community won legal protections and popular tolerance never before imaginable (Mello, Avelar and Maroja 2012). Fátima, my PT-affiliated Piauiense associate, comments on the latter:

> We always knew they were among us, but they were in secret. Now they are showing themselves. There are some who even walk through the streets together. Their social mobilisation has been effective and there are many laws passed during the time of the PT that protect their rights. They are safer now.

On the facts (though not the evaluation) of this matter, my Pentecostal assistant, agreed.

> There were already many (gays) here, but under the table. But now these laws of the PT incentivise people to be gay … They sit in the plaza holding hands … Their parents tolerate it. It's against the bible. And it's nauseating. It devastates the family. The family, as we know, is born from the man and the woman.

While I doubt most Piauienses would posit a moral equivalence between gay people and murderous criminals, they have long viewed both figures as marginals and have noted that, during the PT, the government showed increased 'tolerance' towards them. This is what my Pentecostal assistant means when he calls the PT *corrupto*. It's not a reference to kickbacks or tricky accounting, but to the PT's re-routing of value (public monies, legal protections, etc.) away from 'good citizens' and towards those 'marginals' who siphon value (wealth, esteem, state protection, etc.) away from the channel running between highly-positioned Christian fathers (Bolsonaro) to their more capillary counterparts (ordinary Christian fathers). Interweaving anti-gay and law-and-order themes into their anti-corruption rhetoric, the new right (in Piauí and in general) excoriates the PT for encouraging 'parents (that) tolerate' these enemies of the family, and for hamstringing stronghanded fathers who want to set the nation's children on the straight and narrow.

In this way, Bolsonaro's discourse and policies find friendly reception in the patronal moral imagination – a gradient of care and munificence running downward from parents to (respectful) children who, in turn, send obedience and respect upward. Crucially (and ironically), this same local moral imagination (when differently inflected) has made Piauienses highly receptive to leftist figurations of redistributive policy qua the munificence of present fathers.

## Conclusion

Here I have argued that a robust analytic framework for studying and comparing culturally particular folk models of corruption helps us to make sense of Brazilian politics. To build this framework, I've argued that normative moral orders can be regarded as culturally idealised gradations of value co-varying with (and flowing across) degrees of moral worth. Corruption then refers to those practices that degrade this gradient via the improper movement of value. I've sought to explain the orientations of rural Piauienses towards both left-wing (Lula, the PT, etc.) and right-wing (Bolsonaro, the new right, etc.) politics at the national level, as functions of Piauienses' local models of self-governance and corruption. The latter form the reception matrix through which Piauienses assess left-wing and right-wing politicians at the national level.

In this way, rural Piauienses' historically entrenched models of local self-governance (patronage) can be seen as projections of transgenerational and patriarchal kin relations in which munificence (money, blessings, lands, etc.) flow downward (generationally and morally) at the discretion of senior kin (prototypically fathers), expected to be 'present' in the lives of their respectful junior dependents. Within this local idiom, corruption amounts to the absence of a father, such as a father's re-channelling of resources from this moral circuit to destinations outside it, or another agents' sabotaging of a good father's munificence. Such practices short-circuit the reproductive cycles of families, crops, livestock, etc., undermining basic moral order.

Both Lula and Bolsonaro appeal, intentionally or not, to this patronal moral framework, though in different ways. Piauienses (like many other Brazilians) believe Lula to be a caring, 'present father' whose policies put food on the table for the most deserving of 'children', the honest poor. They perceive Bolsonaro as a strong father who exercises legitimate violence over disrespectful and wayward children, bringing them back into proper patters of peaceful, heteronormative obedience. From the same rural Piauiense standpoint, both Lula's channelling of resources and protections to 'marginal' (LGBT and criminal) populations, as well as Bolsonaro's sabotage of Lula's paternal munificence, constitute forms of corruption.

In the event, Lula and the PT proved far more successful at garnering Piauiense support and galvanising opposition to Bolsonaro's new right. Local support for Bolsonaro (in both 2018 and 2022) was mainly limited to those people closely associated with Pentecostal churches and law enforcement. But my analysis suggests that this equilibrium is delicate and that Brazil's 'new right' will find increasing appeal with the northeastern population. If the left doesn't want that to happen, it should continue to support redistributive policy and find a way to cast its pro-LGBT and human rights-guided criminal justice policies within the sort of paternalist discourses I heard in Piauí, affirming that such people 'never cease to be part of our family'.

## Acknowledgements

I would like to express my gratitude to Andreza Aruska de Souza Santos and Katerina Hatzikidi for inviting me to be part of this important project and for editing and discussing my contribution with me.

## Note

1 https://www.facebook.com/permalink.php?story_fbid=pfbid02bobg6ofAmkDBdrNg5825Eok3p3Vb6Fjjg96gofUJTnvJTAkjuEyuXYRLZvyRdT44l&id=1602376756480655.

## References

Anderson, P. 2019. *Brazil Apart 1964–2019*. New York: Verso.
Ansell, A. 2014, *Zero Hunger: Political culture and antipoverty policy in northeast Brazil*. Chapel Hill, NC: University of North Carolina.
Ansell, A. 2018. 'Impeaching Dilma Rousseff: The double life of corruption allegations on Brazil's political right', *Culture, Theory and Critique* 59(4): 312–31. https://doi.org/10.1080/14735784.2018.1499432.
Ansell, A. 2022. 'On calling Donald Trump corrupt'. In *Corruption and Illiberal Politics in the Trump Era*, edited by D. Goldstein and K. Drybread, 43–62. New York: Routledge.
Bratsis, P. 2003. 'The construction of corruption, or rules of separation and illusions of purity in bourgeois societies', *Social Text* 4(77): 9–33. Accessed 24 January 2023. https://muse.jhu.edu/article/50296.
Buarque de Holanda, S. 2012 [1936]. *Roots of Brazil*. Translated from the Portuguese by G. Harvey Summ. Notre Dame, IN: The University of Notre Dame Press.
Prado Júnior, C. 1957. *Formação do Brasil contemporâneo: Colônia*. São Paulo: Brasiliense.
DaMatta, R. 1991 [1979]. *Carnivals, Rogues and Heroes: An interpretation of the Brazilian dilemma*. Notre Dame, IN: The University of Notre Dame Press.

Dullo, E. 2015. 'A Sensibilidade secular da política brasileira', *Debates do NER* 16(27): 178–98. https://doi.org/10.22456/1982-8136.56478.

Felizardo, N. 2022. 'Fome e fé: Pastores estão virando votos para o Bolsonaro na cidade mais petista em 2018', *The Intercept Brazil* (February) [online]. Accessed 12 May 2022. Available at https://theintercept.com/2022/02/09/guaribas-pastores-votos-bolsonaro-cidade-mais-petista/.

French, J. and A. Fortes. 2012. 'Nurturing hope, deepening democracy and combating inequalities in Brazil: Lula, the Workers' Party and Dilma Rousseff's 2010 election as President', *Labor Studies in Working Class History of the Americas* 9(1): 7–28. https://doi.org/10.1215/15476715-1461059.

Fukuyama, F. 2014. *Political Order and Political Decay: From the industrial revolutionary to globalization of democracy*. New York: Farrar, Straus and Giroux.

Garrett, G. 2022. 'Em baixa no Nordeste, Bolsonaro viaja a reduto de Lula e Ciro em fevereiro', *Exame* (Jan.) [online]. Accessed 12 May 2022. Available at https://exame.com/brasil/em-baixa-no-nordeste-bolsonaro-viaja-a-reduto-de-lula-e-ciro-em-fevereiro/.

Greenwald, G., L. Demori and B. Reed. 2019. 'How and why the *Intercept* is reporting on a vast trove of materials about Brazil's operation Car Wash and justice minister Sergio Moro', *The Intercept* (9 June) [online]. Accessed 12 May 2022. Available at https://theintercept.com/2019/06/09/brazil-archive-operation-car-wash/.

Heredia, B. and M. Palmeira. 2006. 'O Voto como Adesão'. In *Imaginários sociais em movimento: Oralidade e escrita em contextos multiculturais*, edited by J. Henriques, I. Pordeus Júnior and F. Laplantine, 281–98. Fortaleza, Brazil: Pontes Editores.

Holston, J. 2008. *Insurgent Citizenship: Disjunctions of democracy and modernity in Brazil*. Princeton, NJ: Princeton University Press.

Kockelman, P. 2016. 'Grading, gradients, degradation, grace Part 1: Intensity and causality', *Hau: Journal of Ethnographic Theory* 6(2): 389–423. https://doi.org/10.14318/hau6.2.022.

Lebner, A. 2012. 'A Christian politics of friendship on the Brazilian frontier', *Ethnos* 77(4): 496–517. https://doi.org/10.1080/00141844.2011.610512.

L'Estoile, B. 2014, 'Money is good, but a friend is better. Uncertainty, orientation to the Future and "the Economy"', *Current Anthropology* 55(9): S62–S73. https://doi.org/10.1086/676068.

Lowy, M. 1996. *War of Gods: Religion and politics in Latin America*. New York: Verso.

*Lula, Son of Brazil* [feature film]. 2009. Directed by Fabeo Barreto. Rio de Janeiro: Luiz Barreto Produções.

Mello, L., R. B. de Avelar and D. Maroja. 2012. 'Por onde andam as políticas públicas para a população LGBT no Brasil', *Sociedade e Estado* 27(2): 289–312. https://doi.org/10.1590/S0102-69922012000200005.

Muir, S. and A. Gupta. 2018. 'Rethinking the anthropology of corruption: An introduction', *Current Anthropology* 59(S18): S4–S15. https://doi.org/10.1086/696161.

Muniz, R.C., F. M. Ferradas, G. Gomez and L. J. Pegler. 2021. 'Covid-19 in Brazil in an era of necropolitics: Resistance in the face of disaster', *Disasters* 45(S1): S97–S118. https://doi.org/10.1111/disa.12528.

*O Globo*, 2018. 'Bolsonaro diz ao JN que criminoso não é 'ser humano normal' e defende policial que "matar 10, 15 ou 20"'.

Papp, A. C. 2022. 'Auxílio Brasil de R$ 600 começa 18 de agosto; vale-gás será pago em 3 meses', *CNN Brasil* (27 November) [online]. Accessed 7 March 2024. Available at https://www.cnnbrasil.com.br/economia/auxilio-brasil-de-r-600-comeca-18-de-agosto-vale-gas-sera-pago-em-3-meses/.

Piliavsky, A. 2021. *Nobody's People: Hierarchy as hope in a society of thieves*. Stanford, CA: Stanford University Press.

Resende, S. and G. Garcia. 2022. 'Auxílio Brasil: Senado aprova valor mínimo permanente de R$ 400', *O Globo Política*, 4 May 2002. [online]. Accessed 12 May 2022. Available at https://g1.globo.com/politica/noticia/2022/05/04/auxilio-brasil-senado-aprova-valor-minimo-permanente-de-r-400.ghtml.

Rossi, A. 2022. 'Nordeste dá 1º lugar a Lula; votação de Bolsonaro na região cresce 1,3 mil', *UOL Notícias/Eleições 2022*, 3 October 2022. Accessed 7 March 2024. Available at https://noticias.uol.com.br/eleicoes/2022/10/03/nordeste-da-1-lugar-a-lula-votacao-de-bolsonaro-na-regiao-cresce-13-mi.htm.

Rothstein, B. 2011. *The Quality of Government Corruption, Social Trust, and Inequality in International Perspective*. Chicago, IL: The University of Chicago Press.

Soares, J. 2018. 'Bolsonaro diz que policial que mata "10, 15 ou 20" deve ser condecorado', *O Globo*. 28 August 2018. [online]. Accessed 12 May 2022. Available at https://oglobo.globo.com/politica/bolsonaro-diz-que-policial-que-mata-10-15-ou-20-deve-ser-condecorado-23019806.

Soares, L. E. and M. K. Guindani. 2017. 'Direitos humanos nos governos do PT'. In *Cinco mil dias: O Brasil na era do Lulismo*, edited by J. Medeiros and G. Maringoni, 191–206. São Paulo, SP: Boitempo.

Tenente, L. 2022. 'Eleito presidente, Lula vence Bolsonaro no Nordeste; veja análise por região', *O Globo*. 31 October 2022. [online]. Accessed 30 June 2023. Available at https://g1.globo.com/politica/eleicoes/2022/eleicao-em-numeros/noticia/2022/10/31/eleito-presidente-lula-so-venceu-bolsonaro-no-nordeste-veja-analise-por-regiao.ghtml.

UOL. 2018. 'Caos durante greve de caminhoneiros agita debate sobre intervenção militar', *UOL Notícias*. 31 May 2018. [online]. Accessed 12 May 2022. Available at https://noticias.uol.com.br/ultimas-noticias/afp/2018/05/31/caos-durante-greve-de-caminhoneiros-agita-debate-sobre-intervencao-militar.htm?cmpid=copiaecola.

UOL. 2019. 'Bolsonaro chama Bolsa Família de "condução coercitiva" e diz que programa era usado para angariar votos', *UOL Economia*. 16 August 2019. [online]. Accessed 13 May 2022. Available at https://economia.uol.com.br/noticias/reuters/2019/08/16/bolsonaro-chama-bolsa-familia-de-conducao-coerciva-e-diz-que-programa-era-usado-para-angariar-votos.htm?cmpid=copiaecola.

UOL. 2021. 'Bolsonaro: Beneficiários do Bolsa Família "não sabem fazer quase nada"', *UOL Economia*. 28 October 2021. [online]. Accessed 13 May 2022. Available at https://economia.uol.com.br/noticias/redacao/2021/10/28/bolsonaro-beneficiarios-bolsa-familia.htm?cmpid=copiaecola.

Veja. 2018. 'Bolsonaro: "Policial que não mata não é policial"', *Veja Política*. 23 April 2018. [online]. Accessed 12 May 2022. Available at https://veja.abril.com.br/politica/bolsonaro-policial-que-nao-mata-nao-e-policial/.

Villela, J. 2004. 'O Dinheiro e suas diversas faces nas eleições municipais em Pernambuco', *Mana* 11(1): 267–96. https://doi.org/10.1590/S0104-93132005000100009.

Werneck, N. 2021. 'Veja vídeo: Bolsonaro defendeu tortura para quem fica em silêncio em CPI', *Estado de Minas: Política*. 18 May 2021. [online]. Accessed 12 May 2022. Available at https://www.em.com.br/app/noticia/politica/2021/05/18/interna_politica,1267678/veja-video-bolsonaro-defendeu-tortura-para-quem-fica-em-silencio-em-cpi.shtml.

# 10
# Idealism, pragmatism and disenchantment in Brazilian elections: politicians and the votes of the poor

Flávio Eiró

To contribute to the understanding of Brazil's recent rearrangement of political forces, this chapter will discuss the ways in which political candidates imagine and perform politics in Recife and Olinda, in the state of Pernambuco. Interviewing and accompanying different politicians and their advisors during the 2018 and 2020 elections, I look at politics 'from the other side', in contrast to most of the anthropological work on politics which has mainly studied voters' and residents' preferences and engagement with politicians (Auyero 1999; Eiró and Koster 2019; Hunter and Power 2007), as well as their brokers (Auyero 2001; Koster 2012). In recent years municipal and state-level candidates and their staff had to navigate a new political scenario, the result of the unexpected emergence of Jair Bolsonaro as a presidential candidate, elected president and, later, as former president, defeated in his bid for re-election. Some political commentators and academics resist identifying the 2018 electoral cycle as containing something fundamentally novel to Brazilian politics. They point out that the then candidate Jair Bolsonaro was not the first to claim the position of an outsider to politics in the run for the presidency. Others have observed that Bolsonaro was not an isolated phenomenon. He rather surfed a successful wave of far-right politics, drawing upon similar agendas (adapted to national contexts) that flirted with authoritarianism, moral conservatism and neoliberal economic principles (Mudde 2010; Pasieka 2017; Pinheiro-Machado and Scalco 2020).

This provides the context against which this chapter will zoom in on how politicians interpret the ways the urban poor engage with politics. In so doing, it builds on ethnographic research carried out in

Recife and Olinda during the 2018 and 2020 elections. Since 2012 I have been researching how the poor (in both urban and rural contexts) engage with politics in northeast Brazil (the Nordeste region), first in the countryside of Bahia and Pernambuco and later in a middle-size urban centre in Ceará. In 2018 I turned my focus to politicians' perspective on that relationship, to understand how they interpret the ways in which the urban poor engage with an increasingly turbulent political landscape. I critically examine the tensions politicians experience in, on the one hand, attending to people's direct needs and, on the other, in performing what they consider to be a 'truly noble politics'. I also reflect here on my own experience of conducting fieldwork amidst a global pandemic, with the ethical and practical challenges that this posed.

## The ethnography and the 2018–2020 electoral cycles

In order to analyse this phenomenon I followed four election cycles (2018–24) in Olinda and Recife, although this chapter focuses mainly on the first two. In 2018 state and presidential elections took place in October. In order to make better use of the one and a half months I spent there, I drew upon contacts established prior to my arrival. To that end, I relied on recommendations and introductions made by a colleague,[1] as well as on my own network in Brazil, to gain access to politicians – something that I expected to be the most difficult part of my fieldwork. Contrary to my expectations, I was able quickly to establish a few important collaborations, giving me access to the ins and outs of some electoral campaigns.

    Those I encountered were mainly politicians or employees of political parties who had an academic affinity and interest. They saw in our relationship an opportunity to discuss theories of the state and politics, as well as to engage in constant comparisons between Brazilian and European politics. As a Brazilian who has lived in Europe for almost a decade, I provided them with an interesting perspective on both our professions. In this scenario I was constantly asked to give my own opinion on the developments in national politics, something I experienced so openly for the first time during fieldwork. The abjection Bolsonaro provoked in these politicians, from Left and Centre parties – as I will describe later – made them assume (accurately) that I would share a similar feeling. I was not asked to take sides on local political matters, since I did not vote in the state; instead I (honestly) assumed ignorance of the history and details of such topics.

In 2020 my fieldwork had been drastically reduced in order to avoid unnecessary exposure to Covid-19. I tried to compensate for this by maintaining intense online contact with my main interlocutors. During the weeks I spent in Pernambuco in 2020, my priority was to maintain contact with more than one campaign team at a time. I rotated between them, depending on the public activities that were scheduled and the politicians' availability. Furthermore, my sample was not diverse in terms of political parties. As my access and time were limited, I focused my attention on politicians from two parties: the Workers' Party (PT) and the Brazilian Democratic Movement (MDB). While the first is the main left-leaning party in the country, having occupied the presidential office from 2003 to 2016, the second is consistently the largest; its flexible centrist (lack of) ideology allows it to align itself to ruling parties as local and national alliances require. The MDB is known for participating in the coalitions of all federal administrations since the country's re-democratisation in 1985. As is the case for most parties in Brazil, regional differences are substantial in political parties' identities and strategies. This can result in conflicting simultaneous alliances.

The Covid-19 pandemic and the agitated political scenario in Brazil, two years after Bolsonaro's election, make up the extraordinary circumstances of this research. This is the clear impression I had when arriving in Pernambuco a few weeks before the 2020 elections. With an alternated cycle of four years in relation to presidential, gubernatorial and national congress and state assemblies, municipal elections had been delayed by one month, taking place exceptionally in November. The decision to maintain fieldwork plans in these circumstances was not an easy one. The political scenario in Brazil, which included the contested responses to the pandemic in different levels of government, was the defining factor for my return. Having conducted my first fieldwork there during the 2018 elections, it seemed important to give continuity to my research at that moment – not least because Bolsonaro's administration politicised the pandemic as much as possible in order to benefit allied politicians, among other goals.

Upon arriving in Pernambuco, it took me some time to get used to the relatively normal pattern of life. There was a constant presence of masks, indoors and outdoors, yet all commercial establishments were open and public transport was as crowded as I had experienced two years before. If some sense of normality permeated daily life, however, the same could not be said for the upcoming elections. The main change came a few weeks before voting day, when the state electoral court (TRE-PE) banned campaign gatherings of more than 20 people. The core of municipal electoral campaigns being street rallies – a traditional display of strength (Eiró 2018; Palmeira 1992) – the 2020 candidates felt crippled by this prohibition. Some focused on online campaigning; others on strolls through residential neighbourhoods with small teams. A common strategy I observed consisted of candidates themselves handing out flyers to cars and pedestrians at traffic lights. Instead of hiring workers to wave flags on busy crossings, flags stood alone on pavements, their poles buried in heavy bases. In fact such flags became the most visible sign of elections in the city, competing for people's attention at crossings, avenues, squares, playgrounds and beaches. Some candidates even defied the rules and faced the risk of fines.

In reflecting on my experience in conducting ethnographic research during the Covid-19 pandemic, my top priority was the health and safety of my collaborators. I thus adhered to all national and local public health guidelines and created my own set of protocols. Although this guide was specific to my circumstances, it may offer insight to other researchers navigating similar situations. To minimise the risk of Covid-19 transmission, I asked collaborators if I could join them on already planned open-air activities – mainly campaigning.

My goal was to avoid creating situations in which research participants would be exposed to the virus because of my wish to interview them. A few of them were isolating for the full duration of my fieldwork, so we kept in touch via video and voice messages. When meeting face-to-face, physical distancing and mask-wearing were always the norm. The exception to this was when participants asked me to meet them in open-air restaurants, where masks were not mandatory.

Based on the information I possessed at the time, I presented participants with my risk assessment before engaging with them. This included my recent testing history and general health perception. I reminded them that none of this guaranteed that I did not have the virus, and that I preferred to talk outdoors. After they had indicated that they were comfortable with the situation, I explained what participating in my research entailed and assured them of anonymity. Such assurance relates to the main ethical challenge I encountered: respecting participants' privacy and confidentiality. On a couple of occasions I was made aware of an acquaintance's positive Covid-19 status, as well as their desire to keep that information confidential. In these situations I had to balance my ethical obligation to maintain confidentiality with my responsibility to ensure the safety of others who might have been exposed to the virus. I self-isolated when necessary and asked others who were potentially exposed to do the same, without divulging any specific information.

Overall my experience conducting ethnographic research during the pandemic was challenging. However, by following proper protocols and prioritising the safety of my collaborators, I was able to continue my work while keeping all those involved as safe as possible.

## The state and the politics of the poor

While the fast-growing field of anthropology of the state has focused on bureaucracies (Bierschenk and De Sardan 2019; Dubois 2010), development projects (Ferguson 1990) and welfare provision (Thelen et al. 2014; Koch 2021), to give some examples, my ethnographic entry point into studying the state consists of elections and electoral politics (see also Barreira 1998; Björkman 2014; Banerjee 2014). Especially in Brazil, studies that deal with poorer people's involvement in electoral politics touch upon the phenomenon of clientelism (Gay 1998; Palmeira 1992). Some use the term explicitly; others prefer to avoid it, as 'clientelism' comes with normative and emic meanings that can be restricting in analytical work (for example, Ansell 2014; de L'Estoile 2014). Let us now turn to the way in which this phenomenon is seen and studied in Northeast Brazil.

### Reciprocity and economic rationality

A division that frames clientelism studies opposes reciprocity and economic rationality as analytical lenses. Although the division persists roughly along disciplinary lines (notably opposing anthropology and political science respectively), I subscribe to the proposal of Benoit de L'Estoile (2014), who recommends viewing these (and other) perspectives as *frames of reference* – available to people both to make sense of their reality and to be used in response to it, even if in apparent contradictory ways. Taking these two perspectives as ideal types is a helpful analytical tool, as long as they do not become straightjackets into which people, groups, or even countries are fitted or competing explanatory models.

In Brazilian anthropological literature the distribution of goods and the brokering of public services provide an opportunity for politicians to demonstrate they are 'men of their word' (*homens de palavra*): people that are able and willing to fulfil the promises they make. Indeed, their trustworthiness is important for the establishment of a moral 'commitment' (*adesão*) between voters and politicians (Heredia and Palmeira 2006). Emphasising the reciprocity aspect, Aaron Ansell (2014) uses the term 'intimate hierarchy' as an alternative to 'clientelism' in the context of Northeast Brazil. Although clientelism also comprises emotional and symbolic traits, this term seeks to highlight the existence of moral equality in a context of material inequality. Ansell observed how voters and politicians make use of family values in order to distinguish between moral and immoral relations and exchanges.

The other ideal type refers to the economic rationality of such interactions (for example, Nichter 2014; Szwarcberg 2013). In this view, clients instrumentally assess political candidates in terms of what they have to offer. Those involved try to maximise their gains, without the need of a personalised relationship or commitment. Such instrumentalisation of relationships between political candidates and voters is not necessarily seen by the first group *in opposition* to a more personal relationship.

In fact, politicians and campaign workers made no such distinction, since their focus on living up to their promises and protecting their credibility did not concern motivations. This echoes the findings of my previous research, where urban residents in northeast Brazil would refuse to vote for candidates known for not fulfilling longer-term promises *regardless* of their high bids and promises (Eiró and Koster 2019). In so doing they combined an economic rationale with an emphasis on morality.

## Disenchantment

Engaging with this body of literature is useful to understand yet another form of relation between politicians and voters – one that is in fact opposed to frames of reference that motivate or justify them. It is the denial of entering these relationships, or rupturing them based on *disenchantment* with traditional politics.

This attitude is connected to the break of trust associated with reciprocity and economic rationality – something that structures these relationships in terms of expectations and obligations. This disenchantment with politics feeds from a worldwide distrust in traditional politics that has gained momentum in the 2010s, favouring a diverse group of self-proclaimed political outsiders. Such framing – and by referring to it as such I am emphasising its shared nature, one that can be explained as a social and cultural event – helped to guide the choices of people frustrated at seeing their hopes hampered by empty promises. Although disappointment with and distrust of politicians have for a long time been an important aspect of how residents of low-income neighbourhoods see and talk about politics (for example, Leal Nunes 2012; Bursztyn 1990), in the 2018 elections these feelings were even more prominent. Many people complained about the previous government's' involvement in corruption scandals, which many felt were unprecedented and which provoked much anger.

It is important to take into account that for many of these voters the PT's coming to power (2003–16) included a promise of a general improvement of politics, including less corruption, that for many was not realised. This disenchantment with politics under the PT was especially strong among the lower-middle classes (such as those living in lower-income neighbourhoods but who had stable formal jobs or owned commercial establishments). Many of these voters felt somehow left behind by social policies that targeted the poorest in society.

## Between idealist and pragmatic politics

In 2018 I saw how this disenchantment motivated people in low-income neighbourhoods throughout Recife to vote for the 'outsider candidate', the one who represented a kind of rupture with the status quo. Bolsonaro was able to capture this sentiment (or to be captured by it) by presenting himself as anti-establishment and the only one carrying the truthful will of 'the people' – a classic move for populist politicians from all sides of the political spectrum (Mudde and Rovira Kaltwasser 2017; Panizza 2005). This context obviously affects the way other politicians understand politics and their role in the changing political landscape.

In the following three subsections, we turn to politicians themselves, analysing how they navigate both *idealism* and *disenchantment* in politics. The first zooms in on the dilemmas faced by an MDB politician as he seeks to balance his ideals with voters' demands for services that he can provide. The second discusses the implications of this dilemma for a programmatic PT affiliate, whose justifications for practices she deems undemocratic rely on the stigmatisation of poorer people's ways of doing politics. The third centres around a PT politician and his strategies to construct programmatic politics in these contexts.

### Service (noun): the action of helping or doing work for someone

In 2018 I came across the term '*prestar serviço*' ('service providing') in my fieldwork. The term was frequently used by my informants – first-time candidates, established politicians and campaign staff – to describe their own work. Although this was the first time I heard it used in that specific context, *'prestar serviço'* is a common expression in Brazil. It means to 'come to the aid of someone', 'offer support' or 'be at someone's service'. In the political context the expression was used to refer to services offered by elected representatives to their (potential) constituency. It encompasses the obligations towards one's constituency in the shape of small favours or services to be brokered.

The first person to explain the expression to me was Fernando,[2] an experienced Pernambucan politician. He had been *vereador* (an elected municipal councillor) in a small city in the metropolitan area of Recife and had held high positions in the state government, but was then the right-hand of an elected federal deputy from the MDB. Thinking back to his time in elected office, he explained to me how a *vereador* often gets trapped in this kind of work, which emerges from a relationship of 'dependency':

> This relationship of dependency exists, so there are whole families there, there are neighbourhoods and such, and many times you are, let's say, someone who offers assistance for four years. A *vereador* is often that, he is a *prestador de serviço* (service provider). He does not legislate, he does not oversee government [*fiscaliza*], he only *presta serviço* (provides service) to the community, uses the power he has for that.[3]

I have got to know Fernando as an idealistic politician. Aged in his late forties, he had a university degree in economics and was versed in local and national politics. For him, the 'political praxis' of *prestar serviço* does not fit the image and ideal of a decent, public-spirited politician, although he does accept it as an inevitable part of the work. Fernando used the term 'praxis' to emphasise the *realpolitik* aspect that made engaging in this practice not an option. He also used the term to identify the relationship politicians have with 'dependent communities' – a euphemism for low-income or very poor neighbourhoods – who rely the most on the type of small favours that a politician can grant.

Another experienced politician I met was Beatriz, then an established PT state deputy. She told me how she had developed a strategy to reduce the amount of these small favours: she only 'helped' organisations, not individuals. Her intention was that these organisations, mostly NGOs, would then organise residents around an issue to improve their lives. This she sees as a goal of politics, an outcome consistent with her party's identity and origins in popular movements, and contrary to personal, short-term demands. However, Beatriz recognises that her policy has limits, and so she often ends up *prestando serviço* (providing service) to individuals as well:

> What we agreed to here [in her office], since the first term, is that we will not respond to individual demands. Of course, you make gestures of solidarity, you have to. For example, this week I will buy a wheelchair for a person who since the first term supports us [*está com a gente*]. The woman has cancer, just started chemotherapy. She is very weak, can't walk. I enrolled her [to receive public assistance], but the institution said she is in fifth place … Lung cancer does not wait in fifth place.

Such acts are part of politicians' understanding of the moral economy that regulates their interactions with poorer voters. My collaborators would often justify their actions, sometimes in anticipation of a negative judgement they believed I was making of them, using terms as care (*cuidado*) and responsibility towards voters on low incomes. They understand that their trustworthiness and honesty are measured by the promises they make and how (and if) these are fulfilled. In their perception, the moral obligation to help those in need is inherent to their work and position in society. They never challenged the essence of this obligation, even when they were not enthusiasts of it or if their own moral values collided with the practical implications of such acts. Such a conflict of values was not rare to find among my collaborators, rooted in a particular view of citizenship and politics that we will consider next.

## Poor people's politics

The resistance of politicians and their staff to engage in *prestar serviço* is deeply rooted in the negative assessment they make of the way poor people see and 'do politics', including something as basic as the understanding of what elected positions entail. Beatriz, for instance, complained about how her electorate does not understand why she is not among them often enough. She referred to a constant need to explain to her voters that she has a lot of work at the state council; she even has formal limits to her absence in plenary sessions and the chamber of deputies, at risk of seeing her salary reduced if she does not justify them. 'People don't understand, they think we need to be on the streets the whole time,' she observes. Beatriz also emphasises that a state deputy has demands all over the state, unlike *vereadores*, whose geographical reach is the city. Fernando added that his electorate would be on his back if he delayed delivering goods or services promised. If he refused to do it he would quickly be labelled as elitist, someone who does not care [*não dá atenção*].

In Recife in 2018 I also met Adriana, an experienced campaign organiser for the PT. Aged in her early forties, Adriana had started her political activism career very young and held several high-level positions in the campaigns and offices of her party's elected politicians. This gave her not only a historical perspective on the party evolution, but also a personal involvement and passion that she did not try to hide. Adriana explained to me how hard it is to run the campaign of her candidate for federal deputy with so few resources, dependent as she was on grassroots organisations and volunteer work. For her, competing with bigger parties – those holding offices, for example – is unfair because the PT 'doesn't play with the same weapons'. 'Even if they would like to, they wouldn't know how, nor have the same resources to do so,' she added.

Those familiar with Brazilian politics will see some irony in what Adriana says. The PT is in fact one of the largest parties in the country and at the time of the interview had held presidential office for 13 years (from 2003 to 2016). Nevertheless, it is important to consider that not all candidates from large parties have access to the same resources. In the case of the PT, for example those located in less strategic areas or with slimmer chances of winning will not receive many resources to compete with well-funded political machines (Merton 1949), to whom dominating local politics is its only purpose.

This harsh competition and recurring failure, experienced in the case of Adriana's campaign in 2018, is understood and framed as a result of the degrading of the political citizenship of PT's traditional voters, the poor. Adriana was nostalgic about a time when 'families would gather behind a name', with poor people more committed to an individual politician or party. She also resents the fact that the voters manifest a more immediate mindset, not valuing the past achievements that she is proud to recall. As a consequence she now finds it hard to rely on the 'conscience vote'. She told me how her inability to 'conquer' votes by reason, ideology and loyalty made her feel hopeless, as this left no other way than through distribution of resources to achieve electoral success.

Adriana's framing of the issue is one that relies on a long history of clientelism as a normative label in Brazil, used to accuse political opponents of not practising a noble form of politics, of playing 'dirty' (Gay 1998; Leal Nunes 2012). Adriana then justifies the use of means that would certainly be framed by others as clientelistic (or vote-buying), something that she disapproves of herself, as a short-term solution to a larger problem. When I asked whether she felt betrayed that many former PT voters were turning to Bolsonaro in 2018, Adriana pointed out what the party could have done differently to avoid that: 'To do more politics. In all senses'.

She explained that running a good administration was not enough on its own to generate gratitude in the electorate. In her view the party had stopped doing what they did best: talking, discussing politics with people, engaging with voters. Furthermore, Adriana believes that the votes from low-income neighbourhoods 'oscillate too much' because voters there are susceptible to the 'machine of the state'. Adriana blames vote-buying, which she sees as the main factor in electing some politicians.

Adriana's interpretation should be read through the lens of the material conditions that shape poor people's politics, as suggested by Auyero (1999). He analyses clientelist practices as actions embedded in the conditions of extreme material and symbolic destitution. Instead of seeing clients as people who vote and support political candidates solely *in exchange* for favours and services, Auyero focuses on the relational and experiential matrix that links patrons, brokers and (some) clients in ongoing problem-solving networks.

This shift of perspective avoids blaming political culture for poverty where clientelism is a sign of civic underdevelopment and should be eliminated. Instead it perceives poverty to be the main factor determining what kind of relationship will be established between citizens and political candidates. Although Adriana did not go so far in her own analysis of the electoral behaviour of the poor, her perspective links such 'problem-solving networks' as a gap-filling capacity of clientelism where the state is absent. Instead of normalising clientelism as an expression of an inherent characteristic of certain people, Auyero reconstructs the fabric that facilitates it.

If Adriana (and other politicians I met) avoided placing an explicit blame on poor people's culture for the 'need' of clientelism, they do rank different types of political work in normative terms. Being realists, they understand that 'pure' and noble political work is not enough to gain the support of low-income residents; it must be complemented with another type of work that she deems less worthy. By making this distinction, politicians are also assessing the political citizenship of the people they wish to represent, at times flirting with an essentialist view of poor people's political culture.

Such a view is long present in social sciences' interpretations of politics. Among the most influential of these is the work of Banfield (1958), for whom certain 'cultures' contain values and norms that are inherently opposed to collective action and therefore not in the interest of the public good. Similarly, my interlocutors would often frame poor people's engagement with politics as being inherently apolitical, centred on individual interests rather than abstract political orientations or collective interests. They reduce these practices to a self-centred economic rationality, contributing to the reproduction of a discourse of stigmatisation of 'poor people's politics'.

## The right way of doing (Leftist) politics

In 2020 I met Augusto, a well-educated man in his early thirties who was running for *vereador* for the first time. Although he has had an impressive 20-year activist career, he only entered party politics in 2015, when he joined the PT and volunteered in a campaign for *vereador* in 2016. He launched his own candidacy later. Augusto describes to me how he took up 'a daunting challenge'. Since 2016, all members of the municipal council in his municipality are centre or right-wing, something that he sees as a consequence of the turbulent political context of 2015–16 that culminated in Dilma Rousseff's impeachment. Certainly these events harmed the popularity of left-wing parties'. Structurally Augusto blames the tradition of 'assistentialism' of centre and right-wing parties, a term used throughout Latin America to disqualify social policies (see Nagels 2016). For Augusto, this tradition is not far removed from vote buying, shown in the systematic distribution of goods and favours in exchange for votes.

In order to compete with that political machine, Augusto tells me passionately how he believes in the 'winning hearts and minds' approach. In the 2020 campaign he focused his efforts on the search for voters who are 'sick and tired of this type of politics', who are aware that a 'vote sold is a street that doesn't get paved, rubbish that is not collected, a sewage system that is not extended'. As he describes this potential voter to me, he immediately acknowledges that his interpretation of the political scenario, in which there are so many frustrated voters, can be based on his own idealism. This is reflected in his actual strategy of gaining votes, undertaken somewhat against his own wishes, which he summarised in one word: *presença*.

For Augusto, the only way to beat assistentialist politics with fewer resources is to be present, to show up, to remember people and to make them feel they matter. This constitutes a constant physical manifestation of a 'commitment' (*compromisso*) and the establishment of a genuine partnership. He goes as far as to use the expression 'tactile strategies' to reach lower classes, relating literally to the physical proximity, the hugging and touching characteristic of electoral campaigns in Brazil, even during a pandemic (see Chapter 9 by Aaron Ansell for a complementary discussion on *presença*).

To make his point, Augusto also contrasts this 'tactile voter' with the 'opinion vote' from higher social classes. It is here that Augusto's idealism about politics, in particular his overestimation of poor voters' commitment to a progressive left-wing politics, conflicts with a rigid and normative vision of how the poor actually do politics. For Augusto, the main difference between tactile and opinion voters is that the latter need to be convinced, but only once, whereas for the former the candidate's recurring *presença* is crucial, providing a constant reminder of their commitment. Once again the operationalisation of such views of poor voters relate to delicate practices.

Just like Beatriz, Augusto also believes that the Left should not 'brush off' urgent demands from voters as an illegitimate way of doing politics: for him, it is a justifiable attitude given the circumstances of precarity in which many exist. To adopt such a posture would be to assume a position of moral superiority that he says he is 'tired of' in the Left. However, he does see this kind of interaction to be a lesser form of political engagement, and his solution is to make this moment an educational one. In deciding to respond to some of these demands, he still explains, overtly and repeatedly, that he is doing what he believes 'the state should be doing'. It is because of the state's shortcomings that these people find themselves forced to resort to him; in his political acting (notably as future elected office holder) he fights so that the state will fill these gaps and people will not have to resort to such 'undignified' ways of having their rights met. To summarise, Augusto believes that a politician should 'look out for urgent needs' of voters *if* such actions are embedded in a process of 'political construction' – that is, framed as part of a collective political project, not as personal benefit to a close supporter.

Augusto's discursive attempt to re-politicise such actions brought me back to how he (and my other interlocutors) justified their politics in opposition to politicians who had too many resources and supposedly lacked an ideological framing of their actions. These idealist politicians saw such actions from others as short-term and self-interested; they even resented voters who accepted them. Trying to understand what they have in common, I ask Augusto if he does not believe that a trusting relationship between voters and politicians could be established with the support of the distribution of goods – or perhaps even because of them, as a sign of commitment, but without an explicit ideological framing.

I am not sure whether he was uncomfortable with the question or the idea itself, but Augusto struggled to answer. He admitted it to be possible. A few hours before we had talked about how the Left tends to patronise low-income voters as 'not-knowing better', so I suspect Augusto was trying to reconcile these ideas when answering my question. To conclude, he says that not much is left for politicians like him to do except to try and convince voters of their political project and to involve them as active players in it, thus 'winning hearts and minds'.

## Conclusion

In this chapter, my aim was to gain a deeper understanding of how Brazilian politicians perceive electoral politics and assess voters in low-income neighbourhoods. While the classic frames of reciprocity and economic rationality were present in their discourse, this chapter also showed how these individuals navigated the tension between being idealist politicians, keen to work towards collective benefits, and being *prestadores de serviço*, providers of direct favours to individual voters. Through their discourse, it became evident the image of the state as a provider of services is central to how politicians perceive low-income voters' engagement with electoral politics. However, such views are often considered inferior, leaving politicians and campaign workers to reproduce cultural essentialist views that portray people in poverty as inherently bad citizens.

The rapid political changes that have occurred in Brazil since 2016 have been particularly disruptive to the way these politicians *do* politics. This disruption goes beyond a simple sympathy for an 'outsider' as a form of protest to encompass a real disenchantment with politics among the poor. This undermines the most direct form of establishing trust, through direct contact and the exchange of symbolic goods that build trust between politicians and voters. Politicians from the mainstream Centre and Left struggle to make sense of this scenario. As a result these participants showed clear frustration with voters who they considered to have always helped, or with whom they share real political goals.

The material discussed in this chapter poses a challenge for clientelism studies, often divided into approaches of reciprocity or economic rationality. Here I highlight the disruption of the moral economy that regulated relationships between politicians and the poor, which should encourage researchers to avoid the rigid adoption of one of these approaches as an explanatory model. Instead, clientelism studies should focus on building a repertoire of frames of reference available to individuals to make sense of and to structure these relationships. This study both reveals the complexity of political interactions in Brazil and calls for further research to explore the multiple frames of reference that govern political relationships.

## Acknowledgements

This project has received funding from the European Research Council (ERC) under the European Union's Horizon 2020 research and innovation program (grant agreement No. 679614).

## Notes

1 I am indebted to Martijn Koster (PI of the Brokers project which financed this research), who introduced me into this network, built by the decade-long ethnographic research of low-income neighbourhoods of Recife. His collaborators – residents, community leaders and political party Staffers – generously transferred some of their trust of him to me, saving me valuable time.
2 All interviewees' names are pseudonyms. When possible, I omitted the municipality they served (mainly either Olinda or Recife), but the identification of political parties, as well as the interviewees' level of work (municipality, state or federal), were maintained.
3 All quotes and interview excerpts were translated from Portuguese to English by the author.

## References

Ansell, A. 2014. *Zero Hunger*. Chapel Hill, NC: University of North Carolina Press.
Auyero, J. 1999. '"From the client's point(s) of view": How poor people perceive and evaluate political clientelism', *Theory and Society* 28: 297–334. Accessed 24 January 2025. Available at https://www.jstor.org/stable/3108473.
Auyero, J. 2001. *Poor People's Politics*. Durham, NC: Duke University Press.
Banerjee, M. 2014. *Why India Votes?* Abingdon, Oxon: Routledge.
Banfield, E. C. 1958. *The Moral Basis of a Backward Society*. New York: Free Press.
Barreira, I. A. F. 1998. *Chuvas de papéis. Ritos e símbolos de campanhas eleitorais no Brasil*. Rio de Janeiro: Relume Dumará.
Bierschenk, T. and de Sardan, J. P. O. 2019. 'How to study bureaucracies ethnographically?', *Critique of Anthropology* 39(2): 243–57. https://doi.org/10.1177/0308275x19842918.
Björkman, L. 2014. '"You can't buy a vote": Meanings of money in a Mumbai election', *American Ethnologist* 41(4): 617–34. https://doi.org/10.1111/amet.12101.
Bursztyn, M. 1990. *O país das alianças: Elites e continuísmo no Brasil*. Petrópolis: Vozes.

Dubois, V. 2010. *The Bureaucrat and the Poor: Encounters in French Welfare Offices*. Farnham, Surrey: Ashgate Publishing.
Eiró, F. 2018. 'Anti-poverty programs and vote-buying strategies'. In *Corruption and Norms*, edited by I. Kubbe and A. Engelbert, 133–52. Cham, Switzerland: Springer International Publishing.
Eiró, F. and M. Koster. 2019. 'Facing bureaucratic uncertainty in the Bolsa Família program: Clientelism beyond reciprocity and economic rationality', *Focaal* 85: 84–96. https://doi.org/10.3167/fcl.2019.850108.
Ferguson, J. 1990. *The Anti-Politics Machine: Development, depoliticisation, and bureaucratic power in Lesotho*. Cambridge: Cambridge University Press.
Gay, R. 1998. 'Rethinking clientelism: Demands, discourses and practices in contemporary Brazil', *European Review of Latin American and Caribbean Studies* 65, 7–24. Accessed 24 January 2025. Available at https://www.jstor.org/stable/25675795.
Heredia, B. M. A. and M. Palmeira. 2006. 'O voto como adesão', *Teoria e Cultura* 1(1): 35–58.
Hunter, W. and T. J. Power. 2007. 'Rewarding Lula: Executive power, social policy and the Brazilian elections of 2006', *Latin American Politics and Society* 49(1): 1–30. https://doi.org/10.1111/j.1548-2456.2007.tb00372.x.
Koch, I. 2021. 'The guardians of the welfare state: Universal credit, welfare control and the moral economy of frontline work in austerity Britain', *Sociology* 55(2): 243–62. https://doi.org/10.1177/0038038520936981.
Koster, M. 2012. 'Mediating and getting "burnt" in the gap: Politics and brokerage in a Recife slum, Brazil', *Critique of Anthropology* 32, 479–97. https://doi.org/10.1177/0308275X12456643.
De L'Estoile, B. 2014. 'Money is good, but a friend is better', *Current Anthropology* 55: S62–S73. https://doi.org/10.1086/676068.
Leal Nunes, V. 2012. *Coronelismo, enxada e voto: O município e o regime representativo no Brasil*. São Paulo: Companhia das Letras.
Merton, R. K. 1949. *Social Theory and Social Structure*. Glencoe, IL.: The Free Press.
Mudde, C. 2010. 'The populist radical right: A pathological normalcy', *West European Politics* 33(6): 1167–86. https://doi.org/10.1080/01402382.2010.508901.
Mudde, C. and C. Rovira Kaltwasser. 2017. *Populism: A very short introduction*. Oxford: Oxford University Press.
Nagels, N. 2016. 'The social investment perspective, conditional cash transfer programmes and the welfare mix: Peru and Bolivia', *Social Policy and Society* 15(3): 479–93. https://doi.org/10.1017/S1474746416000105.
Nichter, S. 2014. 'Political clientelism and social policy in Brazil'. In *Political clientelism, patronage, and development*, edited by D. A. Brun and L. Diamond, 135–57. Cambridge: Cambridge University Press.
Palmeira, M. 1992. 'Voto: Racionalidade ou significado', *Revista Brasileira de Ciências Sociais* 7(20): 26–30.
Pasieka, A. 2017. 'Taking far-right claims seriously and literally: Anthropology and the study of right-wing radicalism', *Slavic Review* 76(S1): S19–29. https://doi.org/10.1017/slr.2017.154.
Panizza, F. 2005. 'Introduction'. In n Panizza, F. (ed.) *Populism and the Mirror of Democracy*, edited by F. Panizza, 1–31. London: Verso.
Pinheiro-Machado, R. and L. M. Scalco. 2020. 'From hope to hate', *HAU: Journal of Ethnographic Theory* 10: 21–31. https://doi.org/10.1086/708627.
Szwarcberg, M. 2013. 'The microfoundations of political clientelism: Lessons from the Argentine case', *Latin American Research Review* 48: 32–54. https://doi.org/10.1353/lar.2013.0024.
Thelen, T., L. Vetters and K. von Benda-Beckmann. 2014. 'Introduction to stategraphy: Toward a relational anthropology of the State', *Social Analysis* 58(3): 1–19. https://doi.org/10.3167/sa.2014.580302.

# 11
# Afterword
Flávia Biroli, 13 August 2024

In many Latin American countries, including Brazil, Social Sciences research evolved institutionally and professionally by interacting with the opportunities and challenges set by democratisation. By that, I don't mean the specific timeline of the transition from the military regimes of the 1960s and 1970s to plural democratic regimes in the 1980s. I rather refer to longer, more multifaceted processes which consist of disputes over the institutionalisation of rights and policy, the scope of participation and the translation of political citizenship into social guarantees. The obstacles to consolidating democracy in the face of authoritarian legacies and tremendous social inequalities were acknowledged by researchers of distinct theoretical affiliation. Nevertheless, until the beginning of the twentieth century many of us still presumed that the binary distinction between democracy and authoritarianism made sense – as the field was strongly informed by the change from one regime to another, marked by the 1988 democratic Constitution and the return to competitive elections. Authoritarianism was approached as a political legacy that had lost its grip in the present or that had become circumscribed to marginal events, actors and platforms with limited impact on the core of the disputes.

This book shows that we have plenty of reasons to change the route and rethink this framework. It joins an increasing body of research focusing on the current authoritarian threats to democracy. Their global and local expressions require attention and are deeply implicated in political changes at different levels. That is why the multi-dimensional scope of the analysis presented in these chapters makes a precious contribution to scholarship beyond Brazilian or Latin American Studies. How do changes in national political dynamics connect with transnational organisations that promote, and often fund, illiberal platforms and leadership? On the other hand, what does the increase in the support for undemocratic alternatives tell us about the living experience of democracy in local communities? Moreover, how can we connect the political opportunities for authoritarianism – and resistance – with structural inequalities that shape the perspectives of the citizens?

In Brazil, the ambivalences of liberal democracy are vivid in the deep-rooted inequalities of class, race and gender that determine access to opportunities and legal guarantees. Neoliberal adjustments have clearly enhanced their effects, as they have compromised the capacity of the state. Despite this, during the government of Centre to Left parties, policy that challenged hierarchies of class and status, and regional disparities, triggered reactions. On the other hand, democracy fell short of producing enduring structural change. Possibly the most studied case of the 'turn to the left' in Latin America, Brazil has seen the growth of a far right that openly states its malaise with liberal democracy, diversity and social justice. Such politics tap into different kinds of resentment, encouraging authoritarian movements and subjectivities. In the new atmosphere that emerged, romanticising military dictatorships and demanding a coup to restore the order became a recurring feature of protests and news.

The election of the far-right president Jair Bolsonaro in 2018 also made Brazil a subject for investigation into the causes of, and implications of the advancement of, authoritarianism in the Americas. Similarities with the performance and practices of leaders such as Viktor Orbán in Hungary, Recep Tayyip Erdoğan in Turkey, Donald Trump in the United States and Nayib Bukele in El Salvador, among others, help researchers to investigate whether we could talk of a conceptual 'family', and how international conservative and radical right networks tap into local dynamics. Moreover, resistance in Brazil was significant in many ways, as discussed in this book, and Bolsonaro ultimately lost his re-election attempt. This result gave researchers the opportunity to consider how authoritarian movements and platforms adapt under changing political contexts.

The book approaches these dynamics thoughtfully, doing justice to their complexity. The authors focus on distinct aspects of authoritarianism in Brazil – the local and the global, leadership and electoral support, institutional impact and diffuse mobilisation, political leadership and economic interests. Its main contribution relies in unpacking the elements and levels in which authoritarianism in contemporary Brazil takes shape. The editors of the volume bravely put together studies that activate varied disciplinary and theoretical tools to investigate both the circumstantial and the structural. The set of studies presented in this book thus confronts the new – the emergence, the novel context of political alignments and risks. Yet they do not miss what was already there – the opportunities for illiberal and authoritarian alternatives to be nurtured in a deeply unequal social context, in which resentment and insecurities take form under long-lasting hierarchies of power that constitute the lived experiences of democracy.

In their introduction Hatzikidi and de Souza Santos clarify that the book is as much about authoritarianism as it is about disputes over the meanings of democracy. Now that we are past the moment of surprise (or horror) with the present appeal of authoritarianism, we can understand the opportunities found by far-right movements and contribute to discussing the future of democracy. Facing its paradoxes is more valuable than romanticising it, as this brings us closer to dealing with failed promises, achievements and unfulfilled potential.

# Index

accountability 6, 9, 76, 77, 93, 94, 97, 101, 104
anti-democratic
  project 38
  radical right 48
  shifts 16
  subjectivities 2
anti-intellectualism 3
Anvisa 22, 101, 112, 114, 118, 121
armed forces 5, 8, 9, 13, 20, 23, 43, 70
authoritarianism
  affordances 16, 87, 88, 93, 97, 98, 101
  dispositions 11, 12, 17, 152, 153, 166, 182
  modalities 12, 17, 129, 130, 145, 146
  playbook 10
  roots 3–4
autonomy 6–8, 22, 73, 81, 91–7, 103–4
  bureaucratic autonomy 16, 65, 75
  and corporate autonomy 87, 93, 94, 96, 97, 98, 100, 101, 103
  and physician's autonomy 87, 88, 91, 93, 94, 96, 97, 100, 101, 103

Bolsa Família 179, 183–4
Bolsonarismo 18, 32, 38–41, 49, 54, 58, 146
bureaucracy 8, 6, 52, 65, 66–8, 74, 80, 83, 152
Butantan 22, 109, 110, 113, 116–18

Christian values 13, 130, 136–7, 139, 142
civil society 23

Clientelism 175–6, 197–8, 202–3, 207
Conservative
  Evangelicals 129, 142, 143
  leaders 47
  morals 100, 132
  values 48, 56, 133
conspiracy theories 7, 11–12, 18, 49, 50–2, 58, 167–8
contestation 1, 23, 82, 102
corruption
  anti-corruption 72, 173, 174, 187
  enemy of 185
  fight corruption 5, 72
  folk model 14, 174, 176, 177, 179, 188
  liberal model of 176
  model of corruption 174, 176–7, 179
  and moral governance 174
  new right model 176
  patronal figures 176
  practice 181, 188
  scandal 19, 130, 143, 199
  self-governance 188
  systematic 143
  transculturally 175–6
Covid-19
  clinical trials 112, 122
  Covid kit 89, 92, 96, 101
  and early treatment 88–91, 96–9, 101, 113
  health protocol 89, 93, 94
  immunisation 109, 114, 115
  and malgovernance 90
  Pandemic 2, 6, 19, 21, 22, 36–8, 42, 49, 57, 77, 87, 184, 195
  and Supreme Court 22, 23, 89
  treatment 97, 98
  vaccination 7, 107–11, 113–23
CPI 89, 90, 93, 95, 97–9, 101

democracy
  consolidation 23
  de-democratisation 3–4
  excesses 8
  representative 8, 45
dictatorship
  civil/military (1964–1985) 3, 20, 31, 35, 39, 210
  democracy 35
  Estado Novo 4
  military regime 3, 5, 31, 173, 209
  Southern Cone 47
disenchantment 3, 4, 193, 195, 197, 198, 199, 206
discipline 8, 23, 83, 103, 141, 185–6
dissent
  acts of dissent 6
  Democratic dissent 36
  forms of dissent 1, 2, 7
  manifesting dissent 103
  physicians 7, 92, 94
  silenced 96
  social science literature 66
  strategies of dissent and resistance 6, 19, 79
  subversive action 6, 75, 76, 80, 81
  tide of dissent 102
  voices 74
  within organisations 6, 66

elections
  Conservative uprisings 36, 129
  ethnography 193, 197
  Evangelical political activism 130, 132, 136, 137, 140
  legislation 41, 195
  re-election 38, 68, 107, 193, 210
  and spiritual warfare 2, 139, 140, 144
elections 2022 and 2018 32, 39, 131, 184, 186, 193, 194
  anti-system 32, 34
  electronic voting system 11, 13
  evangelicals 132, 143
  Lula 37, 39, 40, 41, 129
  re-election 38, 193
  spiritual battlefield 13
  *voto impresso* 10

establishment, the 17, 45, 58, 145, 197, 205
Estado Novo 3–4
ethnography 1, 14, 158, 174, 193–4, 196–7

family
  and Christianity 56, 144
  patriarchal family hierarchy 13, 176
  of the radical right 8, 47, 48
  and the state 175, 182
  traditional family 48, 57, 139, 143, 146
  values 133, 139, 142, 185, 198
far right
  alliances 1
  Brazilian far right 59
  international meetings 48
  politics 193
  the far right 5, 6, 32, 35, 38, 39, 40, 41, 43, 44
Federal Highway Police 8, 9
Fiocruz 110, 112, 115, 117–18
freedom
  and autonomy 87, 93–4, 95, 104
  of expression 143
  family and faith 54, 55
  and limitation 95, 103
  limitless 87, 100, 101, 103, 104
  and religion 140–1, 144
  unbridled 87, 93, 103
  of worship 144

good citizen 12, 14, 15, 54, 185, 187

hierarchy 8, 13, 23, 75, 76, 100, 103, 176, 198

ideology
  gender 133, 136, 142, 166, 186
  good versus evil / moral ideology 14, 140
  'Regime of truth' 11
illiberal backlash 3
intimidation 6, 19, 20, 21, 22, 73, 80, 92, 96, 103

Lula
  administration 49, 83
  alliances 59
  corruption 174, 181
  election 21, 24, 43, 131
  evil forces 13, 139
  government 39, 41, 43, 179, 180
  impeachment 39, 174
  imprisonment 182, 185
  and the left 129, 139
  morally upright patronal leader 14, 174
  Northeastern voters 184, 188
  paternalism 14, 179, 185, 188
  second round 53, 175

Ministry of Health 16, 90, 101, 109, 114, 117, 121, 123

National Congress 9, 10, 195
Neoliberalism 2, 31, 48, 100, 102
Northeast Brazil 194, 197, 198

patronage 66, 174–9, 182, 185–6, 188
Piauí 14, 174–5, 177–80, 182–3, 185–9
pluralism 133, 145
  *Pemedebismo* 32–5, 37, 41–3
  PMDB 34, 42, 180
polarisation 2, 4, 18, 39, 129, 138
politics
  local 2, 174, 194, 202
  low-income voters 14, 206
  municipal 14, 174
  political control 6, 16, 65–7, 70, 73, 80–3
  political elites 15, 23, 43, 114
populism
  administrations 66, 82
  backlash 44
  Bolsonaro's populism 18
  discursive articulation 17
  ideological orientation 17
  leaders 65, 80
  narratives 18
  politicians 199
  populist politics 17, 18

right wing populism 110, 174
  worldwide 130
Prevent Senior 6, 9, 93, 94, 97, 101, 103
procurement 107, 109, 110, 115–17, 121–2
protests 3, 19, 21
  June 2013 3, 19, 36, 45
privilege 22, 141, 167
PT 3, 19, 23, 33, 50, 53, 133, 143–4, 173, 179, 195
  and Bolsonaro 176, 182
  and Christophobia 144
  disenchantment with politics 198
  and evangelicals 144
  and the northeast 184
  and PSDB 33
  sex and gender 167
  social policies 181
  support 175, 179
  *vereador* 200, 204
  voters 203
public interest 65–9, 78, 81–2
public security
  insecurity 4
  security policies 133
public servants 6, 20, 22, 66, 81

Radical right
  administration 49, 52
  in Brazil 47, 50
  global family of the radical right 8, 58
  government 50, 55
  Jair Bolsonaro 48, 49
  in Latin America 47
  leaders 48, 49
  Nativism 48
  parties 48, 53
  Vox Party 51, 53
Recife 193–4, 199–200, 202
religion
  freedom of religion 140
  guiding force 47, 134
  mainstream 159, 160
  new political actors 130, 131
  political mobilisation 141

Rousseff, Dilma
    impeachment 4, 50, 68, 69, 130, 180, 185, 204
    second term 41, 180
    successor 174, 179, 180

Supreme Court 10, 21–3, 41, 89–90, 174

technocracy 6, 66, 68
truth, regime of 10, 107, 129, 139, 145

Universal Church of the Kingdom of God/ IURD 12, 151, 156, 160

vaccines
    AstraZeneca 108–10, 112, 115–18
    BioNTech 110, 116
    CoronaVac 108–9, 111, 114–16, 118
    Pfizer 108–9, 111, 115–16, 122
    vaccination hesitancy 7, 121
violence
    communist ideologies 142
    criminal incidence 21
    criminality 187
    electoral 129
    excessive 9
    family 163
    police 9, 21
    strong father 188
    structures 4
    urban 130, 133
voting 10, 11, 13, 21, 129, 132, 136, 139, 185, 195